THE PERMANENT REVOLUTION

and

RESULTS AND PROSPECTS

Trotsky in his cell in the period preceding the September, 1906, trial of the leaders of the St. Petersburg Soviet. (The photograph was taken by the lawyer Elisseev.)

Leon Trotsky

The Permanent Revolution

and

Results

and

Prospects

merit publishers

873 Broadway
New York, N.Y. 10003

CONTENTS

6

Introduction

By Peter Camejo

The first socialist revolution occurred in Russia, which was both a semi-imperialist and a semi-colonial country. Marx had anticipated that one or more of the advanced countries of Western Europe would lead the way in abolishing capitalism. The Yugoslav, Chinese, and Cuban revolutions have since shown that the Russian experience was not unique.

Was Marx all wrong? Why have the more backward countries been the first to have socialist revolutions? Will the rest of the colonial world also take the road to socialism?

These are some of the questions raised and answered by Leon Trotsky's theory of permanent revolution. This book includes Trotsky's original presentation of his views in *Results and Prospects*. published in 1906, soon after the crushing of the 1905 revolution. The second part of this work was written twenty-three years later as an answer to an attack upon the theory of permanent revolution by the Soviet journalist Karl Radek.

Trotsky's arguments, like many of Lenin's writings, are here presented in polemical form and refer to a period of history unfamiliar to the current generation. At times his very vocabulary can be confusing. Not only does he assume a knowledge of Marxist terminology, but some of the terms he uses have changed their common meaning over the several decades that have elapsed since he wrote this material.

In his introduction to the 1930 edition of *Permanent Revolution*, Trotsky wrote: "A different form of exposition of the questions that interest us might, of course, have been selected. But this form was never created by the author, and was not selected by him of his own accord. It was imposed upon him partly by the opponent's will and partly by the very course of political development. Even the truths of mathematics, the most abstract of the sciences, can best be learned in connection with the history of their discovery. This applies with even greater force to the more concrete, i.e., historically-conditioned truths of Marxist politics. The history of the origin and development of the prognoses of the revolution under the conditions of pre-revolutionary Russia will, I think, bring the reader much closer and far more concretely to the essence of the revolutionary tasks of the world proletariat than a scholastic and pedantic exposition of these political ideas, torn out of the conditions of struggle which gave them birth."

Trotsky's point is well taken. But if the reader does not understand either the context or the terminology, the advantages of the polemical approach in the original document may be lost. The following introduction is designed to aid readers who are unacquainted either with Trotsky's ideas or the intricacies of pre-1917 Russian revolutionary history.

*   *   *

According to Marx, fundamental changes in the mode of production have resulted in the evolution of society in general, and class societies in particular. Slavery was succeeded by feudalism; Western European feudalism gave birth to capitalism. Capitalism, he predicted, would in turn give way to socialism, which would proceed to create a classless society.

Marx's prevision of a socialist society presupposed the development of the highly industrialized and mechanized production fostered by capitalism. He therefore held that the socialist revolution would most likely begin in those countries where such preconditions for socialism as a powerful industry and a well-organized proletariat had already been created. Marx correctly forecast the overthrow of capitalism by the working masses. He "erred" in not foreseeing how the consequences of the manner in which capitalism spread across the globe were to affect the order of emergence of the anti-capitalist regimes.

During and after their establishment in Europe, capitalist forces and relations invaded the rest of the world in forms very different from those of their original appearance on that continent. Capitalism won power in Western Europe through a series of revolutionary onslaughts against feudalism. The oppositional bourgeois-democratic forces there, in alliance with the artisans and peasants, successfully struggled for land reform, swept aside the impediments to industrialization, and consolidated the nation. In their confrontations with the throne, the church, and the nobility, they achieved civil liberties, parliamentary democracy, and a whole set of institutions which were progressive and enlightened compared with the old regime.

But Holland, England, France, and other powers that were reshaped by their own bourgeois-democratic revolutions, did not share their blessings or extend their gains to the overseas peoples they dominated. With the penetration of French capitalism, its representatives did not create a New France, dedicated to "liberty, equality and fraternity," in Vietnam. They did not permit Vietnam to become an independent and industrialized nation, to have a land reform for the peasantry, or to set up a parliamentary democracy. On the contrary, whatever was socially, economically, and politically progressive in the bourgeois revolutions of Europe was deliberately withheld and blocked from being implanted in Vietnam through the agency of French capitalism.

Thus, as capitalism expanded into the more backward regions of the world, the democratic revolution did not follow or go along with it. The chief exports of imperialism were more intense exploitation and oppression on top of the old. Under the auspices of imperialism, archaic pre-capitalist forms were not rooted out but adapted to capitalist relations. Colonialism wove all kinds of degrading human relations, from caste discrimination to child labor, into its pattern. This happened when the Belgian imperialists took over the Congo; the English, India; the United States, the Caribbean and Latin America; and when all the great powers from England to Japan laid hands on China.

In those countries which had a belated capitalist development, the bourgeoisie was too small, weak, corrupt, and cowardly to resist imperialism. As accomplices of the feudal landlords on the one hand and the foreign capitalists on the other, they were unable and unwilling to lead the workers and peasants in any consistent, thoroughgoing struggle for national liberation, land reform, and social revolution.

After noting these facts, Trotsky posed the following question: If the national bourgeoisie is opposed to the democratic revolution, how can it come about and who will lead it to victory?

He observed that it was not the feudalists who primarily controlled the huge estates and facilities in the colonial countries. In Vietnam, Cuba, the Congo, and elsewhere, it was the imperialist monopolists who stood in the way of self-determination, land reform, and modernization. Just because the advanced powers had already developed immense productive capacities along capitalist lines, the poorer colonial nations, forced to compete in the world market, could not easily industrialize themselves.

Did this then mean that the battle for the redistribution of the land, self-determination, industrialization, and democratization had to be given up as hopeless by the colonial and semi-colonial peoples? Not at all, declared

Trotsky. What it meant was that colonial peoples could not realize these demands in the same ways that they had been won in the older capitalist countries. The colonial peoples would have to adopt new methods and strike out on a new path. The fulfillment of the democratic tasks formerly carried out by the revolutionary and liberal bourgeoisie would have to be achieved by anti-capitalist forces and methods.

What would the new alignment of social classes have to be? The national bourgeoisie, which headed the democratic struggles and regimes in Europe and North America, could not play that same role in the colonial countries. It was tied for life or death to the imperialists, since the abolition of control by foreign capital would immediately endanger its own existence and privileges.

In order to carry through the democratic revolution, workers and peasants would have to join together to throw out both the foreign overlords and the national bourgeoisie submissive to them. In that event the plebeian classes would themselves have to take power. Thus the anti-imperialist movement for democracy would lead, not to the conquest of supremacy by the native owning classes, but to an altogether exceptional outcome. A resolute struggle for power by the worker-peasant masses would be inexorably oriented in an anti-capitalist, pro-socialist direction.

This perspective at once posed the further question: Which class among the insurgent population would assume the commanding position in the revolution and the regime that issued from it — the workers or the peasants? Trotsky explained that only the workers could fill that role.

Their political primacy in the partnership was determined not only by the urban location and concentration of the wageworkers in the chief industrial, transportation, and agricultural enterprises, but by the heterogeneous composition and divided aims of the peasantry. The peasantry was composed of relatively comfortable proprietors, who hired others to work their land, and of layers of poorer and poorer small cultivators, with land-less agricultural workers at the bottom of the heap.

However massive their numbers or angry their moods, the peasants were not independent, integrated, and united enough to lead an anti-capitalist revolution which would project a new social order. The richer peasants had the mentality of private proprietors and, like all small pro-ducers, kept pressing for higher prices for their produce. Those engaged in subsistence farming wanted more land. The agricultural workers were under the thumbs of the well-to-do peasants for whom they toiled.

These socio-economic factors inclined the peasantry as a whole, and sections of it, to waver between the capitalists and the workers. The triumph of the democratic revolution is possible only if the peasants rally to the support of the working class in struggle against the foreign and native capitalists. The alternative is sharply posed: either the workers will lead the peasants to power through a socialist revolution or imperialism will maintain its hold directly or indirectly through the reactionary, anti-democratic national bourgeoisie.

The first premise of the theory of permanent revolution is that in the imperialist epoch the workers are the pre-destined leaders of both the democratic and the socialist revolutions in the backward countries. These two types of revolution, which were separated in the West, are com-bined there in time and in space.

The twofold character of the colonial revolutions is manifested when the workers come to power at the head of the insurgent people. The struggle for such democratic aims as land reform, national independence and unifica-tion, and the eradication of feudalism becomes interlinked with anti-capitalist moves and measures. In order to defend its positions against capitalist counter-revolution, the representatives of the revolution must nationalize mines, plantations, and industries; control prices and foreign trade; aid agricultural workers; etc. Even if such measures encounter resistance from the upper layers of the peasantry, they are indispensable for national progress, for satisfying the needs of the masses and laying the foundations of a new society.

Trotsky agreed with Marx that socialism is impossible without the high productivity created by capitalism. But he separated the question of beginning the socialist revolution from that of consummating the revolution. It was one thing to achieve a socialist revolution and another to build a socialist society.

Could a country that had not yet undertaken or completed its bourgeois-democratic revolution, where the economy was underdeveloped and the working class a minority in relation to the peasantry, have a victorious socialist revolution? Trotsky was the first to answer "yes" to this crucial question. It was not only possible but mandatory, he explained, because that was the only way that the democratic revolution could be realized.

The permanence of the revolution consisted first of all in the fact that the struggle for democracy irresistibly grows over into the movement for socialism under the leadership of the proletariat and its revolutionary party.

Trotsky originated his theory in connection with the problems presented by the coming Russian revolution. He agreed with the other Russian Marxists that the revolution had to be bourgeois in the sense that the tasks to be realized, such as the transformation of agrarian relations, the overthrow of czarism, etc., belonged historically to the bourgeois revolution. He added the amendment, however, that because of the peculiarities of Russia's development, first outlined in *Results and Prospects*, the working class would take the lead in the democratic struggle in alliance with the peasantry and, after conquering power against the landlords and capitalists, would go forward to institute socialist measures.

The problem of the transition from the democratic to the socialist stage of the revolution, he explained, was only one aspect of revolutionary strategy. Two further elements made up the concept of permanent revolution. The second dealt with the ceaseless transformation of social relations and institutions that would take place after the conquest of power.

The third involved the international character of the socialist revolution. The working class could take power and begin the building of socialism within a national framework. But because of the world character of the productive forces and the world scope of the class struggle, the revolution cannot be consummated or socialism become effective except on an international basis. Despite its ebbs and flows, the world revolution constituted a permanent process which would not end until capitalism was abolished in its strongholds and the prerequisites for the new society were brought into being.

Socialism by definition is a society where the state and its repressive agencies have begun to wither away, where abundance ensures equality, where full democracy flourishes. So long as imperialism exists and threatens the post-capitalist states with aggression and destruction, they must maintain strong armies and a strong state. The power of the state is further fortified in the transitional period by the inadequate productive capacities and poverty of the backward countries, which can lead to ultra-bureaucratic regimes.

Marx, Lenin, and Trotsky did not conceive of a socialist society except as a world system which would have not only a higher level of production and consumption but far more freedoms than the most advanced and liberal capitalisms. It could not be erected, as the Stalinists were to teach, in a single country—and a backward one at that!

*   *   *

The Cuban revolution is a splendid example of the logic of the permanent revolution. The leaders of the July 26th Movement originally envisaged a democratic regeneration of Cuba. Their program called for land reform, self-determination, and an end to Batista's tyranny. They explicitly stated that they did not intend to nationalize either native or foreign-owned holdings.

What actually happened? As soon as they came to power, the Fidelistas ran into opposition from both the national bourgeoisie and the American. This was not because they represented a future socialist danger but simply because they took their promises for democratic reforms seriously and set out to put them into effect. Their land reform involved the expropriation of both native and foreign capital.

The capitalists counterattacked. They launched a hue and cry against the dissolution of the old police and army, protesting against the trials and executions of the Batista henchmen, who had murdered 20,000 Cubans. They stopped buying Cuba's products. They cut the sugar quota and then imposed a total trade embargo. At one point they refused to refine oil. Attempts were made to shut down factories and in some cases to dismantle them. Finally, they mounted an invasion to reverse the democratic reforms, as they had done so successfully in Guatemala in 1954.

In order to accomplish and safeguard their reforms, the Fidelistas, who remained true to their democratic program, had to take a series of steps which went beyond bourgeois limits. They had to arm the workers and peasants to defend Cuba from U. S. aggression and to protect their social gains. They had to nationalize the major industries to prevent the economy from being paralyzed by the private owners. They had to place foreign trade under government control and turn for help to other non-capitalist economies, in order to survive economically in face of the reprisals by American capitalism.

Some reactionary commentators claim that Fidel Castro's earlier political declarations were nothing but camouflage and that he really was conspiring from the first to take Cuba toward socialism. All the evidence indicates it was the vindictive, menacing actions of the imperialist and national bourgeoisies that compelled him

to make a definitive choice — back to imperialist sub-
jugation or forward to socialism.

Today the Cubans recognize that the road to emancipation they have had to take is the only one for the rest
of Latin America. They adhere to the logic of the theory
of the permanent revolution, even if they have not yet
explicitly adopted it.

*   *   *

The United States itself provides a living example of
the pertinence of the theory of permanent revolution in
the strivings of the Afro-Americans for self-determination.
They represent an oppressed nationality of many millions,
which is demanding the democratic rights and equality
that it failed to receive following the Civil War.

The freedmen wanted a land reform after their emancipation. They asked for forty acres for each ex-slave
family. Since there were approximately one million black
families in the South, this would have totaled forty million
acres. The ex-slaveowners possessed 360 million acres, so
that the expropriation of only one-ninth of their property
would have sufficed to carry through the land reform.
In addition to the Western territories with their endless
expanse of homestead lands, there were also forty-four
million acres of public land available in five Southern
states alone.

However, the triumphant Northern capitalists not only
denied this reform but, once they had disarmed their
planter rivals, collaborated with the Southern white su-
premacists in thrusting the mass of freedmen back into
servitude. They snatched political liberties away from the
Afro-Americans, re-legalized racism, and reduced the freedmen to the status of a doubly exploited social caste.

That part of the democratic revolution which was aborted
in the eighteen-sixties and eighteen-seventies has been put
on the agenda a century later, after the bulk of the Afro-
Americans have become urbanized and proletarianized.
Their drive for self-determination today will have to be

fought and won, not by reliance upon the capitalists, but only by an uncompromisingly militant battle against them. It represents a twofold movement, that of a subject people against its oppressors and that of a section of the working class against its exploiters. This explains why the struggle of the blacks for liberation acquires a more and more pronounced anti-capitalist edge and why it is one of the crucial components of the developing socialist revolution in the United States.

*   *   *

Throughout this work the terms "democracy" and "dictatorship" are used in a Marxist sense, which differs from the way they are commonly understood in the United States. This may create some confusion in the reader's mind.

The average American identifies democracy with the institutions he is most familiar with, such as free elections, party contests, parliaments, due process of law, and civil liberties. The Marxist definition embraces all this but gives a wider and deeper significance to the term. It goes beyond and behind the forms of democracy to find out what its specific class essence is. In this work the word democracy is used as the equivalent of the words bourgeois revolution or bourgeois democracy.

Marxists acknowledge that the bourgeois revolutions, which overturned monarchical and clerical regimes, considerably expanded human rights. Although the parliamentary republics promised all power to the people, they did not and could not make good on these claims, because they remained under the domination of the capitalists. A genuine democracy would ensure that the decision-making powers in economic, political, and other spheres of life were vested in the working masses, not in a small minority of rich owners.

Similarly, in ordinary usage, dictatorship refers to a type of rule where the government is in the hands of a single individual or a tight, tyrannical group. Marxists use the term not only in this restricted political sense but in a more fundamental way. There are social as well as political dictatorships. The social dictatorship of the capitalists defends the institutions of private property and the right to production for profit. This kind of social dictatorship can be exercised through a variety of political forms. Thus the German capitalists ruled by totalitarian means in Nazi Germany and maintain their domination through a parliamentary republic in West Germany today.

This brings us to the much maligned and misinterpreted phrase, "dictatorship of the proletariat." Does this mean that socialists intend to set up totalitarian tyrannies over the majority and against their will, as the capitalist demagogues insist? Nothing of the sort.

Trotsky in *Results and Prospects,* like Marx in *The Communist Manifesto* and Lenin in *State and Revolution,* looked upon the rule of the revolutionary workers as an immense extension of democracy. The dictatorial side of the proletarian power was directed only against counter-revolutionary attempts to restore the property or the minority control of the rich. The working masses who made the revolution and got rid of the profiteers would democratically control both the government and the economy and thereby enjoy far more freedoms than ever before.

The complex term, "the democratic dictatorship of the proletariat and peasantry," which often recurs in these pages, can be understood only in connection with the controversies that developed within the social-democratic movement in Russia regarding the nature and prospects of the future revolution. The various tendencies held three different positions on this question.

While all of them agreed that Russia faced a bourgeois-democratic revolution, they parted company on the political conclusions they drew from this proposition.

The Mensheviks maintained that the natural consequence of this situation would be the transfer of power to the bourgeoisie and the opening of a prolonged period of parliamentarism during which the pre-conditions for socialism would be prepared. They awarded leadership of the revolution in advance to the Russian capitalists.

The Bolsheviks asserted that the chief task of the revolution would be establishment of a democratic republic headed, not by the bourgeoisie, but by an alliance of the workers and peasantry under the form of "the democratic dictatorship of the proletariat and peasantry."

Trotsky held a third point of view: the revolution would begin as a bourgeois revolution in regard to its tasks but could be won only through the conquest of power by the proletariat standing at the head of the urban and rural masses. The workers' regime would have to resort almost at once to more and more radical measures of a socialist character and seek support in an extension of the revolution to Western Europe.

The concept of the "democratic dictatorship" advanced by Lenin was ambiguous. It did not spell out what the relationship would be between the two classes making the revolution. After February 1917, this cloudiness in Lenin's formulation permitted the emergence of two divergent policies among the Bolshevik leaders. Some, such as Kamenev and Stalin, who headed the party before Lenin arrived from exile, utilized it to justify giving critical support to the provisional government of Prince Lvov. (Kerensky became the head of this government in the midsummer of 1917.)

When Lenin returned in April, he adamantly opposed the bourgeois government and launched instead the slogan and perspective of "all power to the soviets" (workers' councils). He actually discarded the old formulation on the ground that events had rendered it obsolete by settling in the most decisive manner the reactionary role of the bourgeoisie and the political relations between the workers and peasants. The workers had to take power to save the country from ruin.

The 1917 revolution wiped out the theoretical differences

between Lenin and Trotsky on this issue; their basic agreement was certified by their close collaboration in leading the revolution from then on. For the next seven years Lenin's formulation was relegated to the past history of the evolution of revolutionary theory in Russia. Then, after his death in 1924, it was suddenly resurrected in a new context and for a different purpose.

*   *   *

This brings us to the sequence of developments that produced the second work in this collection, Trotsky's reply to Karl Radek, written during the former's exile at Alma-Ata. It is Trotsky's most extensive historical-theoretical defense of his conception of permanent revolution.

Radek, who belonged to the original Left Opposition and was also exiled to Siberia, wavered in 1928-29 and then went over to Stalin. He was later framed up in the Moscow Trials and died in prison.

When the privileged bureaucratic caste that is still in power in the Soviet Union today began its ascension under Stalin in the nineteen-twenties, it met the most principled and staunch resistance from the Left Opposition led by Trotsky. The personal heroism, revolutionary equalitarianism, and internationalism exemplified by Che Guevara in our generation was at that time personified by Trotsky.

The Soviet bureaucracy was primarily concerned with maintaining, protecting, and expanding its privileges and power rather than extending the revolution on a world scale. Like the American trade union bureaucrats, they wanted to co-exist with capitalism rather than to fight against it for the interests of the working class, and were willing to make dirty, opportunistic deals with the class enemy to further their ends.

Stalin, the leader of the Soviet bureaucracy, codified its narrow nationalistic outlook in the theory of "socialism in one country." This innovation not only flew in the face of the traditions of Marxism and the teachings of Bolshevism, but was diametrically opposed to the internationalist essence of the permanent revolution.

In the fierce factional fights within Russian and world Communism, Stalin's propagandists and allies tried to discredit Trotsky by playing up the pre-1917 disagreements between him and Lenin on the approaching revolution. Lenin's formulation was counterposed to Trotsky's as evidence of irreconcilable differences between them.

The inherent vagueness of Lenin's prescription, what Trotsky called "its algebraic character," had an advantage for the bureaucratic backsliders from Bolshevism. It enabled them to misuse selected quotations wrenched out of context from Lenin's writings on the bourgeois-democratic character of the revolution to justify open political support to the bourgeoisie in colonial countries. Under the false cover of loyalty to Leninism, the Stalinist upholders of the line of socialism in one country began to give a Menshevik coloration and content to their policy by subordinating the struggles of the worker-peasant masses to the bourgeoisie.

What this meant concretely was demonstrated in the second Chinese revolution of 1925-27, when the young Communist Party was instructed by Stalin's Third International to join the Kuomintang and subject itself to the leadership of General Chiang Kai-shek. Shortly before he slaughtered thousands of Chinese Communists and workers, Chiang was hailed as a sterling revolutionary and made an honorary member of the highest body of the world Communist movement. (Trotsky was the sole Russian leader to vote against this action.)

It will seem incredible today that anyone once considered Chiang Kai-shek, that infamous agent of Chinese capitalism and tool of imperialism, to be a revolutionary — and in Moscow at that. This points up the continuing relevance of Trotsky's criticisms of the Menshevik nature of Stalinism. They have more than a historic interest.

They directly and forcefully apply to the most burning current political problems.

Chiang represents a type of bourgeois political leader which the Stalinists have hailed and supported time and again with the most catastrophic results. General Kassim of Iraq was one such figure; Premier Sukarno of Indonesia was another.

The policy of pinning hopes on the progressive bourgeoisie, which is bound up with the theory of socialism in one country, has had three different incarnations. First was the debacle of backing Chiang. The second was the Popular Front announced by Dimitrov in 1935, which called for "collective security" to stop facism by subordinating the workers' movement to a political alliance with the liberal bourgeoisie. This led to the reinforcement of reaction in France and the triumph of Franco in Spain. In the early nineteen-forties Stalin's followers in Cuba applauded the victory of Batista as a vindication of their policy.

The third version is the notion of "peaceful co-existence" advanced by Khrushchev and his associates, which denotes that while the Russians are building communism in one country, the main job of the Communist parties in the capitalist world is to attach themselves to some liberal-sounding capitalist politicians or parties that can be made sympathetic to Moscow. One fruit of this line was the support given by the American Communist Party to Kennedy in 1960 and Johnson in 1964.

Another variant of the same course is the Maoist "bloc of four classes," not least amongst them the national bourgeoisie. This is linked with the Menshevik conception of the "two-stage" revolution: first comes the democratic stage, in which the workers and peasants work together with the bourgeoisie; and then comes the socialist stage, in which they part company. The trouble is that the cunning representatives of the bourgeoisie do not wait until the second phase matures before they turn to crush the revolution. This is precisely what happened in Indonesia in 1965, when the national bourgeois regime of Sukarno, supported by both Peking and Moscow, capitulated to the military and paved the way for the present bloody dictatorship.

*   *   *

However much some New Lefts may dismiss the issues in the Stalin-Trotsky conflict as outmoded, they are very much alive in contemporary world politics. That is the immense value of a work like this. One of the greatest contributions to revolutionary theory ever written, it is above all useful as a guide to action, not only in the colonial areas, but in advanced countries like the United States. Trotsky penned these pages to clarify the fundamental problems of revolutionary strategy in our time. They should be read in that spirit.

July 1, 1969

TRANSLATOR'S NOTE

The Permanent Revolution was published in Berlin, in Russian, in 1930. An English version appeared in New York in 1931. The present translation was made by the late John G. Wright and revised by Brian Pearce.

Results and Prospects was published in St. Petersburg in 1906. An English version was put out (under title *A Review and Some Perspectives*) in Moscow in 1921, with a special introduction included which the author had written for the Russian edition of 1919. The present translation has been made from the original by Brian Pearce.

Notes by the author are followed by the letters 'L.T.' All other notes are by the translator. References have been supplied to the fourth (Russian) edition, and to English versions of Lenin's works wherever available.

B.P.

Results and Prospects

COMMUNIST LIBRARY.

WORKERS OF ALL COUNTRIES UNITE!

A REVIEW
AND SOME
PERSPECTIVES

BY L. TROTSKY

TRANSLATED FROM THE RUSSIAN
BY J. FINEBERG.

PUBLISHED BY THE COMMUNIST INTERNATIONAL.

MOSCOW — 1921.

Facsimile of the cover of the English version of 'Results and Prospects'—Moscow 1921

PREFACE TO THE RE-ISSUE OF THIS WORK PUBLISHED IN MOSCOW IN 1919

The character of the Russian Revolution was the fundamental question in relation to which the various ideological trends and political organizations of the Russian revolutionary movement grouped themselves. Even in the social-democratic movement itself this question aroused serious disagreements from the moment events gave it a practical character. From 1904 onwards these differences took the shape of two fundamental trends, Menshevism and Bolshevism. The Menshevik point of view was that our revolution would be a *bourgeois* revolution, i.e., that its natural consequence would be the transfer of power to the bourgeoisie and the creation of conditions for bourgeois parliamentarism. The point of view of Bolshevism, while recognizing the inevitability of the bourgeois character of the coming revolution, put forward as the task of the revolution the establishment of a democratic republic by means of the dictatorship of the proletariat and the peasantry.

The social analysis of the Mensheviks was extremely superficial and in essence reduced itself to crude historical analogies—the typical method of 'educated' philistines. Neither the fact that the development of Russian capitalism had created extraordinary contradictions at both its poles, reducing the role of bourgeois democracy to insignificance, nor the experience of subsequent events, restrained the Mensheviks from an indefatigable search for 'true', 'real' democracy, which would place itself at the head of the 'nation' and establish parliamentary and so far as possible democratic conditions for capitalist development. Always and

everywhere the Mensheviks strove to find signs of the development
of bourgeois democracy, and where they could not find them they
invented them. They exaggerated the importance of every
'democratic' declaration and demonstration, at the same time
belittling the forces of the proletariat and the prospects before its
struggle. So fanatically did they strive to find this leading
bourgeois democracy, in order to secure the 'legitimate' bourgeois
character of the Russian Revolution alleged to be required by the
laws of history, that during the Revolution itself, when no leading
bourgeois democracy was to be found, the Mensheviks themselves
undertook, with more or less success, to carry out its duties.

Petty-bourgeois democracy without any Socialist ideology,
without any Marxian class preparation, could not, of course, have
acted differently under the conditions of the Russian Revolution,
than did the Mensheviks in the role of the 'leading' party of the
February Revolution. The absence of any serious social
foundation for bourgeois democracy told on the Mensheviks
themselves, because they very soon outlived themselves, and in
the eighth month of the Revolution were thrown aside by the
class struggle.

Bolshevism, on the contrary, was by no means imbued with
faith in the power and strength of revolutionary bourgeois
democracy in Russia. From the very beginning, it acknowledged
the decisive importance of the working class for the coming
Revolution, but as to the programme of the Revolution itself the
Bolsheviks limited it at first to the interests of the many millions
of peasants, without and against whom the Revolution could not
have been carried through to the end by the proletariat. Hence
their acknowledgement (for the time being) of the *bourgeois*-
democratic character of the Revolution.

As regards the estimation of the inner forces of the Revolution
and its prospects, the author, at that period, adhered neither to one
nor to the other of the main trends in the Russian Labour
movement. The standpoint he then supported can be outlined
as follows: the Revolution, having begun as a bourgeois
revolution as regards its first tasks, will soon call forth powerful
class conflicts and will gain final victory only by transferring
power to the only class capable of standing at the head of the

oppressed masses, namely, to the proletariat. Once in power, the proletariat not only will not want, but will not be able to limit itself to a bourgeois democratic programme. It will be able to carry through the Revolution to the end only in the event of the Russian Revolution being converted into a Revolution of the European proletariat. The bourgeois-democratic programme of the Revolution will then be superseded, together with its national limitations, and the temporary political domination of the Russian working class will develop into a prolonged Socialist dictatorship. But should Europe remain inert the bourgeois counter-revolution will not tolerate the government of the toiling masses in Russia and will throw the country back—far back from a democratic workers' and peasants' republic. Therefore, once having won power, the proletariat cannot keep within the limits of bourgeois democracy. It must adopt the tactics of *permanent revolution*, i.e., must destroy the barriers between the minimum and maximum programme of Social Democracy, go over to more and more radical social reforms and seek direct and immediate support in revolution in Western Europe. This position is developed and argued in the work now reissued, which was originally written in 1904-1906.

In maintaining the standpoint of the permanent revolution during a period of 15 years, the author nevertheless fell into error in his estimation of the contending factions of the social-democratic movement. As both of them started out from the standpoint of *bourgeois* revolution, the author was of the opinion that the divergencies existing between them would not be so deep as to justify a split. At the same time, he hoped that the further course of events would clearly prove the weakness and insignificance of Russian bourgeois democracy, on the one hand, and on the other, the objective impossibility of the proletariat limiting itself to a democratic programme. This he thought would remove the ground from under factional differences.

Having stood outside both of the two factions in the period of emigration, the author did not fully appreciate the very important circumstance that in reality, along the line of the disagreement between Bolsheviks and Mensheviks, there were being grouped inflexible revolutionaries on the one side and, on the other, elements which were becoming more and more opportunist and accommodating. When the Revolution of 1917 broke out, the Bolshevik Party constituted a strong centralized organization uniting all the best elements of the advanced workers and revolutionary intellectuals, which—after some internal struggle— frankly adopted tactics directed towards the socialist dictatorship of the working class, in full harmony with the entire international situation and class relations in Russia. As to the Menshevik faction, it had, by that time, just ripened sufficiently to be able to assume, as I said before, the duties of bourgeois democracy.

In offering to the public this reprint of his book at the present time, the author not only desires to explain the theoretical principles which rendered it possible for him and other comrades, who for many years had stood outside the Bolshevik Party, to join their fate with the fate of that party at the beginning of 1917 (such a personal explanation would not provide a sufficient reason for the reprinting of the book), but also to recall the social-historical analysis of the motive forces of the Russian Revolution from which followed the conclusion that the seizure of political power by the working class could and must be the task of the Russian Revolution, long before the proletarian dictatorship had become an accomplished fact. The fact that it is possible for us now to re-issue without alteration this pamphlet written in 1906 and conceived in its fundamental lines already in 1904, is sufficient proof that Marxist theory is not on the side of the Menshevik substitutes for bourgeois democracy but on the side of the party which actually carries out the dictatorship of the working class.

The final test of a theory is experience. Irrefutable proof of our having correctly applied Marxist theory is given by the fact that the events in which we are now participating, and even our methods of participation in them, were foreseen in their fundamental lines some 15 years ago.

As an appendix we reprint an article which was published in the Paris *Nashe Slovo* for October 17th, 1915, entitled 'The Struggle for Power'. This article had a polemical purpose and was a criticism of the programmatic 'Letter' addressed to 'Comrades in Russia' by the leaders of the Mensheviks. In it we drew the conclusion that the development of class relations during the ten years after the revolution of 1905 had yet further undermined the Menshevik hope for a bourgeois democracy, and that thereby, obviously, the fate of the Russian Revolution was more than ever bound up with the question of the dictatorship of the proletariat . . . In the face of the battle of ideas of all these many preceding years, one must indeed be a blockhead to speak of the 'adventurism' of the October Revolution!

Talking of the attitude of the Mensheviks to the Revolution, one cannot but mention the Menshevik degeneration of Kautsky, who in the 'theories' of Martov, Dan and Tsereteli now finds the expression of his own theoretical and political decay. After October 1917, we heard from Kautsky that, although the conquest of political power by the working class should be regarded as the historic task of the Social-Democratic Party, nevertheless, as the Russian Communist Party had failed to come to power through the particlar door and according to the particular timetable fixed for it by Kautsky, the Soviet Republic ought to be handed over for correction to Kerensky, Tsereteli and Chernov. Kautsky's reactionary-pedantic criticism must have come the more unexpectedly to those comrades who had gone through the period of the first Russian Revolution with their eyes open and had read Kautsky's articles of 1905-1906. At that time Kautsky (true, not without the beneficial influence of Rosa Luxemburg) fully understood and acknowledged that the Russian Revolution could not terminate in a bourgeois-democratic republic but must inevitably lead to the proletarian dictatorship, because of the level attained by the class struggle in the country itself and because of the entire international situation of capitalism. Kautsky then frankly wrote about a workers' government with a social-democratic majority. He did not even think of making the real course of the class struggle depend on the changing and superficial combinations of political democracy.

At that time, Kautsky understood that the Revolution would begin for the first time to rouse the many millions of peasants and urban petty-bourgeoisie and that not all at once but gradually, layer by layer, so that when the struggle between the proletariat and the capitalist bourgeoisie reached its climax, the broad peasant masses would still be at a very primitive level of political development and would give their votes to intermediary political parties reflecting only the backwardness and the prejudices of the peasant class. Kautsky understood then that the proletariat, led by the logic of the revolution toward the conquest of power, could not arbitrarily postpone this act indefinitely, because by this self-abnegation it would merely clear the field for counter-revolution. Kautsky understood then that, once having seized revolutionary power, the proletariat would not make the fate of the revolution depend upon the passing moods of the least conscious, not yet awakened masses at any given moment, but that, on the contrary, it would turn the political power concentrated in its hands into a mighty apparatus for the enlightenment and organization of these same backward and ignorant peasant masses. Kautsky understood that to call the Russian Revolution a bourgeois revolution and thereby to limit its tasks would mean not to understand anything of what was going on in the world. Together with the Russian and Polish revolutionary Marxists, he rightly acknowledged that, should the Russian proletariat conquer power before the European proletariat, it would have to use its situation as the ruling class not for the rapid surrender of its positions to the bourgeoisie but for rendering powerful assistance to the proletarian revolution in Europe and throughout the world. All these world-wide prospects, imbued with the spirit of Marxian doctrine, were not made dependent either by Kautsky or by us upon how and for whom the peasants would vote at the elections to the so-called Constituent Assembly in November and December 1917.

Now, when the prospects outlined 15 years ago have become reality, Kautsky refuses to grant a birth-certificate to the Russian Revolution for the reason that its birth has not been duly registered at the political office of bourgeois democracy. What an astonishing fact! What an incredible degradation of Marxism! One can say with full justice that the decay of the Second International has found in this philistine judgment on the Russian Revolution by one of its greatest theoreticians a still more hideous expression than in the voting of the War credits on August 4, 1914.

For decades Kautsky developed and upheld the ideas of social revolution. Now that it has become reality, Kautsky retreats before it in terror. He is horrified at the Russian Soviet power and takes up a hostile attitude towards the mighty movement of the German Communist proletariat. Kautsky resembles to the life a miserable schoolmaster, who for many years has been repeating a description of spring to his pupils within the four walls of his stuffy schoolroom, and when at last, at the sunset of his days as a teacher, he comes out into the fresh air, does not recognize spring, becomes furious (in so far as it is possible for this schoolmaster to become furious) and tries to prove that spring is not spring after all but only a great disorder in nature, because it is taking place against the laws of natural history. It is well that the workers do not trust even to the most authoritative pedants, but trust the voice of spring!

We, disciples of Marx, together with the German workers, stand by our conviction that the spring of revolution has arrived fully in accordance with the laws of social nature, and at the same time in accordance with the laws of Marxist theory, for Marxism is not a schoolmaster's pointer rising above history, but a social analysis of the ways and means of the historic process which is really going on.

I have left the text of the two works—that of 1906 and that of 1915—without any alterations. Originally I intended to supply the text with notes which would bring it up to date; but on looking through the text I had to renounce this intention. If I wanted to go into details, I should have to double the size of the book, for which I have no time at present—and, besides, such a 'two-storeyed' book would hardly be convenient for the reader. And, what is more important, I consider that the train of ideas in its main ramifications very nearly approaches the conditions of our time, and the reader who takes the trouble to get more thoroughly acquainted with this book will easily be able to supplement the exposition it gives with the necessary data taken from the experience of the present Revolution.

L. TROTSKY

March 12, 1919. The Kremlin

RESULTS AND PROSPECTS

The Revolution in Russia came unexpectedly to everybody but the Social Democrats. Marxism long ago predicted the inevitability of the Russian Revolution, which was bound to break out as a result of the conflict between capitalist development and the forces of ossified absolutism. Marxism estimated in advance the social character of the coming revolution. In calling it a bourgeois revolution, Marxism thereby pointed out that the *immediate objective* tasks of the revolution consisted in the creation of 'normal conditions for the development of bourgeois society as a whole'.

Marxism has proved to be right, and this is now past the need for discussion or proof. The Marxists are now confronted by a task of quite another kind: to discover the 'possibilities' of the developing revolution by means of an analysis of its internal mechanism. It would be a stupid mistake simply to identify our revolution with the events of 1789-93 or of 1848. Historical analogies, by which liberalism lives and is nurtured, cannot take the place of social analysis.

The Russian Revolution has a quite peculiar character, which is the result of the peculiar trend of our entire social and historical development, and which in its turn opens before us quite new historical prospects.

I. THE PECULIARITIES OF RUSSIAN HISTORICAL DEVELOPMENT

If we compare social development in Russia with social development in the other European countries—bracketing the latter together in respect of that which their history has in common and which distinguishes it from the history of Russia— we can say that the main characteristic of Russian social development is its comparative primitiveness and slowness.

We shall not dwell here on the natural causes of this primitiveness, but the fact itself remains indubitable: Russian social life has been built up on a poorer and more primitive economic foundation.

Marxism teaches that the development of the forces of production determines the social-historical process. The formation of economic corporations, classes and estates is only possible when this development has reached a certain level. Estate* and class differentiation, which is determined by the development of the division of labour and the creation of more specialized social functions, presupposes that the part of the population employed on immediate material production produces a surplus over and above its own consumption: it is only by alienating this surplus that non-producing classes can arise and take shape. Furthermore,

---

*i.e., a section of pre-capitalist society possessing formally laid-down rights and duties. Cf. the 'third estate', i.e., those who were neither nobles nor clergy, in pre-revolutionary France. (Trans.)

the division of labour among the producing classes themselves is possible only at a certain degree of development of agriculture, capable of ensuring the supply of agricultural produce to the non-agricultural population. These fundamental propositions of social development were already clearly formulated by Adam Smith.

Hence it follows that, although the Novgorod period of our history coincides with the beginning of the European Middle Ages, the slow pace of economic development caused by the natural-historical conditions (less favourable geographical situation, sparse population) was bound to hamper the process of class formation and to give it a more primitive character.

It is difficult to say what shape Russian social development would have taken if it had remained isolated and under the influence of inner tendencies only. It is enough to say that this did not happen. Russian social life, built up on a certain internal economic foundation, has all the time been under the influence, even under the pressure, of its external social-historical milieu.

When this social and state organization, in the process of its formation, came into collision with other, neighbouring organizations, the primitiveness of the economic relations of the one and the comparatively high development of the others played decisive parts in the ensuing process.

The Russian state, which grew up on a primitive economic basis, entered into relations and came into conflict with state organizations built upon higher and more stable foundations. Two possibilities presented themselves: either the Russian State was to succumb in its struggle with them, as the Golden Horde had succumbed in its struggle with the Moscow State, or it was to overtake them in the development of economic relations and absorb a great deal more vital forces than it could have done had it remained isolated. The economy of Russia, however, was already *sufficiently* developed to prevent the former happening. The State did not break down but started growing under the terrible pressure of economic forces.

Thus, the main thing was not that Russia was surrounded by enemies on all sides. This alone does not explain the position.

Indeed, this would apply to any other European country, except, perhaps, England. In their mutual struggle for existence, these states depended upon more or less identical economic bases and therefore the development of their state organizations was not subject to such powerful *external* pressure.

The struggle against the Crimean and Nogai Tatars called forth the utmost exertion of effort. But this was, of course, not greater than the exertion of effort during the hundred years' war between France and England. It was not the Tatars who compelled Old Russia to introduce firearms and create the standing regiments of Streltsi; it was not the Tatars who later on forced her to form knightly cavalry and infantry forces, but the pressure of Lithuania, Poland and Sweden.

As a consequence of this pressure on the part of Western Europe, the State swallowed up an inordinately large part of the surplus produce; i.e., it lived at the expense of the privileged classes which were being formed, and so hampered their already slow development. But that was not all. The State pounced upon the 'necessary product' of the farmer, deprived him of his livelihood, caused him to flee from the land upon which he had not even had time to settle—and thus hampered the growth of the population and the development of the productive forces. Thus, inasmuch as the State swallowed up a disproportionately large part of the *surplus* product, it hampered the already slow differentiation between estates; inasmuch as it took away an important part of the *necessary* product it destroyed even those primitive production bases upon which it depended.

But in order to exist, to function, and therefore, above all, to alienate the part of the social product it required, *the State needed a hierarchical organization of estates*. This is why, while undermining the economic foundations of its development, it simultaneously strove to force the development of these foundations by Government measures, and—like any other State—strove to turn this development of estates to its own advantage. Milyukov, the historian of Russian culture, sees in this a direct contrast to the history of Western Europe. But there is no contrast here.

The estates-monarchy of the Middle Ages, which grew into bureaucratic absolutism, constituted a state form reinforcing certain definite social interests and relations. But this state form itself, once it had arisen and was in being, had its own interests (dynastic, court, bureaucratic . . .) which came into conflict not only with the interests of the lower but even with those of the higher estates. The dominating estates, which constituted the socially indispensable 'middle wall' between the masses of the people and the State organization, exercised pressure on the latter and made their own interests the content of the State's practical activity. At the same time, the State power, as an independent force, also looked upon the interests of the higher estates from *its own* point of view. It developed resistance to their aspirations and tried to subject them to itself. The actual history of the relations between State and estates proceeded along resultant lines, determined by the correlation of forces.

A process identical in fundamentals took place in Russia.

The State strove to make use of the developing economic groups, to subject them to its own specialized financial and military interests. The dominating economic groups, as they arose, strove to use the State to consolidate their advantages in the form of estate privileges. In this play of social forces, the resultant went much more in favour of the State power than was the case in the history of Western Europe. The exchange of services between the State power and the upper social groups, at the expense of the working masses, which finds its expression in the distribution of rights and obligations, of burdens and privileges, was less advantageous to the nobility and clergy in Russia than in the mediaeval estates-monarchies of Western Europe. This is beyond doubt. Nevertheless, it would be a great exaggeration and contrary to all sense of proportion to say that while in the West the estates created the State, in Russia the State power created the estates in its own interests (as Milyukov does).

Estates cannot be created by State action, by law. Before one or another social group can take shape as a privileged estate with the help of the State power, it must have developed economically with all its social advantages. Estates cannot be manufactured according to a previously established scale of ranks or according to the code of the Légion d'Honneur. The State power can but assist, with all its resources, the elementary economic process which brings forward higher economic formations. As indicated above, the Russian State consumed a comparatively large share of the forces of the nation, thus hampering the process of social crystallization, but it needed this process for its own purposes. It is natural, therefore, that under the influence and the pressure of its more differentiated Western milieu, a pressure that was transmitted through the military-state organization, the State in its turn strove to force the development of social differentiation on a primitive economic foundation. Furthermore, the very need for forcing, caused by the weakness of the social-economic formations, made it natural that the State in its efforts as guardian should have tried to use its preponderant power to direct the very development of the upper classes according to its own discretion. But on the way to the achievement of great success in this direction, the State first found itself baulked by its own weakness and the primitive character of its own organization, which was due, as we have seen, to the primitiveness of the social structure.

Thus, the Russian State, erected on the basis of Russian economic conditions, was being pushed forward by the friendly, and even more by the hostile, pressure of the neighbouring State organizations, which had grown up on a higher economic basis. From a certain moment—especially from the end of the seventeenth century—the State strove with all its power to accelerate the country's natural economic development. New branches of handicraft, machinery, factories, big industry, capital, were, so to say, artificially grafted on the natural economic stem. Capitalism seemed to be an offspring of the State.

From this standpoint it could be said that all Russian science is the artificial product of government effort, an artificial grafting on the natural stem of national ignorance.*

Russian thought, like the Russian economy, developed under the direct pressure of the higher thought and more developed

---

*It is sufficient to recall the characteristic features of the original relations between the State and the school to realize that the latter was, at the very least, just as 'artificial' a product of the State as the factory was. The educational efforts of the State illustrate this 'artificiality'. Pupils who played truant were put in chains. The whole school was in chains. Study was a form of service. Pupils were paid wages, etc., etc.—L.T.

economies of the West. Since, owing to the natural-economy character of economic conditions, i.e., the poor development of foreign trade, relations with other countries bore a predominantly State character, the influence of these countries found expression in fierce struggle for the existence of the State before expressing itself in direct economic competition. Western economics influenced Russian economics through the intermediary of the State. In order to be able to survive in the midst of better-armed hostile countries, Russia was compelled to set up factories, organize navigation schools, publish textbooks on fortification, etc. But if the general course of the internal economy of this enormous country had not been moving in this same direction, if the development of economic conditions had not created the demand for general and applied science, all the efforts of the State would have been fruitless. The national economy, which was naturally developing from natural economy to money-commodity economy, responded only to those measures of the Government which corresponded to its development and only to the extent that they corresponded to it. The history of Russian industry, of the Russian currency system, and of State credit, are the best possible evidence for the above opinion.

'The majority of the branches of industry (metal, sugar, petroleum, distilling, even the textile industry),' writes Professor Mendeleyev, 'were originated under the direct influence of Government measures, sometimes even with the help of large Government subsidies, but especially because the Government always consciously followed the policy of Protection. In the reign of Alexander, the Government frankly inscribed this policy on its banner. . . . The higher Government circles, fully accepting the principles of Protection in application to Russia, proved to be more advanced than our educated classes as a whole.' (D. Mendeleyev, *Towards the Understanding of Russia*, St. Petersburg, 1906, p. 84).

The learned panegyrist of industrial Protection forgets to add that the policy of the Government was dictated not by any concern to develop industrial forces, but purely by fiscal and in part military-technical considerations. For this reason, the policy of Protection was often opposed, not only to the fundamental interests of industrial development but even to the private interests of various groups of businessmen. Thus, the cotton-mill owners openly declared that 'the high duties on cotton are being maintained not with a view to encouraging cotton-growing but exclusively for fiscal interests'. As in the 'creation' of estates the Government was pursuing, above all, the aims of the State, so also in 'planting' industry, its main concern was directed towards the requirements of the State Exchequer. There is no doubt, however, that the autocracy played no small part in transplanting the factory system of production on to Russian soil.

At the moment when developing bourgeois society began to feel a need for the political institutions of the West, the autocracy proved to be armed with all the material might of the European States. It rested upon a centralized bureaucratic machine which was quite useless for establishing new relations but was able to develop great energy in carrying out systematic repressions. The enormous distances of the country had been overcome by the telegraph, which imparts confidence to the actions of the administration and gives relative uniformity and rapidity to its proceedings (in the matter of repressions). The railways render it possible to throw military forces rapidly from one end of the country to the other. The pre-revolutionary governments of Europe hardly knew railways and telegraphs. The army at the disposal of absolutism was colossal—and if it proved useless in the serious trials of the Japanese War, it was nevertheless good enough for internal domination. Not only the Government of France before the great Revolution, but even the Government of 1848, knew nothing similar to the Russian army of today.

While exploiting the country to the utmost by means of its fiscal and military machine, the Government brought its yearly budget up to the huge figure of two milliard roubles. Supported by its army and its budget, the autocratic government made the European Stock Exchange its exchequer, and the Russian taxpayer thus became a hopeless tributary of this European Stock Exchange.

Thus, in the eighties and nineties of the nineteenth century, the Russian Government confronted the world as a colossal military-bureaucratic and fiscal—Stock-Exchange organization of invincible power.

The financial and military might of the absolute monarchy overwhelmed and blinded not only the European bourgeoisie but also Russian liberalism, which lost all faith in the possibility of trying conclusions with absolutism in an open measurement of strength. The military and financial might of absolutism seemed to exclude any chance whatever for the Russian Revolution. But in reality just the opposite proved to be the case.

The more a government is centralized and the more independent it is of society, the sooner it becomes an autocratic organization standing above society. The greater the financial and military forces of such an organization are, the longer and more successfully can it continue its struggle for existence. The centralized State with its budget of two milliards, its debt of eight milliards and its army of many millions of men under arms, could continue to exist long after it had ceased to satisfy the most elementary needs of social development—not only the needs of internal administration but even the needs of military security, for the maintenance of which it was originally formed.

The longer such a state of affairs dragged on, the greater became the contradiction between the needs of economic and cultural development and the policy of the Government, which had developed its mighty 'milliard-fold' inertia. After the epoch of the 'great patchwork reforms'—which not only did not eliminate these contradictions but on the contrary for the first time vividly revealed them—had been left behind, it became ever more difficult, and psychologically ever more impossible, for the Government voluntarily to take the path of parliamentarism. The only way out of these contradictions which its situation indicated to society was through the accumulation of sufficient steam within the boiler of absolutism to burst it.

Thus, the administrative, military and financial power of absolutism, thanks to which it could exist in spite of social development, not only did not exclude the possibility of revolution, as was the opinion of the liberals, but, on the contrary, made revolution the only way out; furthermore, this revolution was guaranteed in advance an all the more radical character in proportion as the great might of absolutism dug an abyss between itself and the nation. Russian Marxism can justly be proud of having alone explained the direction of this development and foretold its general forms,* while the liberals fed themselves on the most utopian 'practicalism' and the revolutionary 'Narodniki' lived on phantasmagoria and a belief in miracles.

The entire preceding social development made revolution inevitable. What, then, were the forces of this revolution?

---

*Even such a reactionary bureaucrat as Professor Mendeleyev cannot but admit this. Speaking about the development of industry, he observes: ' The socialists perceived something here and even partly understood it, but went astray, following their Latinism [!], recommending resort to force, pandering to the brutal instincts of the mob and striving towards revolutions and power,' (*Towards the Understanding of Russia*, p. 120).

II. THE TOWNS AND CAPITAL

Urban Russia is a product of very recent history; more precisely, of the last few decades. At the end of the reign of Peter I, in the first quarter of the eighteenth century, the town population numbered somewhat more than 328,000, i.e., about 3 per cent of the total population of the country. At the end of the same century, it amounted to 1,301,000, about 4.1 per cent of the total population. By 1812 the urban population had risen to 1,653,000, which was equivalent to 4.4 per cent of the total. By the middle of the nineteenth century it was still no more than 3,482,000— 7.8 per cent of the total. Finally, according to the last census (1897) the population of the towns numbered 16,289,000, i.e., about 13 per cent of the total population.*

If we consider the town as a social-economic formation and not merely as an administrative unit, we must admit that the above figures do not give a true picture of urban development: the history of the Russian State shows us numerous instances where charters were granted to or withdrawn from towns for reasons which were far from scientific. Nevertheless, these figures do clearly show the insignificance of the towns in pre-Reform Russia and their feverishly rapid growth during the last decade. According to the calculations of Mikhailovsky, the increase in the

---

* These figures are taken from Milyukov's *Essays*. The urban population of *all* Russia, including Siberia and Finland, was given by the 1897 census as 17,122,000, or 13.25 per cent of the total (Mendeleyev, *Towards the Understanding of Russia*, St. Petersburg, 1906, 2 vols., table on p. 90).

urban population between 1885 and 1887 was equivalent to 33.8 per cent, i.e., more than double the increase in the population of Russia as a whole (15.25 per cent), and nearly three times the increase in the rural population (12.7 per cent). If we add to this the industrial villages and hamlets, the rapid growth of the urban (in the sense of non-agricultural) population appears more clearly still.

But the modern Russian towns differ from the old ones not only in the number of their inhabitants but also in their social type: they are centres of commercial and industrial life. The majority of our old towns played hardly any economic role; they were military and administrative centres or fortresses, their inhabitants were employed in one or another form of State service and lived at the expense of the exchequer, and in general the city was an administrative, military and tax-collecting centre.

When a non-service population settled within the precincts of the town or on its outskirts, for protection against enemies, this did not in the slightest degree interfere with their continuing with their former agricultural pursuits. Even Moscow, the largest town in old Russia, was, according to M. Milyukov, simply 'a royal manor, a considerable portion of the population of which was connected in one way or another with the court, either as members of the suite, as guards, or as servants. Out of over 16,000 households, according to the census of 1701, not more than 7,000, that is, 44 per cent, were settlers and craftsmen, and even these lived in the State suburb and worked for the palace. The remaining 9,000 belonged to the clergy (1,500) and the ruling estate'. Thus, the Russian towns, like the towns under the Asiatic despotisms, and in contrast to the craft and trading towns of the European Middle Ages, played only the role of *consumers*. In the same period the towns of the West more or less successfully established the principle that craftsmen had no right to live in the villages, but the Russian towns never strove after such aims. Where, then, were manufacturing industry and the crafts? In the country, attached to agriculture.

The low economic level, with the intense depredations of the State, did not permit of any accumulation of wealth or social division of labour. The shorter summer in comparison with the

West allowed a longer winter leisure. Owing to these factors, manufacturing industry was never separated from agriculture and was not concentrated in the towns, but remained in the country-side as an occupation auxiliary to agriculture. When, in the second half of the nineteenth century, capitalist industry began to develop widely, it did not encounter any urban crafts but, in the main, only village handicraft. 'For the one and a half million factory workers, at the most, that there are in Russia', writes M. Milyukov, 'there are still not less than four million peasants engaged in domestic manufactures in their own villages, who continue to carry on at the same time their agricultural occupations. This is the very class from which . . . the European factories arose, but which did not in the slightest degree participate . . . in the setting up of Russia's factories.'

Of course, the further growth of the population and of its productivity created a basis for the social division of labour. This naturally applied also to the urban crafts. As a result, however, of the economic pressure of the advanced countries, this basis was seized by large-scale capitalist industry, so that the town handicrafts had no time to develop.

The four million rural craftsmen comprised the very element which, in Europe, formed the nucleus of the town population, entered the guilds as masters or journeymen, and subsequently found themselves more and more left outside the guilds. It was precisely the craftsman class that constituted the bulk of the population in the most revolutionary quarters of Paris during the Great Revolution. This fact alone—the insignificance of our urban crafts—had immeasurable consequence for our revolution.*

The essential economic feature of the modern town lies in the fact that it works up raw materials supplied by the country. For that reason conditions of transport are decisive for it. Only the introduction of railways could so greatly widen the sources of supply for the town as to make it possible to concentrate such large masses of people. The necessity for concentrating the

---

*At a time when uncritical comparison between the Russian revolution and the French revolution of 1789 had become commonplace, Parvus very sagaciously pointed out this fact as being responsible for the particular destiny of the Russian revolution.—L.T.

population arose out of the growth of large factory industry. The nucleus of the population of a modern town, at least of a town possessing some economic and political significance, is the sharply differentiated class of wage-workers. It was this class, as yet substantially unknown during the period of the Great French Revolution, that was destined to play the decisive role in our revolution.

The factory industrial system not only brings the proletariat to the forefront but also cuts the ground from under the feet of bourgeois democracy. In previous revolutions the latter found its support in the urban petty-bourgeoisie: craftsmen, small shopkeepers, etc.

Another reason for the disproportionately large political role played by the Russian proletariat is the fact that Russian capital is to a considerable extent of foreign origin. This fact, according to Kautsky, resulted in the growth of the number, strength and influence of the proletariat being out of proportion to the growth of bourgeois liberalism.

As we have said above, capitalism in Russia did not develop out of the handicraft system. It conquered Russia with the economic culture of the whole of Europe behind it, and before it, as its immediate competitor, the helpless village craftsman or the wretched town craftsman, and it had the half-beggared peasantry as a reservoir of labour-power. Absolutism assisted in various ways in fettering the country with the shackles of capitalism.

In the first place it converted the Russian peasant into a tributary of the Stock Exchanges of the world. The absence of capital within the country and the government's constant need for money created a field for usurious foreign loans. From the reign of Catharine II to the ministry of Witte and Durnovo, the Amsterdam, London, Berlin and Paris bankers systematically strove to convert the autocracy into a colossal Stock-Exchange speculation. A considerable part of the so-called internal loans, i.e., loans realized through the home credit departments, were in no way distinguished from foreign loans, because they were in reality placed with foreign capitalists. Proletarianising and pauperising the peasantry by heavy taxation, absolutism converted the millions of the European Stock Exchange into soldiers and battleships, into prisons and into railways. The greater part of this expenditure was, from the economic point of view, absolutely non-productive. An enormous share of the national product was sent abroad in the form of interest, and enriched and strengthened the financial aristocracy of Europe. The European financial bourgeoisie, whose political influence in parliamentary countries during the last ten years has grown uninterruptedly and has forced the commercial and industrial capitalists into the background, converted, it is true, the Tsarist Government into its vassal; but it could not and did not desire to become a component part of the bourgeois opposition within Russia. It was guided in its sympathies and antipathies by the principles formulated by the Dutch bankers Hoppe and Co., in the conditions for the loan to Tsar Paul in 1798: 'interest must be paid *irrespective of political circumstances*'. The European Stock Exchange was even directly interested in the maintenance of absolutism, for no other government could guarantee such usurious interest. State loans, however, were not the only means whereby European capital was imported into Russia. The very money, payment of which absorbed a good part of the Russian State budget, returned to the territory of Russia in the form of commercial-industrial capital attracted by the untouched natural wealth of the country, and especially by the unorganized labour-power, which so far had not been accustomed to put up any resistance. The latter period of our industrial boom of 1893-99 was also a period of intensified immigration of European capital. Thus it was capital which, as before, remained largely European and which realized its political power in the parliaments of France and Belgium, that mobilised the working class in Russia.

By economically enslaving this backward country, European capital projected its main branches of production and methods of communication across a whole series of intermediate technical and economic stages through which it had had to pass in its countries of origin. But the fewer obstacles it met with in the path of its *economic* domination, the more insignificant proved to be its political role.

The European bourgeoisie developed out of the Third Estate of the Middle Ages. It raised the standard of protest against the pillage and violence carried on by the first two estates, in the name of the interests of the people which it itself desired to exploit. The estates-monarchy of the Middle Ages, in its process of conversion into bureaucratic absolutism, relied on the population of the towns in its struggle against the pretensions of the clergy and the nobility. The bourgeoisie made use of this for its own political elevation. Thus, bureaucratic absolutism and the capitalist class developed simultaneously, and when these two came into conflict, in 1789, the bourgeoisie proved to have the whole nation behind it.

Russian absolutism developed under the direct pressure of the Western states. It copied their methods of government and administration much earlier than economic conditions here permitted the rise of a capitalist bourgeoisie. It already disposed of a tremendous standing army and a centralised, bureaucratic and fiscal machine, and had entered into irredeemable debt to the European bankers, at a time when the Russian towns still played an absolutely insignificant economic role.

Capital intruded from the West with the direct co-operation of absolutism, and in a short period converted a number of old archaic towns into centres of trade and industry, and even created, in a short time, commercial and industrial towns in places that previously had been absolutely uninhabited. This capital frequently appeared in the form of large impersonal shareholding companies. During the ten years of the industrial booms of 1893-1902 the total share capital increased by two milliard roubles, whereas during 1854-92 it had increased by only 900 millions. The proletariat immediately found itself concentrated in tremendous masses, while between these masses and the autocracy there stood a capitalist bourgeoisie, very small in numbers, isolated from the 'people', half-foreign, without historical traditions, and inspired only by the greed for gain.

III.   1789 — 1848 — 1905

History does not repeat itself.   However much one may compare the Russian Revolution with the Great French Revolution, the former can never be transformed into a repetition of the latter.   The 19th century has not passed in vain.

The year 1848 already differs tremendously from 1789.   In comparison with the Great Revolution, the Prussian and Austrian Revolutions surprise one with their insignificant sweep.   In one way they took place too early and in another too late.   That gigantic exertion of strength which is necessary for bourgeois society to settle radically with the lords of the past can only be attained *either by the power of a unanimous nation* rising against feudal despotism, or by the mighty development of the *class struggle* within this nation striving to emancipate itself.   In the first case, which was what happened in 1789-93, the national energy, compressed by the fierce resistance of the old order, was wholly expended in the struggle against reaction; in the second case, which has never yet occurred in history, and which we are considering merely as a possibility, the actual energy necessary for overcoming the dark forces of history is generated within the bourgeois nation by means of an 'internecine' class war.   The severe internal friction, absorbing a great deal of energy and depriving the bourgeoisie of the possibility of playing the chief role, urges its antagonist the proletariat to the forefront, gives the proletariat ten years' experience in a month, places it at the head of affairs, and hands it the tightly-drawn reins of power. This class, determined, knowing no doubts, imparts a mighty sweep to events.

Revolution can be achieved either by a nation gathering itself together like a lion preparing to spring, or by a nation in the process of struggle becoming conclusively divided in order to free the best part of itself for the execution of those tasks which the nation as a whole is unable to carry out. These are two opposite sets of historical conditions, which in their pure form are, of course, possible only in logical contraposition.

A middle course in this, as in so many cases, is worst of all, but it was this middle course that developed in 1848.

In the heroic period of French history we saw a bourgeoisie, enlightened, active, as yet not aware of the contradictions of its own position, upon whom history had imposed the task of leadership in the struggle for a new order, not only against the outworn institutions of France but also against the reactionary forces of the whole of Europe. The bourgeoisie, consistently, in all its factions, regarded itself as the leader of the nation, rallied the masses to the struggle, gave them slogans and dictated their fighting tactics. Democracy bound the nation together with a political ideology. The people—urban petty-bourgeois, peasants and workers—elected bourgeois as their deputies, and the instructions given these deputies by their constituents were written in the language of a bourgeoisie coming to awareness of its messianic mission. During the revolution itself, though class antagonisms were revealed, yet the powerful inertia of the revolutionary struggle consistently threw the more conservative elements of the bourgeoisie off the political path. No stratum was thrown off before it had transferred its energy to the stratum behind it. The nation as a whole continued therefore to struggle for its aims with sharper and more determined methods. When the upper layers of the rich bourgeoisie, breaking away from the national core which had entered into the movement, formed an alliance with Louis XVI, the democratic demands of the nation were directed *against* this bourgeoisie, and this led to universal suffrage and the republic, as the logical, inevitable form of democracy.

The Great French Revolution was indeed a national revolution. And what is more, within the national framework, the world struggle of the bourgeoisie for domination, for power, and for undivided triumph found its classical expression.

Jacobinism is now a term of reproach on the lips of all liberal wiseacres. Bourgeois hatred of revolution, its hatred towards the masses, hatred of the force and grandeur of the history that is made in the streets, is concentrated in one cry of indignation and fear—*Jacobinism*! We, the world army of Communism, have long ago made our historical reckoning with Jacobinism. The whole of the present international proletarian movement was formed and grew strong in the struggle against the traditions of Jacobinism. We subjected its theories to criticism, we exposed its historical limitations, its social contradictoriness, its utopianism, we exposed its phraseology, and broke with its traditions, which for decades had been regarded as the sacred heritage of the revolution.

But we defend Jacobinism against the attacks, the calumny, and the stupid vituperations of anaemic, phlegmatic liberalism. The bourgeoisie has shamefully betrayed all the traditions of its historical youth, and its present hirelings dishonour the graves of its ancestors and scoff at the ashes of their ideals. The proletariat has taken the honour of the revolutionary past of the bourgeoisie under its protection. The proletariat, however radically it may have, in practice, broken with the revolutionary traditions of the bourgeoisie, nevertheless preserves them, as a sacred heritage of great passions, heroism and initiative, and its heart beats in sympathy with the speeches and acts of the Jacobin Convention.

What gave liberalism its charm if not the traditions of the Great French Revolution? At what other period did bourgeois democracy rise to such a height and kindle such a great flame in the hearts of the people as during the period of the Jacobin, *sansculotte*, terrorist, Robespierrian democracy of 1793?

What else but Jacobinism made and still makes it possible for French bourgeois-radicalism of various shades to keep the overwhelming majority of the people and even the proletariat under its influence at a time when bourgeois radicalism in

Germany and Austria has closed its brief history in deeds of pettiness and shame?

What is it if not the charm of Jacobinism, with its abstract political ideology, its cult of the Sacred Republic, its triumphant declarations, that even now nourishes French radicals and radical-socialists like Clemenceau, Millerand, Briand and Bourgeois, and all those politicians who know how to defend the mainstays of bourgeois society no worse than the dull-witted Junkers of Wilhelm II By the Grace of God? They are envied hopelessly by the bourgeois democrats of other countries; and yet they shower calumnies upon the source of their political advantage— heroic Jacobinism.

Even after many hopes had been destroyed, Jacobinism remained in the memory of the people as a tradition. For a long time the proletariat spoke of its future in the language of the past. In 1840, almost half a century after the government of the ' Mountain', eight years before the June days of 1848, Heine visited several workshops in the *faubourg* of Saint-Marceau and saw what the workers, 'the soundest section of the lower classes', were reading. ' I found there', he wrote to a German newspaper, 'several new speeches by old Robespierre and also pamphlets by Marat issued in two-sous editions; Cabet's *History of the Revolution*; the malignant lampoons of Carmenen; the works of Buonarroti, *The Teachings and Conspiracy of Babeuf*, all productions reeking with blood. . . . As one of the fruits of this seed,' prophesies the poet, 'sooner or later a republic will threaten to spring up in France.'

In 1848 the bourgeoisie was already unable to play a comparable role. It did not want and was not able to undertake the revolutionary liquidation of the social system that stood in its path to power. We know now *why* that was so. Its aim was— and of this it was perfectly conscious—to introduce into the old system the necessary guarantees, not for its political domination, but merely for a sharing of power with the forces of the past. It was meanly wise through the experience of the French bourgeoisie, corrupted by its treachery and frightened by its failures. It not only failed to lead the masses in storming the old order, but

placed its back against this order so as to repulse the masses
who were pressing it forward.

The French bourgeoisie succeeded in bringing off its Great
Revolution. Its consciousness was the consciousness of society
and nothing could become established as an institution without
first passing through its consciousness as an aim, as a problem of
political creation. It often resorted to theatrical poses in order to
hide from itself the limitations of its own bourgeois world—but
it marched forward.

The German bourgeoisie, however, from the very start, did
not 'make' the revolution, but dissociated itself from it. Its
consciousness rose against the objective conditions for its own
domination. The revolution could only be carried out not by it
but against it. Democratic institutions represented to its mind
not an aim to fight for but a menace to its welfare.

In 1848 a class was needed that would be able to take charge
of events without and in spite of the bourgeoisie, a class which
would not only be prepared to push the bourgeois forward by its
pressure but also at the decisive moment to throw its political
corpse out of the way. Neither the urban petty-bourgeoisie nor
the peasants were able to do this.

The *urban petty bourgeoisie* was hostile not only to yesterday
but also to the morrow. Still enmeshed in mediaeval relations,
but already unable to stand against 'free' industry, still setting its
imprint on the towns, but already giving way before the middle
and big bourgeoisie, steeped in prejudice, deafened by the noise
of events, exploited and exploiting, greedy and helpless in its
greed, the petty bourgeoisie, left stranded, could not control the
tremendous events of the day.

The *peasantry* was to an even larger extent deprived of
independent political initiative. Shackled for centuries, poverty-
stricken, furious, uniting in itself all the threads of the old
exploitation and the new, the peasantry at a certain moment
constituted a rich source of revolutionary strength; but,
unorganized, scattered, isolated from the towns, the nerve centres
of politics and culture, stupid, limited in their horizons to the
confines of their respective villages, indifferent to everything that
the town was thinking, the peasants could not have any signifi-

cance as a leading force. The peasantry was pacified immediately
its back had been relieved of the burden of feudal obligations,
and repaid the towns, which had fought for its rights, with black
ingratitude. The emancipated peasants became the fanatics of
'order'.

The *intellectual democrats* lacked class power. One moment
this group followed its elder sister, the liberal bourgeoisie, as a
sort of political tail, at another it abandoned the liberal
bourgeoisie at the critical instant in order to expose its own
weakness. It confused itself in unsolved contradictions and
carried this confusion around with it everywhere.

The *proletariat* was too weak, lacked organization, experience
and knowledge. Capitalism had developed sufficiently to render
necessary the abolition of the old feudal relations, but not
sufficiently to bring forward the working class, the product of
the new industrial relations, as a decisive political force. The
antagonism between the proletariat and the bourgeoisie, even
within the national framework of Germany, had gone too far
to allow the bourgeoisie fearlessly to take up the role of national
hegemon, but not sufficiently to allow the working class to take
up that role. The internal friction of the revolution, it is true,
prepared the proletariat for political independence, but at the
time it weakened energy and unity of action, caused a fruitless
expenditure of effort, and compelled the revolution, after its first
successes, to mark time tediously and then, under the blows of
reaction, to retreat.

Austria provided a particularly clear and tragic example of
this unfinished and incomplete character of political relations in
the period of revolution.

The *Viennese proletariat* in 1848 exhibited wonderful heroism
and inexhaustible energy. Again and again it rushed into battle,
urged on only by a hazy class instinct, lacking a general conception of the aims of the struggle, and passing gropingly from
one slogan to another. The leadership of the proletariat,
remarkably enough, passed into the hands of the *students*, the
only active *democratic group* which, owing to its activity, had a
great influence on the masses, and for that reason also upon
events. The students undoubtedly could fight bravely on the

barricades and fraternise honourably with the workers, but they were totally unable to direct the progress of the revolution which had handed them the 'dictatorship' of the street.

The proletariat, unorganized, without political experience and independent leadership, followed the students. At every critical moment the workers invariably offered the 'gentlemen who worked with their heads' the assistance of 'those who worked with their hands'. The students at one moment summoned the workers to battle and at another moment themselves barred their way from the suburbs into the city. Sometimes, using their political authority and relying upon the arms of the Academic Legion, they forbade the workers to put forward their own independent demands. This was a classically clear form of benevolent revolutionary dictatorship *over* the proletariat. What was the outcome of these social relations? Why, this: when, on 26th May, all the workers of Vienna, at the call of the students, rose to their feet in order to resist the disarming of the students (the Academic Legion), when the whole of the population of the capital, covering the entire town with barricades, showed remarkable power and took possession of Vienna, when all Austria was rallying to armed Vienna, when the monarchy was in flight and had lost all importance, when as a result of the pressure of the people the last of the troops had been withdrawn from the capital, when the government of Austria resigned without nominating a successor—there was no political force found to take the helm.

The *liberal bourgeoisie* deliberately refused to take the power secured in such brigand-like fashion; it only dreamed of the return of the Emperor who had fled to the Tyrol.

The *workers* were sufficiently brave to beat the reaction, but were not sufficiently organized and conscious to occupy its place. A powerful labour movement existed, but proletarian class struggle with a definite political aim had not yet been sufficiently developed. The proletariat, incapable of taking the helm, could not accomplish this great historical task and the bourgeois democrats, as often happens, sneaked away at the moment of greatest urgency.

To compel these deserters to fulfil their obligations would have required on the part of the proletariat not less energy and maturity than would have been necessary for the setting up of a provisional workers' government.

Altogether, a position was created concerning which a contemporary accurately said: 'A Republic had actually been set up in Vienna, but unfortunately no one saw this.' The Republic that nobody noticed departed for a long time from the stage, giving place to the Habsburgs . . . An opportunity, once missed, never returns.

From the experience of the Hungarian and German revolutions Lassalle drew the conclusion that from now on revolutions could only find support in the class struggle of the proletariat. In a letter to Marx dated 24th October, 1849, Lassalle writes: ' Hungary had more chances than any other country of bringing its struggle to a successful outcome. Among other reasons this was because the party there was not in a state of division and sharp antagonism as it was in Western Europe; because the revolution, to a high degree, had taken the form of a struggle for national independence. Nevertheless, Hungary was defeated, and precisely as a consequence of the treachery of the *national* party.'

' This, and the history of Germany during 1848-49,' continues Lassalle, 'brings me to the conclusion that no revolution can be successful in Europe, unless it is from the very first proclaimed to be purely socialistic. No struggle can be successful if social questions enter into it only as a sort of hazy element, and remain in the background, and if it is carried on under the banner of national regeneration or bourgeois republicanism.'

We shall not stop to criticise these very decided conclusions. It is undoubtedly true, however, that already in the middle of the nineteenth century the problem of political emancipation could not be solved by the unanimous and concerted tactics of the pressure of the whole nation. Only the independent tactics of the proletariat, gathering strength for the struggle from its class position, and only from its class position, could have secured victory for the revolution.

The Russian working class of 1906 in no way resembles the workers of Vienna of 1848. The best evidence of this is the springing up all over Russia of the Soviets of Workers' Deputies.

These were not previously-prepared conspirative organizations for the purpose of seizure of power by the workers at the moment of revolt. No, these were organs created in a planned way by the masses themselves for the purpose of co-ordinating their revolutionary struggle. And these Soviets, elected by the masses and responsible to the masses, are unquestionably democratic institutions, conducting a most determined class policy in the spirit of revolutionary socialism.

The social peculiarities of the Russian revolution are particularly evident in the question of the arming of the nation. A militia, the National Guard, was the first demand and the first gain of every revolution, in 1789 and in 1848, in Paris, in all the states of Italy, in Vienna and in Berlin. In 1848 the National Guard, i.e, the arming of the propertied and the 'educated' classes, was the demand of the whole of the bourgeois opposition, even of the most moderate, and its object was not only to safeguard the liberties won, or rather, subject to 'conferment', against reversals from above, but also to protect bourgeois private property from attacks by the proletariat. Thus the demand for a militia was clearly a class demand of the bourgeoisie. ' The Italians very well understood', says the English liberal historian of united Italy, 'that an armed civil militia would make the further existence of despotism impossible. Besides this it was a guarantee for the propertied classes against possible anarchy and any sort of disorder from below.'* And the ruling reaction, not having a sufficient number of troops in the centre of operations to deal with 'anarchy', that is with the revolutionary masses, armed the bourgeoisie. Absolutism first allowed the burghers to suppress and pacify the workers and then it disarmed and pacified the burghers.

In Russia the demand for a militia found no support in the bourgeois parties. The liberals cannot help understanding the serious significance of arms; absolutism has given them some object-lessons in this respect. But they also understand the absolute impossibility of creating a militia in Russia apart from or against the proletariat. The Russian workers do not resemble

---

* Bolton King, *History of Italian Unity,* Russ. trans., Moscow 1901, vol. I, p. 220.—L.T.

the workers of 1848 who filled their pockets with stones and armed themselves with picks while the shopkeepers, students and lawyers had royal muskets on their shoulders and swords at their sides.

Arming the revolution, in Russia, means first and foremost arming the workers. Knowing and fearing this, the liberals altogether eschew a militia. They even surrender their position to absolutism without a fight just as the bourgeois Thiers surrendered Paris and France to Bismarck simply to avoid arming the workers.

In that manifesto of the liberal-democratic coalition, the symposium called *The Constitutional State*, Mr. Dzhivelegov, discussing the possibility of revolutions, quite rightly says that ' Society itself, at the necessary moment, must be prepared to stand up in defence of its Constitution'. But as the logical conclusion from this is the demand for the arming of the people, this liberal philosopher finds it 'necessary to add' that 'it is not at all necessary for everyone to bear arms'* in order to prevent reversals. It is only necessary that society itself shall be prepared to offer resistance—in what manner is not indicated. If any conclusion at all can be drawn from this, it is that in the hearts of our democrats the fear of the armed proletariat is greater than the fear of the soldiery of the autocracy.

For that reason the task of arming the revolution falls with all its weight upon the proletariat. The civil militia, the class demand of the bourgeoisie in 1848 is, in Russia, from the very first a demand for the arming of the people and above all for the arming of the proletariat. The fate of the Russian Revolution is bound up with this question.

---

* *The Constitutional State*, a symposium, 1st edition, p. 49.—L.T.

IV. REVOLUTION AND THE PROLETARIAT

Revolution is an open measurement of strength between social forces in a struggle for power. The State is not an end in itself. It is only a machine in the hands of the dominating social forces. Like every machine it has its motor, transmitting and executive mechanism. The driving force of the State is class interest; its motor mechanism is agitation, the press, church and school propaganda, parties, street meetings, petitions and revolts. The transmitting mechanism is the legislative organization of caste, dynastic, estate or class interests represented as the will of God (absolutism) or the will of the nation (parliamentarism). Finally, the executive mechanism is the administration, with its police, the courts, with their prisons, and the army.

The State is not an end in itself, but is a tremendous means for organizing, disorganizing and reorganizing social relations. It can be a powerful lever for revolution or a tool for organized stagnation, depending on the hands that control it.

Every political party worthy of the name strives to capture political power and thus place the State at the service of the class whose interests it expresses. The Social-Democrats, being the party of the proletariat, naturally strive for the political domination of the working class.

The proletariat grows and becomes stronger with the growth of capitalism. In this sense the development of capitalism is also the development of the proletariat towards dictatorship. But the day and the hour when power will pass into the hands of the working class depends directly not upon the level attained by the productive forces but upon relations in the class struggle, upon the international situation, and, finally, upon a number of subjective factors: the traditions, the initiative and the readiness to fight of the workers.

It is possible for the workers to come to power in an economically backward country sooner than in an advanced country. In 1871 the workers deliberately took power in their hands in petty-bourgeois Paris—true, for only two months, but in the big-capitalist centres of Britain or the United States the workers have never held power for so much as an hour. To imagine that the dictatorship of the proletariat is in some way automatically dependent on the technical development and resources of a country is a prejudice of 'economic' materialism simplified to absurdity. This point of view has nothing in common with Marxism.

In our view, the Russian revolution will create conditions in which power can pass into the hands of the workers—and in the event of the victory of the revolution it must do so—*before* the politicians of bourgeois liberalism get the chance to display to the full their talent for governing.

Summing up the revolution and counter-revolution of 1848-49 in the American newspaper *The Tribune*, Marx wrote: ' The working class in Germany is, in its social and political develop- ment, as far behind that of England and France as the German bourgeoisie is behind the bourgeoisie of those countries. Like master, like man. The evolution of the conditions of existence for a numerous, strong, concentrated and intelligent proletarian class goes hand in hand with the development of the conditions of existence for a numerous, wealthy, concentrated and powerful middle class. The working-class movement itself never is independent, never is of an exclusively proletarian character until all the different factions of the middle class, and particularly its most progressive faction, the large manufacturers, have conquered political power, and remodelled the State according to their wants. It is then that the inevitable conflict between the employer and the employed becomes imminent, and cannot be adjourned any longer . . .'*

This quotation is probably familiar to the reader, for it has been considerably abused by the textual Marxists in recent times. It has been brought forward as an irrefutable argument against the idea of a working class government in Russia. 'Like master, like man.' If the capitalist bourgeoisie is not strong enough to take power, they argue, then it is still less possible to establish a workers' democracy, i.e., the political domination of the proletariat.

Marxism is above all a method of analysis—not analysis of texts, but analysis of social relations. Is it true that, in Russia, the weakness of capitalist liberalism inevitably means the weakness of the labour movement? Is it true, for Russia, that there cannot be an independent labour movement until the bourgeoisie has conquered power? It is sufficient merely to put these questions to see what a hopeless formalism lies concealed beneath the attempt to convert an historically-relative remark of Marx's into a supra-historical axiom.

During the period of the industrial boom, the development of factory industry in Russia bore an 'American' character; but in its actual dimensions capitalist industry in Russia is an infant compared with the industry of the United States. Five million persons—16.6 per cent of the economically occupied population— are engaged in manufacturing industry in Russia; for the U.S.A. the corresponding figures would be six million and 22.2 per cent. These figures still tell us comparatively little, but they become eloquent if we recall that the population of Russia is nearly twice that of the U.S.A. But in order to appreciate the actual dimensions of Russian and American industry it should be observed that in 1900 the American factories and large workshops turned out goods for sale to the amount of 25 milliard roubles, while in the same period the Russian factories turned out goods to the value of less than two and a half milliard roubles.†

---

* Marx, *Germany in 1848-50*, Russ. trans., Alexeyeva edition, 1905, pp. 8-9.—L.T. [i.e., *Germany : Revolution and Counter-Revolution*, Ch. I ; *Selected Works of Karl Marx*, 1942 edition, Vol. II, p. 46.]

† D. Mendeleyev, *Towards the Understanding of Russia*, 1906, p. 99.—L.T.

There is no doubt that the numbers, the concentration, the culture and the political importance of the industrial proletariat depend on the extent to which capitalist industry is developed. But this dependence is not direct. Between the productive forces of a country and the political strength of its classes there cut across at any given moment various social and political factors of a national and international character, and these displace and even sometimes completely alter the political expression of economic relations. In spite of the fact that the productive forces of the United States are ten times as great as those of Russia, nevertheless the political role of the Russian proletariat, its influence on the politics of its own country and the possibility of its influencing the politics of the world in the near future are incomparably greater than in the case of the proletariat of the United States.

Kautsky, in his recent book on the American proletariat, points out that there is no direct relation between the political power of the proletariat and the bourgeoisie, on the one hand, and the level of capitalist development on the other. 'Two states exist' he says, 'diametrically contrasted one with the other. In one of them there is developed inordinately, i.e., out of proportion to the level of the development of the capitalist mode of production, one of the elements of the latter, and in the other, another of these elements. In one state—America—it is the capitalist class, while in Russia it is the proletariat. In no other country than America is there so much basis for speaking of the dictatorship of capital, while the militant proletariat has nowhere acquired such importance as in Russia. This importance must and undoubtedly will increase, because this country only recently began to take a part in the modern class struggle, and has only recently provided a certain amount of elbow room for it.' Pointing out that Germany, to a certain extent, may learn its future from Russia, Kautsky continues: ' It is indeed most extraordinary that the Russian proletariat should be showing us our future, in so far as this is expressed not in the extent of the development of capital, but in the protest of the working class. The fact that this Russia is the most backward of the large states of the capitalist world would appear', observes

Kautsky, 'to contradict the materialist conception of history, according to which economic development is the basis of political development; but really', he goes on to say, 'this only contradicts the materialist conception of history as it is depicted by our opponents and critics, who regard it not as a *method of investigation* but merely as a ready-made *stereotype*.'* We particularly recommend these lines to our Russian Marxists, who replace independent analysis of social relations by deductions from texts, selected to serve every occasion in life. Nobody compromises Marxism so much as these self-styled Marxists.

Thus, according to Kautsky, Russia stands on an economically low level of capitalist development, politically it has an insignificant capitalist bourgeoisie and a powerful revolutionary proletariat. This results in the fact that 'struggle for the interests of *all* Russia has fallen to the lot of the *only now-existing strong class in the country*—the industrial proletariat. For this reason the industrial proletariat has tremendous political importance, and for this reason the struggle for the emancipation of Russia from the incubus of absolutism which is stifling it has become converted into a *single combat between absolutism and the industrial proletariat,* a single combat in which the peasants may render considerable support but cannot play a leading role.'

Does not all this give us reason to conclude that the Russian 'man' will take power sooner than his 'master'?

*   *   *

There can be two forms of political optimism. We can exaggerate our strength and advantages in a revolutionary situation and undertake tasks which are not justified by the given correlation of forces. On the other hand, we may optimistically set a limit to our revolutionary tasks—beyond which, however, we shall inevitably be driven by the logic of our position.

It is possible to limit the scope of all the questions of the revolution by asserting that our revolution is *bourgeois* in its objective aims and therefore in its inevitable results, closing our

---

*K. Kautsky, *American and Russian Workers,* Russian translation, St. Petersburg, 1906, pp. 4 and 5.—L.T.

eyes to the fact that the chief actor in this bourgeois revolution is the proletariat, which is being impelled towards power by the entire course of the revolution.

We may reassure ourselves that in the framework of a bourgeois revolution the political domination of the proletariat will only be a passing episode, forgetting that once the proletariat has taken power in its hands it will not give it up without a desperate resistance, until it is torn from its hands by armed force.

We may reassure ourselves that the social conditions of Russia are still not ripe for a socialist economy, without considering that the proletariat, on taking power, must, by the very logic of its position, inevitably be urged toward the introduction of state management of industry. The general sociological term *bourgeois revolution* by no means solves the politico-tactical problems, contradictions and difficulties which the mechanics of a *given* bourgeois revolution throw up.

Within the framework of the bourgeois revolution at the end of the eighteenth century, the objective task of which was to establish the domination of capital, the dictatorship of the *sansculottes* was found to be possible. This dictatorship was not simply a passing episode, it left its impress upon the entire ensuing century, and this in spite of the fact that it was very quickly shattered against the enclosing barriers of the bourgeois revolution. In the revolution at the beginning of the twentieth century, the direct objective tasks of which are also bourgeois, there emerges as a near prospect the inevitable, or at least the probable, political domination of the proletariat. The proletariat itself will see to it that this domination does not become a mere passing 'episode', as some realist philistines hope. But we can even now ask ourselves: is it inevitable that the proletarian dictatorship should be shattered against the barriers of the bourgeois revolution, or is it possible that in the given *world-historical* conditions, it may discover before it the prospect of victory on breaking through these barriers? Here we are confronted by questions of tactics: should we consciously work towards a working-class government in proportion as the development of the revolution brings this stage nearer, or must we at that moment regard political power as a misfortune which the bourgeois revolution is ready to thrust upon the workers, and which it would be better to avoid?

Ought we to apply to ourselves the words of the 'realist' politician Vollmar in connection with the Communards of 1871: ' Instead of taking power they would have done better to go to sleep' . . .?

V. THE PROLETARIAT IN POWER AND THE PEASANTRY

In the event of a decisive victory of the revolution, power will pass into the hands of that class which plays a leading role in the struggle—in other words, into the hands of the proletariat. Let us say at once that this by no means precludes revolutionary representatives of non-proletarian social groups entering the government. They can and should be in the government: a sound policy will compel the proletariat to call to power the influential leaders of the urban petty-bourgeoisie, of the intellectuals and of the peasantry. The whole problem consists in this: *who will determine the content of the government's policy, who will form within it a solid majority?*

It is one thing when representatives of the democratic strata of the people enter a government with a workers' majority, but it is quite another thing when representatives of the proletariat participate in a definitely bourgeois-democratic government in the capacity of more or less honoured hostages.

The policy of the liberal capitalist bourgeoisie, in all its waverings, retreats and treacheries, is quite definite. The policy of the proletariat is even more definite and finished. But the policy of the intellectuals, owing to their socially intermediate character and their political elasticity; the policy of the peasantry, in view of their social diversity, their intermediate position and their primitiveness; the policy of the urban petty-bourgeoisie, once again owing to its lack of character, its intermediate position and its complete lack of political tradition—the policy of these three social groups is utterly indefinite, unformed, full of possibilities and therefore full of surprises.

It is sufficient to try to imagine a revolutionary democratic government without representatives of the proletariat to see immediately the senselessness of such a conception. The refusal of the social-democrats to participate in a revolutionary government would render such a government quite impossible and would thus be equivalent to a betrayal of the revolution. But the participation of the proletariat in a government is also objectively most probable, and permissible in principle, only as a *dominating and leading participation.* One may, of course, describe such a government as the dictatorship of the proletariat and peasantry, a dictatorship of the proletariat, peasantry and intelligentsia, or even a coalition government of the working class and the petty-bourgeoisie, but the question nevertheless remains: who is to wield the hegemony in the government itself, and through it in the country? And when we speak of a workers' government, by this we reply that the hegemony should belong to the working class.

The National Convention, as an organ of the Jacobin dictatorship, was by no means composed of Jacobins alone. More than that—the Jacobins were in a minority in it; but the influence of the *sansculottes* outside the walls of the Convention, and the need for a determined policy in order to save the country, gave power into the hands of the Jacobins. Thus, while the Convention was *formally* a national representation, consisting of Jacobins, Girondists and the vast wavering Centre known as the 'marsh', *in essence* it was a dictatorship of the Jacobins.

When we speak of a workers' government we have in view a government in which the working-class representatives dominate and lead. The proletariat, in order to consolidate its power, cannot but widen the base of the revolution. Many sections of the working masses, particularly in the countryside, will be drawn into the revolution and become politically organized only after the advance-guard of the revolution, the urban proletariat, stands at the helm of state. Revolutionary agitation and organization will then be conducted with the help of state resources. The legislative power itself will become a powerful instrument for revolutionizing the masses. The nature of our social-historical relations, which lays the whole burden of the bourgeois revolution upon the shoulders of the proletariat, will not only create tremendous difficulties for the workers' government but, in the first period of its existence at any rate, will also give it invaluable advantages. This will affect the relations between the proletariat and the peasantry.

In the revolutions of 1789-93 and 1848 power first of all passed from absolutism to the moderate elements of the bourgeoisie, and it was the latter class which emancipated the peasantry (*how*, is another matter) before revolutionary democracy received or was even preparing to receive power. The emancipated peasantry lost all interest in the political stunts of the 'townspeople', that is, in the further progress of the revolution, and placing itself like a heavy foundation-stone at the foot of 'order', betrayed the revolution to the Caesarist or *ancien-régime-*absolutist reaction.

The Russian revolution does not, and for a long time will not, permit the establishment of any kind of bourgeois-constitutional order that might solve the most elementary problems of democracy. All the 'enlightened' efforts of reformer-bureaucrats like Witte and Stolypin are nullified by their own struggle for existence. Consequently, the fate of the most elementary revolutionary interests of the peasantry—even the peasantry *as a whole*, as an *estate*, is bound up with the fate of entire revolution, i.e., with the fate of the proletariat.

The proletariat in power will stand before the peasants as the class which has emancipated it. The domination of the proletariat will mean not only democratic equality, free self-government, the transference of the whole burden of taxation to the rich classes, the dissolution of the standing army in the armed people and the abolition of compulsory church imposts, but also recognition of all revolutionary changes (expropriations) in land relationships carried out by the peasants. The proletariat will make these changes the starting-point for further state measures in agriculture.

Under such conditions the Russian peasantry in the first and most difficult period of the revolution will be interested in the maintenance of a proletarian régime (workers' democracy) at all events not less than was the French peasantry in the maintenance of the military régime of Napoleon Bonaparte, which guaranteed to the new property-owners, by the force of its bayonets, the inviolability of their holdings. And this means that the representative body of the nation, convened under the leadership of the proletariat, which has secured the support of the peasantry, will be nothing else than a democratic dress for the rule of the proletariat.

But is it not possible that the peasantry may push the proletariat aside and take its place? This is impossible. All historical experience protests against this assumption. Historical experience shows that the peasantry are absolutely incapable of taking up an *independent* political role.*

The history of capitalism is the history of the subordination

---

*Does the fact of the rise and development first of the Peasant Union and then of the Group of Toil (Trudoviki) in the Duma run counter to these and subsequent arguments? Not in the least. What is the Peasant Union? A Union that embraces some elements of the radical democracy who are looking for masses to support them, together with the more conscious elements of the peasantry—obviously *not* the lowest strata of the peasantry—on the platform of a democratic revolution and agrarian reform.

As to the agrarian programme of the Peasant Union ('equality in the use of land'), which is the meaning of its existence, the following must be observed: the wider and deeper the development of the agrarian movement and the sooner it comes to the point of confiscation and distribution of land, the sooner will the process of disintegration set in in the Peasant Union, in consequence of a thousand contradictions of a class, local, everyday and technical nature. Its members will exercise their share of influence in the Peasants' Committees, the organs of the agrarian revolution in the villages, but needless to say the Peasants' Committees, *economic-administrative* institutions, will not be able to abolish the *political* dependence of the country upon the town, which forms one of the fundamental features of modern society.

The radicalism and formlessness of the Group of Toil was the expression of the contradictoriness in the revolutionary aspirations of the peasantry. During the period of constitutional illusions it helplessly followed the 'Cadets' (Constitutional Democrats). At the moment of the dissolution of the Duma it came naturally under the guidance of the Social-Democratic Group. The lack of independence on the part of the peasant representatives will show itself with particular clearness at the moment when it becomes necessary to show firm initiative, that is, at the time when power has to pass into the hands of the revolutionaries.—L.T.

of the country to the town. The industrial development of the European towns in due course rendered the further existence of feudal relations in agriculture impossible. But the countryside itself never produced a class which could undertake the revolutionary task of abolishing feudalism. The town, which subordinated agriculture to capital, produced a revolutionary force which took political hegemony over the countryside into its hands and spread revolution in state and property relations into the countryside. As further development has proceeded, the country has finally fallen into economic enslavement to capital, and the peasantry into political enslavement to the capitalist parties. These parties have revived feudalism in parliamentary politics, converting the peasantry into a domain for their electoral hunting expeditions. The modern bourgeois state, by means of taxation and militarism, throws the peasant into the clutches of usurers' capital, and by means of state priests, state schools and the corruptions of barrack life makes him a victim of usurers' politics.

The Russian bourgeoisie will surrender the entire revolutionary position to the proletariat. It will also have to surrender the revolutionary hegemony over the peasants. In such a situation, created by the transference of power to the proletariat, nothing remains for the peasantry to do but to rally to the régime of workers' democracy. It will not matter much even if the peasantry does this with a degree of consciousness not larger than that with which it usually rallies to the bourgeois régime. But while every bourgeois party commanding the votes of the peasantry hastens to use its power in order to swindle and deceive the peasants and then, if the worst comes to the worst, gives place to another capitalist party, the proletariat, relying on the peasantry, will bring all forces into play in order to raise the cultural level of the countryside and develop the political consciousness of the peasantry. From what we have said above, it will be clear how we regard the idea of a 'proletarian and peasant dictatorship'. It is not really a matter of whether we regard it as admissible in principle, whether 'we do or do not desire' such a form of political co-operation. We simply think that it is unrealisable —at least in a direct immediate sense.

Indeed, such a coalition presupposes either that one of the existing bourgeois parties commands influence over the peasantry or that the peasantry will have created a powerful independent party of its own, but we have attempted to show that neither the one nor the other is possible.

VI. THE PROLETARIAN REGIME

The proletariat can only achieve power by relying upon a national upsurge and national enthusiasm. The proletariat will enter the government as the revolutionary representative of the nation, as the recognized national leader in the struggle against absolutism and feudal barbarism. In taking power, however, it will open a new epoch, an epoch of revolutionary legislation, of positive policy, and in this connection it cannot at all be sure of retaining the role of the recognized expressor of the will of the nation. The first measures of the proletariat, cleansing the Augean stables of the old régime and driving out its inmates, will meet with the active support of the whole nation, in spite of what the liberal eunuchs may say about the tenacity of certain prejudices among the masses of the people.

This political cleansing will be supplemented by a democratic reorganization of all social and state relations. The workers' government will be obliged, under the influence of direct pressures and demands, to intervene decisively in all relationships and events . . .

Its first task will have to be the dismissal from the army and administration of all those who are stained with the blood of the people, and the cashiering or disbandment of the regiments which have most sullied themselves with crimes against the people. This will have to be done in the very first days of the revolution, that is, long before it is possible to introduce the system of elected and responsible officials and organize a national militia. But the matter will not end there. Workers' democracy will immediately be confronted by questions of the length of the working day, the agrarian question, and the problem of unemployment.

One thing is clear. Every passing day will deepen the policy of the proletariat in power, and more and more define its *class character*. Side by side with that, the revolutionary ties between the proletariat and the nation will be broken, the class disintegration of the peasantry will assume political form, and the antagonism between the component sections will grow in proportion as the policy of the workers' government defines itself, ceasing to be a general-democratic and becoming a class policy.

Though the absence of accumulated bourgeois-individualistic traditions and anti-proletarian prejudices among the peasantry and intellectuals will assist the proletariat to come into power, it is necessary on the other hand to bear in mind that this absence of prejudices is due not to political consciousness but to political barbarism, social formlessness, primitiveness and lack of character. None of these features can in any way create a reliable basis for a consistent, active proletarian policy.

The abolition of feudalism will meet with support from the *entire* peasantry, as the burden-bearing estate. A progressive income-tax will also be supported by the great majority of the peasantry. But any legislation carried through for the purpose of protecting the agricultural proletariat will not only not receive the active sympathy of the majority, but will even meet with the active opposition of a minority of the peasantry.

The proletariat will find itself compelled to carry the class struggle into the villages and in this manner destroy that community of interest which is undoubtedly to be found among all peasants, although within comparatively narrow limits. From the very first moment after its taking power, the proletariat will have to find support in the antagonisms between the village poor and village rich, between the agricultural proletariat and the agricultural bourgeoisie. While the heterogeneity of the peasantry creates difficulties and narrows the basis for a proletarian policy, the insufficient degree of class differentiation will create obstacles to the introduction among the peasantry of developed class struggle, upon which the urban proletariat could rely. The primitiveness of the peasantry turns its hostile face towards the proletariat.

The cooling-off of the peasantry, its political passivity, and all the more the active opposition of its upper sections, cannot but have an influence on a section of the intellectuals and the petty-bourgeoisie of the towns.

Thus, the more definite and determined the policy of the proletariat in power becomes, the narrower and more shaky does the ground beneath its feet become. All this is extremely probable and even inevitable . . .

The two main features of proletarian policy which will meet opposition from the allies of the proletariat are *collectivism* and *internationalism*.

The primitiveness and petty-bourgeois character of the peasantry, its limited rural outlook, its isolation from world-political ties and allegiances, will create terrible difficulties for the consolidation of the revolutionary policy of the proletariat in power.

To imagine that it is the business of Social Democrats to enter a provisional government and lead it during the period of revolutionary-democratic reforms, fighting for them to have a most radical character, and relying for this purpose upon the organized proletariat—and then, after the democratic programme has been carried out, to leave the edifice they have constructed so as to make way for the bourgeois parties and themselves go into opposition, thus opening up a period of parliamentary politics, is to imagine the thing in a way that would compromise the very idea of a workers' government. This is not because it is inadmissible 'in principle'—putting the question in this abstract form is devoid of meaning— but because it is absolutely unreal, it is utopianism of the worst sort—a sort of revolutionary-philistine utopianism.

For this reason:

The division of our programme into maximum and minimum programmes has a profound and tremendous principled significance during the period when power lies in the hands of the bourgeoisie. The very fact of the bourgeoisie being in power drives out of our minimum programme all demands which are incompatible with private property in the means of production. Such demands form the content of a socialist revolution and presuppose a proletarian dictatorship.

Immediately, however, that power is transferred into the hands of a revolutionary government with a socialist majority, the division of our programme into maximum and minimum loses all significance, both in principle and in immediate practice. A proletarian government under no circumstances can confine itself within such limits. Take the question of the eight-hour day. As is known, this by no means contradicts capitalist relations, and therefore it forms an item in the minimum programme of Social Democracy. But let us imagine the actual introduction of this measure during a period of revolution, in a period of intensified class passions; there is no question but that this measure would then meet the organized and determined resistance of the capitalists in the form, let us say, of lockouts and the closing down of factories.

Hundreds of thousands of workers would find themselves thrown on the streets. What should the government do? A bourgeois government, however radical it might be, would never allow affairs to reach this stage because, confronted with the closing-down of factories, it would be left powerless. It would be compelled to retreat, the eight-hour day would not be introduced and the indignant workers would be suppressed.

Under the political domination of the proletariat, the intro-duction of an eight-hour day should lead to altogether different consequences. For a government that desires to rely upon the proletariat, and not on capital, as liberalism does, and which does not desire to play the role of an 'impartial' intermediary of bourgeois democracy, the closing down of factories would not of course be an excuse for increasing the working day. For a workers' government there would be only one way out: expropriation of the closed factories and the organization of production in them on a socialized basis.

Of course, one can argue in this way: we will suppose that the workers' government, true to its programme, issues a decree for an eight-hour day; if capital puts up a resistance which cannot be overcome by the resources of a democratic programme based on the preservation of private property, the Social Democrats will resign and appeal to the proletariat. Such a solution would be a solution only from the standpoint of the group constituting the membership of the government, but it would be no solution for the proletariat or for the development of the revolution. After the resignation of the Social Democrats, the situation would be exactly as it was at the time when they were compelled to take power. To flee before the organized opposition of capital would be a greater betrayal of the revolution than a refusal to take power in the first instance. It would really be far better for the working-class party not to enter the government than to go in so as to expose its own weakness and then to quit.

Let us take another example. The proletariat in power cannot but adopt the most energetic measures to solve the question of unemployment, because it is quite obvious that the representatives of the workers in the government cannot reply to the demands of unemployed workers with arguments about the bourgeois character of the revolution.

But if the government undertakes to maintain the unemployed —it is not important for us at the moment in what form—this would mean an immediate and quite substantial shift of economic power to the side of the proletariat. The capitalists, who in their oppression of the workers always relied upon the existence of a reserve army of labour, would feel themselves *economically* powerless while the revolutionary government, at the same time, doomed them to *political* impotence.

In undertaking the maintenance of the unemployed, the government thereby undertakes the maintenance of strikers. If it does not do *that*, it immediately and irrevocably undermines the basis of its own existence.

There is nothing left for the capitalists to do then but to resort to the lockout, that is, to close the factories. It is quite clear that the employers can stand the closing down of production much longer than the workers, and therefore there is only one reply that a workers' government can give to a general lockout: the expropriation of the factories and the introduction in at least the largest of them of State or communal production.

Similar problems arise in agriculture by the mere fact of the expropriation of the land. In no way must it be supposed that a proletarian government, on expropriating the privately-owned estates carrying on production on a large scale, would break these up and sell them for exploitation to small producers. The only path open to it in this sphere is the organization of co-operative production under communal control or organized directly by the State. But this is the path to Socialism.

All this quite clearly shows that Social Democrats cannot enter a revolutionary government, giving the workers in advance an undertaking not to *give way* on the minimum programme, and at the same time promising the bourgeoisie not to *go beyond* it. Such a bilateral undertaking is absolutely impossible to realize. The very fact of the proletariat's representatives entering the government, not as powerless hostages, but as the leading force, destroys the border-line between maximum and minimum programme; that is to say, it *places collectivism on the order of the day*. The point at which the proletariat will be held up in its advance in this direction depends upon the relation of forces, but in no way upon the original intentions of the proletarian party.

For this reason there can be no talk of any sort of *special* form of proletarian dictatorship in the bourgeois revolution, of *democratic* proletarian dictatorship (or dictatorship of the proletariat and the peasantry). The working class cannot preserve the democratic character of its dictatorship without refraining from overstepping the limits of its democratic programme. Any illusions on this point would be fatal. They would compromise Social Democracy from the very start.

The proletariat, once having taken power, will fight for it to the very end. While one of the weapons in this struggle for the maintenance and the consolidation of power will be agitation and organization, especially in the countryside, another will be a policy of collectivism. Collectivism will become not only the inevitable way forward from the position in which the party in power will find itself, but will also be a means of preserving this position with the support of the proletariat.

When the idea of uninterrupted revolution was formulated in

the socialist press—an idea which connected the liquidation of absolutism and feudalism with a socialist revolution, along with growing social conflicts, uprisings of new sections of the masses, unceasing attacks by the proletariat upon the economic and political privileges of the ruling classes—our 'progressive' press raised a unanimous howl of indignation. ' Oh! ' it cried, 'we have put up with a lot, but we cannot allow this. Revolution,' it cried, 'is not a road that can be "legalised". The application of exceptional measures is only permissible under exceptional circumstances. The aim of the movement for emancipation is not to make revolution permanent but to lead it as soon as possible into the channel of *law*,' etc., etc.

The more radical representatives of this same democracy do not risk taking up a stand against revolution even from the point of view of already-secured constitutional 'gains'. For them this parliamentary cretinism, preceding the rise of parliamentarism itself, does not constitute a strong weapon in the struggle against the proletarian revolution. They choose another path. They take their stand not on the basis of law but on what seems to them the basis of facts—on the basis of historical 'possibility', on the basis of political 'realism' and, finally . . . finally, even on the basis of ' Marxism'. And why not? That pious Venetian bourgeois, Antonio, very aptly said:

' The devil can quote Scripture to his purpose.'

These radical democrats not only regard the idea of a workers' government in Russia as fantastic, but they even deny the possibility of a socialist revolution in Europe in the historical epoch immediately ahead. ' The pre-requisites of revolution', they say, 'are not yet visible.' Is that true? Certainly there is no question of appointing a dateline for the socialist revolution, but it is necessary to point out its real historical prospects.

VII. THE PRE-REQUISITES OF SOCIALISM

Marxism converted socialism into a science, but this does not
prevent some ' Marxists' from converting Marxism into a Utopia.

Rozhkov, arguing against the programme of socialization and
co-operation, presents the 'necessary pre-requisites of the future
society, firmly laid down by Marx', in the following way: 'Are
there already present,' asks Rozhkov, 'the material objective
pre-requisites, consisting of such a development of technique as
would reduce the motive of personal gain and concern for cash
[?], personal effort, enterprise and risk, to a minimum, and which
would thereby make social production a front-rank question?
Such a level of technique is most closely connected with the
almost complete [!] domination of large-scale production in all
[!] branches of the economy. Has such a stage been reached?
Even the subjective, psychological pre-requisites are lacking, such
as the growth of class-consciousness among the proletariat,
developed to such a level as to achieve the spiritual unity of the
overwhelming mass of the people. We know,' continues Rozhkov,
'of producer associations such as the well-known French glassworks at Albi, and several agricultural associations, also in
France, and yet the experience of France shows, as nothing else
can, that even the conditions of so advanced a country are not
sufficiently developed to permit the dominance of co-operation.
These enterprises are of only the average size, their technical
level is not higher than ordinary capitalist undertakings, *they*

are not at the head of industrial development, do not lead it,
but approach a modest average level.

' Only when the experience of individual productive associations
points to their leading rôle in economic life can we say that we
are approaching a new system, only then can we be sure that
the necessary conditions for its existence have been established.'*

While respecting the good intentions of Comrade Rozhkov,
we regretfully have to confess that rarely even in bourgeois
literature have we met such confusion as he betrays with regard
to what are known as the pre-requisites of socialism. It will be
worthwhile dwelling to some extent on this confusion, if not for
the sake of Rozhkov, at least for the sake of the question.

Rozhkov declares that we have not yet reached 'such a stage
of technical development as would reduce the motive of personal
gain and concern for cash [?], personal effort, enterprise and
risk, to a minimum, and which would make social production
a front-rank question'.

It is rather difficult to find the meaning of this passage.
Apparently Rozhkov wishes to say, in the first place, that modern
technique has not yet sufficiently ousted human labour-power
from industry and, secondly, that to secure this elimination would
require the 'almost' *complete domination* of large state enterprises
in *all* branches of the economy, and therefore the 'almost' *complete
proletarianization of the whole population of the country.* These
are the two pre-requisites to socialism alleged to have been 'firmly
laid down by Marx'.

Let us try and imagine the setting of capitalist relations which,
according to Rozhkov, socialism will encounter when it arrives.
' The almost complete domination of large-scale enterprise in all
branches of industry', under capitalism, means, as has been said,
the proletarianization of all small and medium producers in
agriculture and industry, that is to say, the conversion of the
whole of the population into proletarians. But the complete
domination of machine technique in these large undertakings
would lead to the reduction of the employment of human labour-
power to a minimum, and therefore the overwhelming majority

---

* N. Rozhkov, *On the Agrarian Question*, pp. 21 and 22.—L.T.

of the population of the country—say, 90 per cent—would be
converted into a reserve army of labour living at the expense
of the State in workhouses. We said 90 per cent of the population,
but there is nothing to prevent us from being logical and
imagining a state of affairs in which the whole of production
consists of a single automatic mechanism, belonging to a single
syndicate and requiring as living labour only a single trained
orang-outang. As we know, this is the brilliantly consistent theory
of Professor Tugan-Baranovsky. Under such conditions 'social
production' not only occupies 'front rank' but commands the
whole field. Under these circumstances, moreover, *consumption*
would naturally also become *socialized* in view of the fact that
the whole of the nation, except the 10 per cent who own the
trust, will be living at the public expense in workhouses. Thus,
behind Rozhkov we see smiling the familiar face of Tugan-
Baranovsky. Socialism can now come on the scene. The
population emerges from the workhouses and expropriates the
group of expropriators. No revolution or dictatorship of the
proletariat is of course necessary.

The second economic sign of the ripeness of a country for
socialism, according to Rozhkov, is the possibility of the
domination of co-operative production within it. Even in France
the co-operative glassworks at Albi is not on a higher level than
any other capitalist undertaking. Socialist production becomes
possible only when the co-operatives are *in the forefront of
industrial development,* as the *leading* enterprises.

The entire argument from beginning to end is turned inside
out. The co-operatives cannot take the lead in industrial
progress, not because economic development has not gone far
enough, but because it has gone *too far* ahead. Undoubtedly,
economic development creates the basis for co-operation, but for
what kind of co-operation? For capitalist co-operation, based
on wage-labour — every factory shows us a picture of such
capitalist co-operation. With the development of technique
the importance of such co-operation grows also. But in what
manner can the development of capitalism place the co-operative
societies 'in the front rank of industry'? On what does Rozhkov
base his hopes that the co-operative societies can squeeze out the

syndicates and trusts and take their place in the forefront of industrial development? It is evident that if this took place the co-operative societies would then simply have automatically to expropriate all capitalist undertakings, after which it would remain for them to reduce the working day sufficiently to provide work for all citizens and to regulate the amount of production in the various branches in order to avoid crises. In this manner the main features of socialism would be established. Again it is clear that no revolution and no dictatorship of the working class would be at all necessary.

The third pre-requisite is a psychological one: the need for 'the class-consciousness of the proletariat to have reached such a stage as to unite spiritually the overwhelming majority of the people'. As 'spiritual unity', in this instance, must evidently be regarded as meaning conscious socialist solidarity, it follows therefore that Comrade Rozhkov considers that a psychological pre-requisite of socialism is the organization of the 'overwhelming majority of the population' within the Social-Democratic Party. Rozhkov evidently assumes therefore that capitalism, throwing the small producers into the ranks of the proletariat, and the mass of the proletarians into the ranks of the reserve army of labour, will create the possibility for Social Democracy spiritually to unite and enlighten the *overwhelming majority* (90 per cent?) of the people.

This is as impossible of realization in the world of capitalist barbarism as the domination of co-operatives in the realm of capitalist competition. But if this were realizable, then of course, the consciously and spiritually united 'overwhelming majority' of the nation would crush without any difficulty the few magnates of capital and organize socialist economy without revolution or dictatorship.

But here the following question arises. Rozhkov regards Marx as his teacher. Yet Marx, having outlined the 'essential pre-requisites for socialism' in his *Communist Manifesto*, regarded the revolution of 1848 as the immediate prologue to the socialist revolution. Of course one does not require much penetration after 60 years to see that Marx was mistaken, because the capitalist world still exists. But how could Marx have made *this* error? Did he not perceive that large-scale undertakings did not yet dominate in all branches of industry; that producers' co-operatives did not yet stand at the head of the large-scale enterprises; that the overwhelming majority of the people were not yet united on the basis of the ideas set out in the *Communist Manifesto?* If we do not see these things even now, how is it then that Marx did not perceive that nothing of the kind existed in 1848? Apparently, Marx in 1848 was a Utopian youth in comparison with many of the present-day infallible automata of Marxism!

We thus see that although Comrade Rozhkov by no means belongs among the critics of Marx, nevertheless he completely discards the proletarian revolution as an essential pre-requisite of socialism. As Rozhkov has only too consistently expressed the views shared by a considerable number of Marxists in both trends of our party, it is necessary to dwell on the bases in principle and method of the errors he has made.

One must observe in passing that Rozhkov's argument concerning the destiny of the co-operatives is his very own. We have never and nowhere met socialists who both believed in such a simple irresistible progress of the concentration of production and proletarianization of the people and at the same time believed in the dominating role of producers' co-operative societies prior to the proletarian revolution. To unite these two pre-requisites is much more difficult in economic evolution than in one's head; although even the latter had always seemed to us impossible.

But we will deal with two other 'pre-requisites' which constitute more typical prejudices. Undoubtedly, the concentration of production, the development of technique and the growth of consciousness among the masses are essential pre-requisites for socialism. But these processes take place simultaneously, and not only give an impetus to each other, but also retard and *limit* each other. Each of these processes at a higher level demands a certain development of another process at a lower level. But the complete development of each of them is incompatible with the complete development of the others.

The development of technique undoubtedly finds its ideal limit in a single automatic mechanism which takes raw materials from the womb of nature and throws them at the feet of man in the form of finished articles of consumption. If the existence of the capitalist system were not limited by class relations and the revolutionary struggle that arises from them, we should have some grounds for supposing that technique, approaching the ideal of a single automatic mechanism within the framework of the capitalist system, would thereby automatically abolish capitalism.

The concentration of production arising from the laws of competition inherently tends towards proletarianizing the whole population. Isolating this tendency, we should be right in supposing that capitalism would carry out its work to the end, if the process of proletarianization were not interrupted by a revolution; but this is inevitable, given a certain relationship of forces, long before capitalism has converted the majority of the nation into a reserve army, confined to prison-like barracks.

Further — consciousness, thanks to the experience of the everyday struggle and the conscious efforts of the socialist parties, undoubtedly grows progressively, and, isolating this process, we could in imagination follow this growth until the majority of the people were included in the trade unions and political organizations, united by a spirit of solidarity and singleness of aim. If this process could really increase quantitatively without being affected qualitatively, socialism could be realized peaceably by a unanimous, conscious 'civil act' some time in the 21st or the 22nd century.

But the whole point lies in the fact that the processes which are historically pre-requisite for socialism do not develop in isolation, but limit each other, and, reaching a certain stage, determined by numerous circumstances—which, however, is far removed from the mathematical limit of these processes—they undergo a qualitative change, and in their complex combination bring about what we understand by the name of social revolution.

We will begin with the last-mentioned process—the growth of consciousness. This takes place, as we know, not in academies, in which it might be possible artificially to detain the proletariat for fifty, a hundred or five hundred years, but in the course of all-round life in capitalist society, on the basis of unceasing class struggle. The growth of the consciousness of the proletariat transforms this class struggle, gives it a deeper and more purposeful character, which in its turn calls out a corresponding reaction on the part of the dominant class. The struggle of the proletariat against the bourgeoisie will reach its dénouement long before large-scale enterprises begin to dominate in all branches of industry.

Further, it is of course true that the growth of political consciousness depends upon the growth of the numbers of the proletariat, and proletarian dictatorship presupposes that the numbers of the proletariat will be sufficiently large to overcome the resistance of the bourgeois counter-revolution. But this does not at all mean that the 'overwhelming majority' of the population must be proletarians and the 'overwhelming majority' of the proletariat conscious socialists. It is clear, of course, that the conscious revolutionary army of the proletariat must be stronger than the counter-revolutionary army of capital, while the intermediate, doubtful or indifferent strata of the population must be in such a position that the regime of proletarian dictatorship will attract them to the side of the revolution and not repel them to the side of its enemies. Naturally, proletarian policy must consciously take this into consideration.

All this in its turn presupposes the hegemony of industry over agriculture and the domination of town over country.

                    *   *   *

We will now endeavour to examine the pre-requisites of socialism in diminishing order of generality and increasing order of complexity.

1. Socialism is not merely a question of equal distribution but also a question of planned production. Socialism, that is, co-operative production on a large scale, is possible only when the development of productive forces has reached the stage at which large enterprises are more productive than small ones. The more the large enterprises outweigh the smaller, i.e., the more developed technique has become, the more advantageous econo-

mically does socialized production become, and, consequently, the higher must the cultural level of the whole population be as a result of equal distribution based upon planned production.

This first objective pre-requisite of socialism has been in existence a long time—ever since the time when social division of labour led to the division of labour in manufacture. It has existed to an even greater extent since the time when manufacture was replaced by factory, machine production. Large undertakings became more and more advantageous, which also meant that the socialization of these large undertakings would have made society more and more wealthy. It is clear that the transition of all the handicraft workshops to the common ownership of all the handicraftsmen would not have made the latter one whit richer, whereas the transfer of manufactures to the common ownership of their detail-workers, or the transfer of the factories into the hands of the workers employed in them—or, it would be better to say, the transfer of all the means of large factory production into the hands of the whole population—would undoubtedly raise the people's material level; and the higher the stage reached by large-scale production, the higher would be this level.

In socialist literature the instance is often quoted of the English Member of Parliament, Bellers* who, in 1696, i.e., a century before the conspiracy of Babeuf, submitted to Parliament a project for establishing co-operative societies which should independently supply all their own requirements. According to this measure, these producers' co-operatives were to consist of from two to three hundred persons. We cannot here test his argument, nor is it necessary for our purpose; what is important is that collective economy, even if it was conceived only in terms of groups of 100, 200, 300 or 500 persons, was regarded as advantageous from the standpoint of production already at the end of the 17th century.

At the beginning of the 19th century Fourier drew up his schemes for producer-consumer associations, 'phalansteries', each consisting of from 2,000 to 3,000 persons. Fourier's calculations

---

*John Bellers was not an M.P., but a Quaker landowner, who published his scheme in the form of an address to Parliament.

were never distinguished by their exactness; but at all events, the development of manufacture by that time suggested to him a field for economic collectives incomparably wider than in the example quoted above. It is clear, however, that both the associations of John Bellers and the 'phalansteries' of Fourier are much nearer in their character to the free economic communes of which the Anarchists dream, the utopianism of which consists not in their 'impossibility' or in their being 'against nature'— the communist communes in America proved that they were possible—but in that they have lagged 100 to 200 years behind the progress of economic development.

The development of the social division of labour, on the one hand, and machine production on the other, has led to the position that nowadays the only co-operative body which could utilise the advantages of collective production on a wide scale is the State. More than that, socialist production, for both economic and political reasons, could not be confined within the restricting limits of individual states.

Atlanticus,* a German Socialist who did not adopt the Marxist point of view, calculated at the end of last century the economic advantages that would accrue from applying socialist economy in a unit such as Germany. Atlanticus was not at all distinguished by flights of fancy. His ideas generally moved within the circle of the economic routine of capitalism. He based his arguments on the writings of authoritative modern agronomists and engineers. This does not weaken his arguments, rather is it his strong side, because it preserves him from undue optimism. In any case, Atlanticus comes to the conclusion that, with proper organization of socialist economy, with employment of the technical resources of the mid-nineties of the 19th century, the income of the workers could be doubled or trebled, and that the working day could be halved.

One should not imagine, however, that Atlanticus was the first to show the economic advantages of socialism. The greater productivity of labour in large undertakings, on the one hand, and, on the other, the necessity for the planning of production,

---

*G. Jaeckh.

as proved by the economic crises, has been much more convincing evidence for the necessity of socialism than Atlanticus's socialistic book-keeping. His service consists only in that he expressed these advantages in approximate figures.

From what has been said we are justified in arriving at the conclusion that the further growth of the technical power of man will render socialism more and more advantageous; that sufficient technical pre-requisites for collective production have already existed for a hundred or two hundred years, and that at the present moment socialism is *technically advantageous* not only on a national but to an enormous extent also on a world scale.

The mere technical advantages of socialism were not at all sufficient for it to be realized. During the 18th and 19th centuries the advantages of large-scale production showed themselves not in a socialist but in a capitalist form. Neither the schemes of Bellers nor those of Fourier were carried out. Why not? Because there were no social forces existent at that time ready and able to carry them out.

2. We now pass from the productive-technical pre-requisites of socialism to the *social-economic* ones. If we had to deal here not with a society split up by class antagonism, but with a homogeneous community which consciously selects its form of economy, the calculations of Atlanticus would undoubtedly be quite sufficient for socialist construction to be begun. Atlanticus himself, being a socialist of a very vulgar type, thus, indeed, regarded his own work. Such a point of view at the present day could be applied only within the limits of the private business of a single person or of a company. One is always justified in assuming that any scheme of economic reform, such as the introduction of new machinery, new raw materials, a new form of management of labour, or new systems of remuneration, will always be accepted by the owners if only these schemes can be shown to offer a commercial advantage. But in so far as we have to do here with the economy of society, that is not sufficient. Here, opposing interests are in conflict. What is advantageous for one is disadvantageous for another. The

egoism of one class acts not only against the egoism of another, but also to the disadvantage of the whole community. Therefore, in order to realize socialism it is necessary that among the antagonistic classes of capitalist society there should be a social force which is interested, by virtue of its objective position, in the realization of socialism, and which is powerful enough to be able to overcome hostile interests and resistances in order to realize it.

One of the fundamental services rendered by scientific socialism consists in that it theoretically discovered such a social force in the proletariat, and showed that this class, inevitably growing along with capitalism, can find its salvation only in socialism, that the entire position of the proletariat drives it towards socialism and that the doctrine of socialism cannot but become in the long run the ideology of the proletariat.

It is easy to understand therefore what a tremendous step backwards Atalanticus takes when he asserts that, once it is proved that, 'by transferring the means of production into the hands of the State, not only can the general wellbeing be secured, but the working-day also reduced, then it is a matter of indifference whether the theory of the concentration of capital and the disappearance of the intermediate classes of society is confirmed or not'.

According to Atlanticus, immediately the advantages of socialism have been proved, 'it is useless resting one's hopes on the fetish of economic development, one should make extensive investigations and start [!] a comprehensive and thorough preparation for the transition from private to state or "social" production'.*

In objecting to the purely oppositional tactics of the Social Democrats and suggesting an immediate 'start' in preparing the transition to socialism, Atlanticus forgets that the Social Democrats still lack the power needed for this, and that Wilhelm II, Bülow and the majority in the German Reichstag, although they have power in their hands, have not the slightest intention of introducing socialism. The socialist schemes of Atlanticus are

---

*Atlanticus, *The State of the Future*, published by 'Dyelo', St. Petersburg, 1906, pp. 22 and 23.—L.T.

no more convincing to the Hohenzollerns than the schemes of Fourier were to the restored Bourbons, notwithstanding the fact that the latter based his political utopianism on passionate fantasies in the field of economic theory, whereas Atlanticus, in his not less utopian politics, based himself on convincing, philistinely-sober book-keeping.

What level must social differentiation have attained in order that the second pre-requisite for socialism may be realized? In other words, what must be the relative numerical weight of the proletariat? Must it make up a half, two-thirds or nine-tenths of the population? It would be an absolutely hopeless undertaking to try to define the bare arithmetical limits of this second pre-requisite for socialism. In the first place, in such a schematic effort, we should have to decide the question of who is to be included in the category 'proletariat'. Should we include the large class of semi-proletarian semi-peasants? Should we include the reserve masses of the urban proletariat—who on the one hand merge into the parasitical proletariat of beggars and thieves, and on the other fill the city streets as small traders playing a parasitical role in relation to the economic system as a whole? This question is not at all a simple one.

The importance of the proletariat depends entirely on the role it plays in large-scale production. The bourgeoisie relies, in its struggle for political domination, upon its economic power. Before it manages to secure political power, it concentrates the country's means of production in its own hands. This is what determines its specific weight in society. The proletariat, however, in spite of all co-operative phantasmagoria, will be deprived of the means of production right up to the actual socialist revolution. Its social power comes from the fact that the means of production which are in the hands of the bourgeoisie can be set in motion only by the proletariat. From the point of view of the bourgeoisie, the proletariat is also one of the means of production, constituting, in conjunction with the others, a single unified mechanism. The proletariat, however, is the only non-automatic part of this mechanism, and in spite of all efforts it cannot be reduced to the condition of an automaton. This position gives the proletariat the power to hold up at will, partially or wholly, the proper functioning of the economy of society, through partial or general strikes. From this it is clear that the importance of a proletariat—given identical numbers—increases in proportion to the amount of productive forces which it sets in motion. That is to say, a proletarian in a large factory is, all other things being equal, a greater social magnitude than a handicraft worker, and an urban worker a greater magnitude than a country worker. In other words, the political role of the proletariat is the more important in proportion as large-scale production dominates small production, industry dominates agriculture and the town dominates the country. If we take the history of Germany or of England in the period when the proletariat of these countries formed the same proportion of the nation as the proletariat now forms in Russia, we shall see that they not only did not play, but by their objective importance could not play, such a role as the Russian proletariat plays today.

The same thing, as we have seen, applies to the role of the towns. When, in Germany, the population of the towns was only 15 per cent of the whole population of the country, as it is in Russia today, there could be no thought of the German towns playing that role in the economic and political life of the country which the Russian towns play today. The concentration of large industrial and commercial institutions in the towns, and the linking of the towns and the provinces by means of a system of railways, has given our towns an importance far exceeding the mere number of their inhabitants; the growth of their importance has greatly exceeded the growth of their population, while the growth of the population of the towns in its turn has exceeded the natural increase of the population of the country as a whole . . . In Italy in 1848 the number of handicraftsmen — not only proletarians but also independent masters—amounted to about 15 per cent of the population, i.e., not less than the proportion of handicraftsmen and proletarians in Russia at the present day. But the role played by them was incomparably less than that played by the modern Russian industrial proletariat.

From what has been said it should be clear that the attempt to define in advance what proportion of the whole population must be proletarian at the moment of the conquest of political power is a fruitless task. Instead of that, we will offer a few rough figures showing the relative numerical strength of the proletariat in the advanced countries at the present time. The occupied population of Germany in 1895 was 20,500,000 (not including the army, state officials and persons without a definite occupation). Out of this number there were 12,500,000 proletarians (including wage-workers in agriculture, industry, commerce and also domestic service); the number of agricultural and workers being 10,750,000. Many of the remaining 8,000,000 are really also proletarians, such as workers in domestic industries, working members of the family, etc. The number of wage-workers in agriculture taken separately was 5,750,000. The agricultural population composed 36 per cent of the entire population of the country. These figures, we repeat, refer to 1895. The eleven years that have passed since then have unquestionably produced a tremendous change—in the direction of an increase in the proportion of the urban to the agricultural population (in 1882 the agricultural population was 42 per cent of the whole), an increase in the proportion of the industrial proletariat to the agricultural proletariat, and, finally, an increase in the amount of productive capital per industrial worker as compared with 1895. But even the 1895 figures show that the German proletariat already long ago constituted the dominant productive force in the country.

Belgium, with its 7,000,000 population, is a purely industrial country. Out of every hundred persons engaged in some occupation, 41 are in industry in the strict sense of the word and only 21 are employed in agriculture. Out of the 3,000,000-odd gainfully employed, nearly 1,800,000, i.e., 60 per cent, are proletarians. This figure would become much more expressive if we added to the sharply differentiated proletariat the social elements related to it—the so-called 'independent' producers who are independent only in form but are actually enslaved to capital, the lower officials, the soldiers, etc.

But first place as regards industrialization of the economy and proletarianization of the population must undoubtedly be accorded to Britain. In 1901 the number of persons employed in agriculture, forestry and fisheries was 2,300,000, while the number in industry, commerce and transport was 12,500,000. We see, therefore, that in the chief European countries the population of the towns predominates numerically over the population of the countryside. But the great predominance of the urban population lies not only in the mass of productive forces that it constitutes, but also in its qualitative personal composition. The town attracts the most energetic, able and intelligent elements of the countryside. To prove this statistically is difficult, although the comparative age composition of the population of town and country provides indirect evidence of it. The latter fact has a significance of its own. In Germany in 1896 there were calculated to be 8,000,000 persons employed in agriculture and 8,000,000 in industry. But if we divide the population according to age-groups, we see that agriculture has 1,000,000 able-bodied persons between the ages of 14 and 40 less than in industry. This shows that it is 'the old and the young' who pre-eminently remain in the country.

All this leads us to the conclusion that economic evolution—the growth of industry, the growth of large enterprises, the growth of the towns, and the growth of the proletariat in general and the industrial proletariat in particular—has already prepared the arena not only for the *struggle* of the proletariat for political power but for the *conquest* of this power.

3. Now we come to the third pre-requisite of socialism, the dictatorship of the proletariat. Politics is the plane upon which the objective pre-requisites of socialism are intersected by the subjective ones. Under certain definite social-economic conditions, a class consciously sets itself a certain aim—the conquest of political power; it unites its forces, weighs up the strength of the enemy and estimates the situation. Even in this third sphere, however, the proletariat is not absolutely free. Besides the subjective factors—consciousness, preparedness and initiative, the development of which also have their own logic—the proletariat in carrying out its policy comes up against a number of objective factors such as the policy of the ruling classes and the

existing State institutions (such as the army, the class schools, the State church), international relations, etc.

We will deal first of all with the subjective conditions: the preparedness of the proletariat for a socialist revolution. It is, of course, not sufficient that the standard of technique has rendered socialist economy advantageous from the point of view of the productivity of social labour. It is not sufficient, either, that the social differentiation based on this technique has created a proletariat which is the main class by virtue of its numbers and its economic role, and which is objectively interested in socialism. It is further necessary that this class should be *conscious* of its objective interests; it is necessary that it should *understand* that there is no way out for it except through socialism; it is necessary that it should combine in an army sufficiently powerful to conquer political power in open battle.

It would be stupid at the present time to deny the necessity for the proletariat to be prepared in this manner. Only old-fashioned Blanquists can hope for salvation from the initiative of conspiratorial organizations which have taken shape independently of the masses; or their antipodes, the anarchists, might hope for a spontaneous, elemental outburst of the masses, the end of which no one can tell. Social-Democrats speak of the conquest of power as the *conscious action of a revolutionary class*.

But many socialist ideologues (ideologues in the bad sense of the word—those who stand everything on its head) speak of preparing the proletariat for socialism in the sense of its being morally regenerated. The proletariat, and even 'humanity' in general, must first of all cast out its old egoistical nature, and altruism must become predominant in social life, etc. As we are as yet far from such a state of affairs, and 'human nature' changes very slowly, socialism is put off for several centuries. Such a point of view probably seems very realistic and evolutionary, and so forth, but as a matter of fact it is really nothing but shallow moralizing.

It is assumed that a socialist psychology must be developed before the coming of socialism, in other words that it is possible for the masses to acquire a socialist psychology under capitalism. One must not confuse here the conscious striving towards socialism with socialist psychology. The latter presupposes the absence of egotistical motives in economic life; whereas the striving towards socialism and the struggle for it arise from the class psychology of the proletariat. However many points of contact there may be between the class psychology of the proletariat and classless socialist psychology, nevertheless a deep chasm divides them.

The joint struggle against exploitation engenders splendid shoots of idealism, comradely solidarity and self-sacrifice, but at the same time the individual struggle for existence, the ever-yawning abyss of poverty, the differentiation in the ranks of the workers themselves, the pressure of the ignorant masses from below, and the corrupting influence of the bourgeois parties do not permit these splendid shoots to develop fully. For all that, in spite of his remaining philistinely egoistic, and without his exceeding in 'human' worth the average representative of the bourgeois classes, the average worker knows from experience that *his simplest requirements and natural desirₑs can be satisfied only on the ruins of the capitalist system.*

The idealists picture the distant future generation which shall have become worthy of socialism exactly as Christians picture the members of the first Christian communes.

Whatever the psychology of the first proselytes of Christianity may have been—we know from the Acts of the Apostles of cases of embezzlement of communal property—in any case, as it became more widespread, Christianity not only failed to regenerate the souls of all the people, but itself degenerated, became materialistic and bureaucratic; from the practice of fraternal teaching one of another it changed into papalism, from wandering beggary into monastic parasitism; in short, not only did Christianity fail to subject to itself the social conditions of the milieu in which it spread, but it was itself subjected by them. This did not result from the lack of ability or the greed of the fathers and teachers of Christianity, but as a consequence of the inexorable laws of the dependence of human psychology upon the conditions of social life and labour, and the fathers and teachers of Christianity showed this dependence in their own persons.

If socialism aimed at creating a new human nature within the limits of the old society it would be nothing more than a new edition of the moralistic utopias. Socialism does not aim at creating a socialist psychology as a pre-requisite to socialism but at creating socialist conditions of life as a pre-requisite to socialist psychology.

VIII.   A WORKERS' GOVERNMENT IN RUSSIA AND SOCIALISM

We have shown above that the objective pre-requisites for a socialist revolution have already been created by the economic development of the advanced capitalist countries.   But what can we say in this connection with regard to Russia?

Can we expect that the transference of power into the hands of the Russian proletariat will be the beginning of the transformation of our national economy into a socialist one?   A year ago we replied to this question in an article which was subjected to a severe crossfire of criticism by the organs of both factions of our party.   In this article we said the following:

' The Paris workers,' Marx tells us, 'did not demand miracles from their Commune.   We, too, must not expect immediate miracles from proletarian dictatorship today.   Political power is not omnipotence.   It would be absurd to suppose that it is only necessary for the proletariat to take power and then by passing a few decrees to substitute socialism for capitalism. An economic system is not the product of the actions of the government.   All that the proletariat can do is to apply its political power with all possible energy in order to ease and shorten the path of economic evolution towards collectivism.

' The proletariat will begin with those reforms which figure in what is known as the minimum programme; and directly from these the very logic of its position will compel it to pass over to collectivist measures.

' The introduction of the eight-hour day and the steeply progressive income-tax will be comparatively easy, although even here the centre of gravity will lie not in the passing of the "act" but in organizing the practical carrying out of the measures. But the chief difficulty will be—and herein lies the transition to collectivism!—in the state organization of production in those factories which have been closed by their owners in reply to the passing of these acts. To pass a law for the abolition of the right of inheritance and to put such a law into effect will be a comparatively easy task. Legacies in the form of money capital also will not embarrass the proletariat or burden its economy. But to act as the inheritor of land and industrial capital means that the workers' state must be prepared to undertake the organizing of social production.

' The same thing, but to a wider degree, must be said of expropriation — with or without compensation. Expropriation with compensation would be politically advantageous but financially difficult, whereas expropriation without compensation would be financially advantageous but politically difficult. But the greatest difficulties of all will be met within the organization of production. We repeat, a government of the proletariat is not a government that can perform miracles.

' The socialization of production will commence with those branches of industry which present the least difficulties. In the first period, socialized production will be like a number of oases, connected with private undertakings by the laws of commodity circulation. The wider the field of social production becomes extended, the more obvious will become its advantages, the firmer will the new political régime feel, and the bolder will the further economic measures of the proletariat become. In these measures it can and will rely not merely upon the national productive forces, but also upon the technique of the whole world, just as in its revolutionary policy it will rely on the experience not only of the class relations within the country but also on the whole historical experience of the international proletariat.'

The political domination of the proletariat is incompatible with its economic enslavement. No matter under what political flag the proletariat has come to power, it is obliged to take the path of socialist policy. It would be the greatest utopianism to think that the proletariat, having been raised to political domination by the internal mechanism of a bourgeois revolution, can, even if it so desires, limit its mission to the creation of republican-democratic conditions for the social domination of the bourgeoisie. The political domination of the proletariat, even if it is only temporary, will weaken to an extreme degree the resistance of capital, which always stands in need of the support of the state, and will give the economic struggle of the proletariat tremendous scope. The workers cannot but demand maintenance for strikers from the revolutionary government, and a government relying upon the workers cannot refuse this demand. But this means paralysing the effect of the reserve army of labour and making the workers dominant not only in the political but also in the economic field, and converting private property in the means of production into a fiction. These inevitable social-economic consequences of proletarian dictatorship will reveal themselves very quickly, long before the democratization of the political system has been completed. The barrier between the 'minimum' and the 'maximum' programme disappears immediately the proletariat comes to power.

The first thing the proletarian régime must deal with on coming into power is the solution of the agrarian question, with which the fate of vast masses of the population of Russia is bound up. In the solution of this question, as in all others, the proletariat will be guided by the fundamental aim of its economic policy, i.e., to command as large as possible a field in which to carry out the organization of socialist economy. The form and tempo of the execution of this agrarian policy, however, must be determined by the material resources at the disposal of the proletariat, as well as by care to act so as not to throw possible allies into the ranks of the counter-revolutionaries.

The *agrarian* question, i.e., the question of the fate of agriculture in its social relations, is not, of course, exhausted by the *land* question, i.e., the question of forms of landownership. There is no doubt, however, that the solution of the land question, even if it does not predetermine agrarian evolution, will at least predetermine the agrarian policy of the proletariat: in other words, what the proletarian regime does with the land must be closely connected with its general attitude to the course and the requirements of agricultural development. For that reason the land question occupies first place.

One solution of the land question, to which the Socialist-Revolutionaries have given a far from irreproachable popularity, is the socialization of all land; a term, which, relieved of its European make-up, means nothing else than the 'equalization of the use of land' (or 'black redistribution'). The programme of the equal distribution of the land thus presupposes the expropriation of all land, not only privately-owned land in general, or privately-owned peasant land, but even communal land. If we bear in mind that this expropriation would have to be one of the first acts of the new regime, while commodity-capitalist relations were still completely dominant, then we shall see that the first 'victims' of this expropriation would be (or rather, would feel themselves to be) the peasantry. If we bear in mind that the peasant, during several decades, has paid the redemption money which should have converted the allotted land into his own private property; if we bear in mind that some of the more well-to-do of the peasants have acquired—undoubtedly by making considerable sacrifices, borne by a still-existing generation—large tracts of land as private property, then it will be easily imagined what a tremendous resistance would be aroused by the attempt to convert communal and small-scale privately-owned lands into state property. If it acted in such a fashion the new régime would begin by rousing a tremendous opposition against itself among the peasantry.

For what purpose should communal and small-scale privately-owned land be converted into state property? In order, in one way or another, to make it available for 'equal' economic exploitation by all landowners, including the present landless peasants and agricultural labourers. Thus, the new régime would gain nothing *economically* by the expropriation of small holdings and communal land, since, after the redistribution, the state or public lands would be cultivated as private holdings. *Politically*, the new régime would make a very big blunder, as it would at once set the mass of the peasantry against the town proletariat as the leader of the revolutionary policy.

Further, equal distribution of the land presupposes that the employment of hired labour will be prohibited by law. The abolition of wage labour can and must be a *consequence* of economic reform, but it cannot be predetermined by juridical prohibition. It is not sufficient to forbid the capitalist landlord to employ wage-labour, it is necessary first of all to secure for the landless labourer the possibility of existence—and a rational existence from the social-economic point of view. Under the programme of equalization of the use of land, forbidding the employment of wage labour will mean, on the one hand, compelling the landless labourers to settle on tiny scraps of land and, on the other, obliging the government to provide them with the necessary stock and implements for their socially-irrational production.

It is of course understood that the intervention of the proletariat in the organization of agriculture will begin not by binding scattered labourers to scattered patches of land, but with the exploitation of large estates by the State or the communes. Only when the socialization of production has been placed well on its feet can the process of socialization be advanced further, towards the prohibition of hired labour. This will render small capitalist farming impossible, but will still leave room for subsistence or semi-subsistence holdings, the forcible expropriation of which in no way enters into the plans of the socialist proletariat.

In any case, we cannot undertake to carry out a programme of equal distribution which, on the one hand, presupposes an aimless, purely formal expropriation of small holdings, and on the other, demands the complete break-up of large estates into small pieces. This policy, being directly wasteful from the economic standpoint, could only have a reactionary-utopian ulterior motive, and above all would politically weaken the revolutionary party.

*   *   *

But how far can the socialist policy of the working class be applied in the economic conditions of Russia? We can say one thing with certainty — that it will come up against political obstacles much sooner than it will stumble over the technical backwardness of the country. *Without the direct State support of the European proletariat the working class of Russia cannot remain in power and convert its temporary domination into a lasting socialistic dictatorship.* Of this there cannot for one moment be any doubt. But on the other hand there cannot be any doubt that a socialist revolution in the West will enable us directly to convert the temporary domination of the working class into a socialist dictatorship.

In 1904, Kautsky, discussing the prospects of social development and calculating the possibility of an early revolution in Russia, wrote: 'Revolution in Russia could not immediately result in a socialist régime. The economic conditions of the country are not nearly mature for this purpose.' But the Russian revolution would certainly give a strong impetus to the proletarian movement in the rest of Europe, and in consequence of the struggle that would flare up, the proletariat might come to power in Germany. 'Such an outcome,' continued Kautsky, 'must have an influence on the whole of Europe. It must lead to the political domination of the proletariat in Western Europe and create for the Eastern European proletariat the possibility of contracting the stages of their development and, copying the example of the Germans, *artificially setting up socialist institutions.* Society as a whole cannot artificially skip any stages of its development, but it is possible for constituent parts of society to hasten their retarded development by imitating the more advanced countries and, thanks to this, even to take their stand in the forefront of development, because they are not burdened with the ballast of tradition which the older countries have to drag along . . . This may happen,' says Kautsky, 'but, as we have already said, here we leave the field of inevitability and enter that of *possibility*, and so things may happen otherwise.'

These lines were written by this German Social-Democratic theoretician at a time when he was considering the question whether a revolution would break out first in Russia or in the West. Later on, the Russian proletariat revealed a colossal strength, unexpected by the Russian Social-Democrats even in their most optimistic moods. The course of the Russian revolu-

tion was decided, so far as its fundamental features were concerned.   What two or three years ago was or seemed *possible*,
approached to the *probable*, and everything points to the fact
that it is on the brink of becoming *inevitable*.

IX. EUROPE AND REVOLUTION

In June 1905 we wrote:

'More than half a century has passed since 1848, half a century of unceasing conquests by capitalism throughout the whole world; half a century of mutual adaptation between the forces of bourgeois reaction and of feudal reaction; half a century during which the bourgeoisie has revealed its mad lust for domination and its readiness to fight savagely for this.

'Just as a seeker after perpetual motion comes up against ever fresh obstacles, and piles up machine after machine for the purpose of overcoming them, so the bourgeoisie has changed and reconstructed its state apparatus while avoiding "extra-legal" conflict with the forces hostile to it. But just as our seeker after perpetual motion eventually comes up against the final insurmountable obstacle of the law of the conservation of energy, so the bourgeoisie must eventually come up against the final insurmountable obstacle in its path: the class antagonism, which will inevitably be settled by conflict.

'Binding all countries together with its mode of production and its commerce, capitalism has converted the whole world into a single economic and political organism. Just as modern credit binds thousands of undertakings by invisible ties and gives to capital an incredible mobility which prevents many small bankruptcies but at the same time is the cause of the unprecedented sweep of general economic crises, so the whole economic and political effort of capitalism, its world trade, its system of monstrous state debts, and the political groupings of nations which draw all the forces of reaction into a kind of world-wide joint-stock company, has not only resisted all individual political crises, but also prepared the basis for a social crisis of unheard-of dimensions. Driving all the processes of disease beneath the surface, avoiding all difficulties, putting off all the profound questions of internal and international politics, and glossing over all contradictions, the bourgeoisie has managed to postpone the dénouement, but thereby has prepared a radical liquidation of its rule on a world-wide scale. The bourgeoisie has greedily clutched at every reactionary force without inquiring as to its origin. The Pope and the Sultan were not the least of its friends. The only reason why it did not establish bonds of "friendship" with the Emperor of China was because he did not represent any force. It was much more adantageous for the bourgeoisie to plunder his dominions than to maintain him in its service as its gendarme, paying him out of its own coffers. We thus see that the world bourgeoisie has made the stability of its State system profoundly dependent on the unstable pre-bourgeois bulwarks of reaction.

'This immediately gives the events now unfolding an international character, and opens up a wide horizon. The political emanicipation of Russia led by the working class will raise that class to a height as yet unknown in history, will transfer to it colossal power and resources, and will make it the initiator of the liquidation of world capitalism, for which history has created all the objective conditions.'*

If the Russian proletariat, having temporarily obtained power, does not on its own initiative carry the revolution on to European soil, it will be *compelled* to do so by the forces of European feudal-bourgeois reaction. Of course it would be idle at this moment to determine the methods by which the Russian revolution will throw itself against old capitalist Europe. These methods may reveal themselves quite unexpectedly. Let us take the example of Poland as a link between the revolutionary East and

---

* See my foreward to F. Lassalle's *Address To the Jury*, published by ' Molot'.—L.T.

the revolutionary West, although we take this as an illustration of our idea rather than as an actual prediction.

The triumph of the revolution in Russia will mean the inevitable victory of the revolution in Poland. It is not difficult to imagine that the existence of a revolutionary régime in the ten provinces of Russian Poland must lead to the revolt of Galicia and Poznan. The Hohenzollern and Habsburg Governments will reply to this by sending military forces to the Polish frontier in order then to cross it for the purpose of crushing their enemy at his very centre —Warsaw. It is quite clear that the Russian revolution cannot leave its Western advance-guard in the hands of the Prusso-Austrian soldiery. War against the governments of Wilhelm II and Franz Josef under such circumstances would become an act of self-defence on the part of the revolutionary government of Russia. What attitude would the Austrian and German proletariat take up then? It is evident that they could not remain calm while the armies of their countries were conducting a counter-revolutionary crusade. A war between feudal-bourgeois Germany and revolutionary Russia would lead inevitably to a proletarian revolution in Germany. We would tell those to whom this assertion seems too categorical to try and think of any other historical event which would be more likely to compel the German workers and the German reactionaries to make an open trial of strength.

When our October ministry unexpectedly placed Poland under martial law, a highly plausible rumour went round to the effect that this was done on direct instructions from Berlin. On the eve of the dispersal of the Duma the government newspapers published, presenting them as threats, communications concerning negotiations between the governments of Berlin and Vienna with a view to armed intervention in the internal affairs of Russia, for the purpose of suppressing sedition. No ministerial denial of any sort could wipe out the effect of the shock which this communication gave. It was clear that in the palaces of three neighbouring countries a bloody counter-revolutionary revenge was being prepared. How could things be otherwise? Could the neighbouring semi-feudal monarchies stand passively by while the flames of revolution licked the frontiers of their realms?

The Russian revolution, while as yet far from being victorious, had already had its effect on Galicia through Poland. 'Who could have foreseen a year ago', cried Daszynski, at the conference of the Polish Social-Democratic Party in Lvov in May this year, 'what is now taking place in Galicia? This great peasant movement has spread astonishment throughout the whole of Austria. Zbaraz elects a Social-Democrat as vice-marshal of the regional council. Peasants publish a socialist-revolutionary newspaper for peasants, entitled "The Red Flag", great mass meetings of peasants, 30,000 strong, are held, processions with red flags and revolutionary songs parade through Galician villages, once so calm and apathetic . . . What will happen when from Russia the cry of the nationalization of the land reaches these poverty-stricken peasants? '. In his argument with the Polish Socialist Lusnia, more than two years ago, Kautsky pointed out that Russia must no longer be regarded as a weighted ball on the feet of Poland, or Poland regarded as an Eastern detachment of revolutionary Europe thrust like a wedge into the steppes of Muscovite barbarism. In the event of the development and the victory of the Russian revolution, the Polish question, according to Kautsky, 'will again become acute, but not in the sense that Lusnia thought. It will be directed not against Russia but against Austria and Germany, and in so far as Poland will serve the cause of revolution its task will be not to defend the revolution against Russia, but to carry it further into Austria and Germany'. This prophecy is much nearer realization than Kautsky may have thought.

But a revolutionary Poland is not at all the only starting-point for a revolution in Europe. We pointed out above that the bourgeoisie has systematically abstained from solving many complex and acute questions affecting both internal and foreign politics. Having placed huge masses of men under arms, the bourgeois governments are unable, however, to cut with the sword through the tangle of international politics. Only a government which has the backing of the nation whose vital interests are affected, or a government that has lost the ground from under its feet and is inspired by the courage of despair, can send hundreds and thousands of men into battle. Under modern conditions of political culture, military science, universal suffrage and universal military service, only profound confidence or crazy adventurism can thrust two nations into conflict. In the Franco-Prussian war of 1870 we had on the one side Bismarck struggling for the Prussianizing of Germany, which after all meant national unity, an elementary necessity recognized by every German, and on the other hand the government of Napoleon III, impudent, powerless, despised by the nation, ready for any adventure that promised to secure for it another 12 months' lease of life. The same division of roles obtained in the Russo-Japanese war. On the one hand we had the government of the Mikado, as yet unopposed by a revolutionary proletariat, fighting for the domination of Japanese capital in the Far East, and on the other an autocratic government which had outlived its time striving to redeem its internal defeats by victories abroad.

In the old capitalist countries there are no 'national' demands, i.e., demands *of bourgeois society as a whole,* of which the ruling bourgeoisie could claim to be the champions. The governments of France, Britain, Germany and Austria are unable to conduct national wars. The vital interests of the masses, the interests of the oppressed nationalities, or the barbarous internal politics of a neighbouring country are not able to drive a single bourgeois government into a war which could have a liberating and therefore a national character. On the other hand, the interests of capitalist grabbing, which from time to time induce now one and now another government to clank its spurs and rattle its sabre in the face of the world, cannot arouse any response among the masses. For that reason the bourgeoisie either cannot or will not proclaim or conduct any national wars. What modern anti-national wars will lead to has been seen recently from two experiences—in South Africa and in the Far East.

The severe defeat of imperialist Conservatism in Britain is not in the last resort due to the lesson of the Boer war; a much more important and more menacing consequence of imperialist policy (menacing to the bourgeoisie) is the political self-determination of the British proletariat, which, once begun, will advance with seven-league strides. As for the consequences of the Russo-

Japanese war for the Petrograd Government, these are so well known that it is not necessary to dwell on them. But even without these two experiences, European governments, from the moment the proletariat began to stand on its own feet, have always feared to place before it the choice of war or revolution. It is precisely this fear of the revolt of the proletariat that compels the bourgeois parties, even while voting monstrous sums for military expenditure, to make solemn declarations in favour of peace, to dream of International Arbitration Courts and even of the organization of a United States of Europe. These pitiful declarations can, of course, abolish neither antagonisms between states nor armed conflicts.

The armed peace which arose in Europe after the Franco-Prussian War was based on a European balance of power which presupposed not only the inviolability of Turkey, the partition of Poland and the preservation of Austria, that ethnographical harlequin's cloak, but also the maintenance of Russian despotism, armed to the teeth, as the gendarme of European reaction. The Russo-Japanese war, however, delivered a severe blow to this artificially maintained system in which the autocracy occupied a foremost position. Russia for a time fell out of the so-called concert of powers. The balance of power was destroyed. On the other hand, Japan's successes aroused the aggressive instincts of the capitalist bourgeoisie, especially the stock exchanges, which play a very big part in contemporary politics. The possibility of a war on European territory grew to a very high degree. Conflicts are ripening everywhere, and if up till now they have been allayed by diplomatic means, there is no guarantee, however, that these means can be successful for long. But a European war inevitably means a European revolution.

During the Russo-Japanese war the Socialist Party of France declared that if the French Government intervened in favour of the autocracy, it would call upon the proletariat to take most resolute measures, even to the extent of revolt. In March 1906, when the Franco-German conflict over Morocco was coming to a head, the International Socialist Bureau resolved, in the event of a danger of war, to ' lay down the most advantageous methods of action for all international socialist parties and for the whole organized working class in order to prevent war or bring it to an end'. Of course this was only a resolution. It requires a war to test its real significance, but the bourgeoisie has every reason to avoid such a test. Unfortunately for the bourgeoisie, however, the logic of international relations is stronger than the logic of diplomacy.

The State bankruptcy of Russia, no matter whether it be the result of the continued management of affairs by the bureaucracy or whether it be declared by a revolutionary government which will refuse to pay for the sins of the old regime, will have a terrible effect upon France. The Radicals, who now have the political destiny of France in their hands, in taking power have also undertaken all the functions of protecting the interests of capital. For that reason there is every ground for assuming that the financial crisis arising from the bankruptcy of Russia will directly repeat itself in France in the form of an acute political crisis which can end only with the transference of power into the hands of the proletariat. In one way or another, either through a revolution in Poland, through the consequences of a European war, or as the result of the State bankruptcy of Russia, revolution will cross into the territories of old capitalist Europe.

But even without the outside pressure of events such as war or bankruptcy, revolution may arise in the near future in one of the European countries as a consequence of the extreme sharpening of the class struggle. We will not attempt to build assumptions now as to which of the European countries will be the first to take the path of revolution; of one thing there is no doubt, and that is that the class contradictions in all European countries during recent times have reached a high level of intensity.

The colossal growth of Social Democracy in Germany, within the framework of a semi-absolutist constitution, will with iron necessity lead the proletariat to an open clash with the feudal-bourgeois monarchy. The question of offering resistance to a political coup d'etat by means of a general strike has in the last year become one of the central questions in the political life of the German proletariat. In France, the transition of power to the Radicals decisively unties the hands of the proletariat, which were for a long time bound by co-operation with the bourgeois parties in the struggle against nationalism and clericalism. The Socialist Party, rich in the deathless traditions of four revolutions, and the conservative bourgeoisie, screening themselves behind the mask of Radicalism, stand face to face. In Britain, where for a century the two bourgeois parties have been regularly operating the see-saw of parliamentarism, the proletariat under the influence of a whole series of factors have just recently taken the path of political separation. While in Germany this process took four decades, the British working class, possessing powerful trade unions and being rich in experience of economic struggle, may in a few leaps overtake the army of continental socialism.

The influence of the Russian revolution upon the European proletariat is tremendous. Besides destroying Russian absolutism, the main force of European reaction, it will create the necessary prerequisites for revolution in the consciousness and temper of the European working class.

The function of the socialist parties was and is to revolutionize the consciousness of the working class, just as the development of capitalism revolutionized social relations. But the work of agitation and organization among the ranks of the proletariat has an internal inertia. The European Socialist Parties, particularly the largest of them, the German Social-Democratic Party, have developed their conservatism in proportion as the great masses have embraced socialism and the more these masses have become organized and disciplined. As a consequence of this, Social Democracy as an organization embodying the political experience of the proletariat may at a certain moment become a direct obstacle to open conflict between the workers and bourgeois reaction. In other words, the propagandist-socialist conservatism of the proletarian parties may at a certain moment hold back the direct struggle of the proletariat for power. The tremendous influence of the Russian revolution indicates that it will destroy party routine and conservatism, and place the question of an open trial of strength between the proletariat and capitalist reaction on the order of the day. The struggle for universal suffrage in Austria, Saxony and Prussia has become acute under the direct influence of the October strikes in Russia. The revolution in the East will infect the Western proletariat with a revolutionary idealism and rouse a desire to speak to their enemies 'in Russian'. Should the Russian proletariat find itself in power, if only as the result of a temporary conjuncture of circumstances in our bourgeois revolution, it will encounter the organized hostility of world reaction, and on the other hand will find a readiness on the part of the world proletariat to give organized support.

Left to its own resources, the working class of Russia will inevitably be crushed by the counter-revolution the moment the peasantry turns its back on it. It will have no alternative but to link the fate of its political rule, and, hence, the fate of the whole Russian revolution, with the fate of the socialist revolution in Europe. That colossal state-political power given it by a temporary conjuncture of circumstances in the Russian bourgeois revolution it will cast into the scales of the class struggle of the entire capitalist world. With state power in its hands, with counter-revolution behind it and European reaction in front of it, it will send forth to its comrades the world over the old rallying cry, which this time will be a call for the last attack: *Workers of all countries, unite!*

X. THE STRUGGLE FOR POWER*

We have before us a leaflet on our programme and tactics entitled: 'The Tasks Confronting the Russian Proletariat—A Letter to Comrades in Russia'. This document is signed by P. Axelrod, Astrov, A. Martynov, L. Martov and S. Semkovsky.

The problem of the revolution is outlined in this 'letter' in very general fashion, clarity and precision disappearing in proportion as the authors turn from describing the situation created by the war to the political prospects and tactical conclusions; the very terminology becomes diffuse and the social definitions ambiguous.

Two moods seem from abroad to prevail in Russia: in the first place, concern for national defence—from the Romanovs to Plekhanov—and secondly, universal discontent—from the oppositional bureaucratic Fronde to the outbreaks of street rioting. These two pervading moods also create an illusion of a future popular freedom which is to arise out of the cause of national defence. But these two moods are in large measure responsible for the indefiniteness with which the question of 'popular revolution' is presented, even when it is formally counterposed to 'national defence'.

The war itself, with its defeats, has not created the revolutionary problem nor any revolutionary forces for its solution.

---

* From *Nashe Slovo* (Paris), October 17, 1915.—L.T.

History for us does not commence with the surrender of Warsaw to the Prince of Bavaria. Both the revolutionary contradictions and the social forces are the same as those which we first encountered in 1905, only very considerably modified by the ensuing ten years. The war has merely revealed in a mechanically graphic way the objective bankruptcy of the regime. At the same time it has brought confusion into the social consciousness, in which 'everybody' seems infected with the desire to resist Hindenburg as well as with hatred towards the regime of 3rd June. But as the organization of a 'people's war' from the very first moment comes up against the Tsarist police, thereby revealing that the Russia of 3rd June is a fact, and that a 'people's war' is a fiction, so the approach to a 'people's revolution' at the very threshold comes up against the socialist police of Plekhanov, whom, together with his entire suite, one might regard as a fiction if behind him there did not stand Kerensky, Milyukov, Guchkov and in general the non-revolutionary and anti-revolutionary national-democrats and national-liberals.

The 'letter' cannot of course ignore the class division of the nation, or that the nation must by means of revolution save itself from the consequences of the war and the present régime. ' The nationalists and Octobrists, the progressists, the Cadets, the industrialists and even part (!) of the radical intelligentsia proclaim with one voice the inability of the bureaucracy to defend the country and demand the mobilization of social forces for the cause of defence . . .' The letter draws the correct conclusion regarding the anti-revolutionary character of this position, which assumes 'unity with the present rulers of Russia, with the bureaucrats, nobles and generals, in the cause of defence of the State'. The letter also correctly points out the anti-revolutionary position of 'bourgeois patriots of all shades'; and we may add, of the social-patriots, of whom the letter makes no mention at all.

From this we must draw the conclusion that the Social-Democrats are not merely the most logical revolutionary party but that they are the only revolutionary party in the country; that, side by side with them, there are not only groups which are less resolute in the application of revolutionary methods, but also non-revolutionary parties. In other words, that the Social-Democratic Party, in its revolutionary way of presenting problems, is quite isolated *in the open political arena*, in spite of the 'universal discontent'. This first conclusion must be very carefully taken into account.

Of course, parties are not classes. Between the position of a party and the interests of the social stratum upon which it rests, there may be a certain lack of harmony which later on may become converted into a profound contradiction. The conduct of a party may change under the influence of the temper of the masses. This is indisputable. All the more reason therefore for us, in our calculations, to cease relying on less stable and less trustworthy elements such as the slogans and tactics of a party, and to refer to more stable historical factors: to the social structure of the nation, to the relation of class forces and the tendencies of development.

Yet the authors of the 'letter' completely avoid these questions. What is this 'people's revolution' in the Russia of 1915? Our authors simply tell us that it 'must' be made by the proletariat and the democracy. We know what the proletariat is, but what is 'the democracy'? Is it a political party? From what has been said above, evidently not. Is it then the masses? What masses? Evidently it is the petty industrial and commercial bourgeoisie, the intelligentsia and the peasantry—it can only be of these that they are speaking.

In a series of articles entitled ' The War Crisis and Political Prospects' we have given a general estimation of the possible revolutionary significance of these social forces. Basing ourselves on the experience of the last revolution, we inquired into the changes which the last ten years have brought about in the relation of forces that obtained in 1905: have these been *in favour* of democracy (the bourgeoisie) or *against* it? This is the central historical question in judging the prospects of the revolution and the tactics of the proletariat. Has bourgeois democracy in Russia become stronger since 1905, or has it still further declined? All our former discussions centred round the question of the fate of bourgeois democracy, and those who are still unable to give a reply to this question are groping in the dark. We reply to this question by saying that *a national bourgeois revolution is impossible in Russia because there is no genuinely revolutionary bourgeois democracy*. The time for national revolutions has passed—at least for Europe—just as the time for national wars has passed. Between the one and the other there is an inherent connection. We are living in an epoch of imperialism which is not merely a system of colonial conquests but implies also a definite régime at home. It does not set the bourgeois nation in opposition to the old régime, but sets the proletariat in opposition to the bourgeois nation.

The petty-bourgeois artisans and traders already played an insignificant role in the revolution of 1905. There is no question that the social importance of this class has declined still further during the last ten years. Capitalism in Russia deals much more radically and severely with the intermediate classes than it does in the countries with an older economic development. The intelligentsia has undoubtedly grown numerically, and its economic rôle also has increased. But at the same time even its former illusory 'independence' has entirely disappeared. The social significance of the intelligentsia is wholly determined by its functions in organizing capitalist industry and bourgeois public opinion. Its material connection with capitalism has saturated it with imperialist tendencies. As already quoted, the 'letter' says, 'even part of the radical intelligentsia . . . demands the mobilization of social forces for the cause of defence'. This is absolutely untrue; not *a part*, but *the whole* of the radical intelligentsia; in fact, one should say, not only the whole radical section, but a considerable, if not the greater part of the socialist intelligentsia. We shall hardly increase the ranks of 'democracy' by painting-up the character of the intelligentsia.

Thus the industrial and commercial bourgeoisie has declined still further while the intelligentsia have abandoned their revolutionary position. Urban democracy as a revolutionary factor is not worth mentioning. Only the peasantry remains, but as far as we know, neither Axelrod nor Martov ever set great hopes upon its independent revolutionary role. Have they come to the conclusion that the unceasing class differentiation among the peasantry during the last ten years has increased this role? Such

a supposition would be flying in the face of all theoretical conclusions and all historical experience.

But in that case, what kind of 'democracy' does the letter
mean? And in what sense do they speak of 'people's revolution'?
The slogan of a constituent assembly presupposes a revolutionary situation. Is there one? Yes, there is, but it is not
in the least expressed in the supposed birth, at last, of a
bourgeois democracy which is alleged to be now ready and able
to settle accounts with Tsarism. On the contrary, if there is
anything that this war has revealed quite clearly, it is the absence
of a revolutionary democracy in the country.

The attempt of the Russia of 3rd June to solve the internal
revolutionary problems by the path of imperialism has resulted
in an obvious fiasco. This does not mean that the responsible
or semi-responsible parties of the 3rd June régime will take
the path of revolution, but it does mean that the revolutionary
problem laid bare by the military catastrophe, which will drive
the ruling class still further along the path of imperialism, doubles
the importance of the only revolutionary class in the country.

The bloc of 3rd June is shaken, rent by internal friction and
conflict. This does not mean that the Octobrists and Cadets are
considering the revolutionary problem of power and preparing
to storm the positions of the bureaucracy and the united nobility.
But it does mean that the government's power to resist revolutionary pressure undoubtedly has been weakened for a certain
period.

The monarchy and the bureaucracy are discredited, but this
does not mean that they will give up power without a fight. The
dispersal of the Duma and the latest ministerial changes showed
whoever needed showing how far from the facts this supposition
is. But the policy of bureaucratic instability, which will develop
still further, should greatly assist the revolutionary mobilization
of the proletariat by the Social Democrats.

The lower classes of the towns and villages will become more
and more exhausted, deceived, dissatisfied and enraged. This
does not mean that an independent force of revolutionary
democracy will operate side by side with the proletariat. For
such a force there is neither social material nor leading personnel;

but it undoubtedly does mean that the deep dissatisfàction of the lower classes will assist the revolutionary pressure of the working class.

The less the proletariat waits upon the appearance of bourgeois democracy, the less it adapts itself to the passivity and limitations of the petty bourgeoisie and peasantry, the more resolute and irreconcilable its fight becomes, the more obvious becomes its preparedness to go to 'the end', i.e., to the conquest of power, the greater will be its chances at the decisive moment of carrying with it the non-proletarian masses. Nothing, of course, will be accomplished by merely putting forward mere slogans such as 'for the confiscation of land', etc. This to a still greater extent applies to the army, by which the government stands or falls. The mass of the army will only incline towards the revolutionary class when it becomes convinced that it is not merely grumbling and demonstrating, but is fighting for power and has some chances of winning it. There is an objective revolutionary problem in the country—the problem of political power—which has been glaringly revealed by the war and the defeats. There is a progressive disorganization of the ruling class. There is a growing dissatisfaction among the urban and rural masses. But the only revolutionary factor which can take advantage of this situation is the proletariat—now to an incomparably greater degree than in 1905.

The 'letter' would appear, in one phrase, to approach this central point of the question. It says that the Russian Social-Democratic workers should take 'the lead in this national struggle for the overthrow of the monarchy of 3rd June'. What 'national' struggle may mean we have just indicated. But if 'take the lead' does not merely mean that the advanced workers should magnanimously shed their blood without asking themselves for what purpose, but means that the workers must take the *political leadership* of the whole struggle, which above all will be a proletarian struggle, then it is clear that *victory in this struggle must transfer power to the class that has led the struggle, i.e, the Social-Democratic proletariat.*

The question, therefore, is not simply one of a 'revolutionary provisional government'—an empty phrase to which the historical process will have to give some kind of content, but of a *revolutionary workers' government,* the conquest of power by the Russian proletariat. The demands for a national constituent assembly, a republic, an eight-hour day, the confiscation of the land of the landlords, together with the demands for the immediate cessation of the war, the right of nations to self-determination, and a United States of Europe will play a tremendous part in the agitational role of the Social Democrats. But revolution is first and foremost a question of power—not of the state form (constituent assembly, republic, united states) but of the social content of the government. The demands for a constituent assembly and the confiscation of land under present conditions lose all direct revolutionary significance without the readiness of the proletariat to fight for the conquest of power; for if the proletariat does not tear power out of the hands of the monarchy nobody else will do so.

The tempo of the revolutionary process is a special question. It depends upon a number of military and political, national and international factors. These factors may retard or hasten developments, facilitate the revolutionary victory or lead to another defeat. But whatever the conditions may be the proletariat must clearly see its path and take it consciously. Above everything else it must be free from illusions. And the worst illusion in all its history from which the proletariat has up till now suffered has always been reliance upon others.

The Permanent Revolution

INTRODUCTION TO THE FIRST (RUSSIAN) EDITION
(PUBLISHED IN BERLIN)

This book is devoted to an issue which is intimately linked with the history of the three Russian Revolutions. But not with that history alone. This issue has played an enormous role in recent years in the internal struggle in the Communist Party of the Soviet Union; it was then carried into the Communist International, played a decisive role in the development of the Chinese Revolution and determined a whole number of most important decisions on problems bound up with the revolutionary struggle of the countries of the East. This issue has to do with the theory of the permanent revolution, which, according to the teachings of the epigones of Leninism (Zinoviev, Stalin, Bukharin, etc.) represents the original sin of 'Trotskyism'.

The question of the permanent revolution was once again raised in 1924 after a long interval and, at first sight, quite unexpectedly. There was no political justification for it; it was a matter of differences of opinion which belonged to the distant past. But there were important psychological motives. The group of so-called 'old Bolsheviks' who had opened up a fight against me began by counterposing themselves to me as the 'Bolshevik Old Guard'. But a great obstacle in their path was the year 1917. However important may have been the preceding history of ideological struggle and preparation, nonetheless, not only with regard to the party as a whole but also with regard to different individuals, this whole preceding preparatory period found its highest and categorical test in the October Revolution. *Not a single one of the epigones stood up under this test.* Without exception, they all at the time of the February 1917 Revolution adopted the vulgar position of democratic Left Wingers. Not a single one of them raised the slogan of the workers' struggle for power. They all regarded the course toward a socialist revolution as absurd or—still worse—as 'Trotskyism'. In this spirit they led the party up to the time of Lenin's arrival from abroad and the publication of his famous April Theses. After this, Kamenev, already in direct struggle against Lenin, openly tried to form a democratic wing of Bolshevism. Later he was joined by Zinoviev, who had arrived with Lenin. Stalin, heavily compromised by his social-patriotic position, stepped to the sidelines. He let the party forget his miserable articles and speeches of the decisive March weeks and gradually edged over to Lenin's standpoint. This is why the question automatically arose: What had any of these leading 'old Bolsheviks' got from Leninism when *not a single* one of them showed himself capable of applying independently the theoretical and practical experiences of the party at a most important and most critical historical moment? Attention had to be diverted from this question at all costs and another question substituted for it. To this end, it was decided to concentrate fire on the permanent revolution. My adversaries did not, of course, foresee that in creating an artificial axis of struggle they would imperceptibly be compelled to revolve it around themselves and to manufacture, by the method of inversion, a new world outlook for themselves.

In its essential features, the theory of the permanent revolution was formulated by me even before the decisive events of 1905. Russia was approaching the bourgeois revolution. No one in the ranks of the Russian Social Democrats (we all called ourselves Social Democrats then) had any doubts that we were approaching a *bourgeois* revolution, that is, a revolution produced by the contradictions between the development of the productive forces of capitalist society and the outlived caste and state relationships of the period of serfdom and the Middle Ages. In the struggle against the Narodniks and the anarchists, I had to devote not a few speeches and articles in those days to the Marxist analysis of the bourgeois character of the impending revolution.

The bourgeois character of the revolution could not, however, answer in advance the question of which classes would solve the tasks of the democratic revolution and what the mutual relationships of these classes would be. It was precisely at this point that the fundamental strategical problems began.

Plekhanov, Axelrod, Zasulich, Martov and, following them, all the Russian Mensheviks, took as their point of departure the idea that to the liberal bourgeoisie, as the natural claimant to power, belonged the leading role in the bourgeois revolution. According to this pattern, the party of the proletariat was assigned the role of Left Wing of the democratic front. The Social Democrats were to support the liberal bourgeoisie against the reaction and at the same time to defend the interests of the proletariat against the liberal bourgeoisie. In other words, the Mensheviks understood the bourgeois revolution principally as a liberal-constitutional reform.

Lenin posed the question in an altogether different manner. For Lenin, the liberation of the productive forces of bourgeois society from the fetters of serfdom signified, first and foremost, a radical solution of the agrarian question in the sense of complete liquidation of the landowning class and revolutionary redistribution of landownership. Inseparably connected with this was the destruction of the monarchy. Lenin attacked the agrarian problem, which affected the vital interests of the overwhelming majority of the population and at the same time constituted the basic problem of the capitalist market, with a truly revolutionary boldness. Since the liberal bourgeoisie, which confronts the worker as an enemy, is intimately bound by innumerable ties to large landed property, the genuine democratic liberation of the peasantry can be realised only by the revolutionary co-operation of the workers and peasants. According to Lenin, their joint uprising against the old society must, if victorious, lead to the establishment of the 'democratic dictatorship of the proletariat and peasantry'.

This formula is now repeated in the Communist International as a sort of supra-historical dogma, with no attempt to analyse the living historical experiences of the last quarter-century—as though we had not been witnesses and participants in the Revolution of 1905, the February Revolution of 1917, and finally the October Revolution. Such a historical analysis, however, is all the more necessary because never in history has there been a régime of the 'democratic dictatorship of the proletariat and peasantry'.

In 1905, it was a question with Lenin of a strategical hypothesis still to be verified by the actual course of the class struggle. The formula of the democratic dictatorship of the proletariat and peasantry bore in large measure an intentionally algebraic character. Lenin did not solve in advance the question of what the political relationships would be between the two participants in the assumed democratic dictatorship, that is, the proletariat and the peasantry. He did not exclude the possibility that the peasantry would be represented in the revolution by an independent party—a party independent in a double sense, not only with regard to the bourgeoisie but also with regard to the proletariat, and at the same time capable of realising the democratic revolution in alliance with the party of the proletariat in struggle against the liberal bourgeoisie. Lenin even allowed the possibility—as we shall soon see—that the revolutionary peasants' party might constitute the majority in the government of the democratic dictatorship.

In the question of the decisive significance of the agrarian revolution for the fate of our bourgeois revolution, I was, at least from the autumn of 1902, that is, from the time of my first flight abroad, a pupil of Lenin's. That the agrarian revolution, and consequently, the general democratic revolution also, could be realised only by the united forces of the workers and the peasants in struggle against the liberal bourgeoisie, was for me, contrary to all the senseless fairy tales of recent years, beyond any doubt. Yet I came out against the formula 'democratic dictatorship of the proletariat and the peasantry', because I saw its shortcoming in the fact that it left open the question of which class would wield the real dictatorship. I endeavoured to show that in spite of its enormous social and revolutionary weight the peasantry was incapable of creating a really independent party and even less capable of concentrating the revolutionary power in the hands of such a party.

Just as in the old revolutions, from the German Reformation of the sixteenth century, and even before that, the peasantry in its uprisings gave support to one of the sections of the urban bourgeoisie and not infrequently ensured its victory, so, in our belated bourgeois revolution, the peasantry might at the peak of its struggle extend similar support to the proletariat and help it to come to power. From this I drew the conclusion that our bourgeois revolution could solve its tasks radically only in the event that the proletariat, with the aid of the multi-millioned peasantry, proved capable of concentrating the revolutionary dictatorship in its own hands.

What would be the social content of this dictatorship? First of all, it would have to carry through to the end the agrarian revolution and the democratic reconstruction of the State. In other words, the dictatorship of the proletariat would become the instrument for solving the tasks of the historically-belated bourgeois revolution. But the matter could not rest there. Having reached power the proletariat would be compelled to encroach even more deeply upon the relationships of private property in general, that is to take the road of socialist measures.

'But do you really believe,' the Stalins, Rykovs and all the other Molotovs objected dozens of times between 1905 and 1917, 'that Russia is ripe for the socialist revolution?' To that I always answered: No, I do not. But world economy as a whole, and European economy in the first place, is fully ripe for the socialist revolution. Whether the dictatorship of the proletariat in Russia leads to socialism or not, and at what tempo and through what stages, will depend upon the fate of European and world capitalism.

These were the essential features of the theory of the permanent revolution at its origin in the early months of 1905. Since then, three revolutions have taken place. The Russian proletariat rose to power on the mighty wave of the peasant insurrection. The dictatorship of the proletariat became a fact in Russia earlier than in any of the immeasurably more developed countries of the world. In 1924, that is, no more than seven years after the historical prognosis of the theory of the permanent revolution had been confirmed with quite exceptional force, the epigones opened up a frenzied attack against this theory, plucking isolated sentences and polemical rejoinders out of old works of mine which I had by then completely forgotten.

It is appropriate to recall here that the first Russian revolution broke out more than half a century after the wave of bourgeois revolutions in Europe and thirty-five years after the episodic uprising of the Paris Commune. Europe had had time to grow unaccustomed to revolutions. Russia had not experienced any. All the problems of the revolution were posed anew. It is not difficult to understand how many unknown and conjectural magnitudes the future revolution held for us in those days. The formulae of all the groupings were, each in their own way, working hypotheses. One must have complete incapacity for historical prognosis and utter lack of understanding of its methods in order now, after the event, to consider analyses and evaluations of 1905 as though they were written yesterday. I have often said to myself and to my friends: I do not doubt that my prognoses of 1905 contained many defects which it is not hard to show up now, after the event. But did my critics see better and further? Not having re-read my old works for a long time, I was ready in advance to admit to defects in them more serious and important than really were there. I became convinced of this in 1928, when the political leisure imposed upon me by exile in Alma-Ata gave me the opportunity to re-read, pencil in hand, my old writings on the problems of the permanent revolution. I hope that the reader, too, will be thoroughly convinced of this by what he reads in the pages that follow.

It is nevertheless necessary, within the limits of this introduction, to present as exact as possible a characterization of the constituent elements of the theory of the permanent revolution, and the most important objections to it. The dispute has so broadened and deepened that it now embraces in essence all the most important questions of the world revolutionary movement.

The permanent revolution, in the sense which Marx attached to this concept, means a revolution which makes no compromise with any single form of class rule, which does not stop at the democratic stage, which goes over to socialist measures and to war against reaction from without; that is, a revolution whose every successive stage is rooted in the preceding one and which can end only in the complete liquidation of class society.

To dispel the chaos that has been created around the theory of the permanent revolution, it is necessary to distinguish three lines of thought that are united in this theory.

First, it embraces the problem of the transition from the democratic revolution to the socialist. This is in essence the historical origin of the theory.

The concept of the permanent revolution was advanced by the great Communists of the middle of the nineteenth century, Marx and his co-thinkers, in opposition to the democratic ideology which, as we know, claims that with the establishment of a 'rational' or democratic state all questions can be solved peacefully by reformist or evolutionary measures. Marx regarded the bourgeois revolution of 1848 as the direct prelude to the proletarian revolution. Marx 'erred'. Yet his error has a factual and not a methodological character. The Revolution of 1848 did not turn into the socialist revolution. But that is just why it also did not achieve democracy. As to the German Revolution of 1918, it was no democratic completion of the bourgeois revolution, it was a proletarian revolution decapitated by the Social Democrats; more correctly, it was a bourgeois *counter-revolution*, which was compelled to preserve pseudo-democratic forms after its victory over the proletariat.

Vulgar 'Marxism' has worked out a pattern of historical development according to which every bourgeois society sooner or later secures a democratic regime, after which the proletariat, under conditions of democracy, is gradually organized and educated for socialism. The actual transition to socialism has been variously conceived: the avowed reformists pictured this transition as the reformist filling of democracy with a socialist content (Jaurès); the formal revolutionists acknowledged the inevitability of applying revolutionary violence in the transition to socialism (Guesde). But both the former and the latter considered democracy and socialism, for all peoples and countries, as two stages in the development of society which are not only entirely distinct but also separated by great distances of time from each other. This view was predominant also among those Russian Marxists who, in the period of 1905, belonged to the Left Wing of the Second International. Plekhanov, the brilliant progenitor of Russian Marxism, considered the idea of the dictatorship of the proletariat a delusion in contemporary Russia. The same standpoint was defended not only by the Mensheviks but also by the overwhelming majority of the leading Bolsheviks, in particular by those present party leaders, without exception, who in their day were resolute revolutionary democrats but for whom the problems of the socialist revolution, not only in 1905 but also on the eve of 1917, still signified the vague music of a distant future.

The theory of the permanent revolution, which originated in 1905, declared war upon these ideas and moods. It pointed out that the democratic tasks of the backward bourgeois nations lead directly, in our epoch, to the dictatorship of the proletariat and that the dictatorship of the proletariat puts socialist tasks on the order of the day. Therein lay the central idea of the theory. While the traditional view was that the road to the dictatorship of the proletariat led through a long period of democracy, the theory of the permanent revolution established the fact that for backward countries the road to democracy passed through the dictatorship of the proleriat. Thus democracy is not a régime that remains self-sufficient for decades, but is only a direct prelude to the socialist revolution. Each is bound to the other by an unbroken chain. Thus there is established between the democratic revolution and the socialist reconstruction of society a permanent state of revolutionary development.

The second aspect of the 'permanent' theory has to do with the socialist revolution as such. For an indefinitely long time and in constant internal struggle, all social relations undergo transformation. Society keeps on changing its skin. Each stage of transformation stems directly from the preceding. This process necessarily retains a political character, that is, it develops through collisions between various groups in the society which is in transformation. Outbreaks of civil war and foreign wars alternate with periods of 'peaceful' reform. Revolutions in economy, technique, science, the family, morals and everyday life develop in complex reciprocal action and do not allow society to achieve equilibrium.

Therein lies the permanent character of the socialist revolution as such.

The international character of the socialist revolution, which constitutes the third aspect of the theory of the permanent revolution, flows from the present state of economy and the social structure of humanity. Internationalism is no abstract principle but a theoretical and political reflection of the character of world economy, of the world development of productive forces and the world scale of the class struggle. The socialist revolution begins on national foundations—but it cannot be completed within these foundations. The maintenance of the proletarian revolution within a national framework can only be a provisional state of affairs, even though, as the experience of the Soviet Union shows, one of long duration. In an isolated proletarian dictatorship, the internal and external contradictions grow inevitably along with the successes achieved. If it remains isolated, the proletarian state must finally fall victim to these contradictions. The way out for it lies only in the victory of the proletariat of the advanced countries. Viewed from this standpoint, a national revolution is not a self-contained whole; it is only a link in the international chain. The international revolution constitutes a permanent process, despite temporary declines and ebbs.

The struggle of the epigones is directed, even if not always with the same clarity, against all three aspects of the theory of the permanent revolution. And how could it be otherwise, when it is a question of three inseparably connected parts of a whole? The epigones mechanically separate the *democratic* and the *socialist* dictatorships. They separate the *national* socialist revolution from the *international*. They consider that, in essence, the conquest of power within national limits is not the initial act but the final act of the revolution; after that follows the period of reforms that lead to the national socialist society. In 1905, they did not even grant the idea that the proletariat could conquer power in Russia earlier than in Western Europe. In 1917, they preached the self-sufficing democratic revolution in Russia and spurned the dictatorship of the proletariat. In 1925-27, they steered a course toward national revolution in China under the leadership of the national bourgeoisie. Subsequently, they raised the slogan for China of the democratic dictatorship of the workers and peasants in opposition to the slogan of the dictatorship of the proletariat. They proclaimed the possibility of the construction of an isolated and self-sufficient socialist society in the Soviet Union. The world revolution became for them, instead of an indispensable condition for victory, only a favourable circumstance. This profound breach with Marxism was reached by the epigones in the process of permanent struggle against the theory of the permanent revolution.

The struggle, which began with an artificial revival of historical reminiscences and the falsification of the distant past, led to the complete transformation of the world outlook of the ruling stratum of the revolution. We have already repeatedly explained that this re-evaluation of values was accomplished under the influence of the social needs of the Soviet bureaucracy, which became ever more conservative, strove for national order and demanded that the already-achieved revolution, which insured privileged positions to the bureaucracy, should now be considered adequate for the peaceful construction of socialism. We do not wish to return to this theme here. Suffice it to note that the bureaucracy is deeply conscious of the connection of its material and ideological positions with the theory of national socialism. This is being expressed most crassly right now, in spite of, or rather because of, the fact that the Stalinist machine of government, under the pressure of contradictions which it did not foresee, is driving to the left with all its might and inflicting quite severe blows upon its Right-Wing inspirers of yesterday. The hostility of the bureaucrats toward the Marxist Opposition, whose slogans and arguments they have borrowed in great haste, is not, as we know, diminishing in the least. The condemnation of the theory of the permanent revolution, and an acknowledgment, even if only indirect, of the theory of socialism in one country, is demanded, first and foremost, of those Oppositionists who raise the question of their re-admission into the party for the purpose of supporting the course toward industrialization, etc. By this the Stalinist bureaucracy reveals the purely *tactical* character of its left turn which goes along with retention of its national-reformist *strategical* foundations. It is superfluous to explain what this means; in politics as in war, tactics are in the long run subordinated to strategy.

The question has long ago gone beyond the specific sphere of the struggle against 'Trotskyism'. Gradually extending itself, it has to-day embraced literally all the problems of the revolutionary world outlook. Either permanent revolution *or* socialism in one country—this alternative embraces at the same time the internal problems of the Soviet Union, the prospects of revolution in the East, and finally, the fate of the Communist International as a whole.

The present work does not examine this question from *all* these sides; it is not necessary to repeat what has been already said in other works. In the *Criticism of the Draft Programme of the Communist International*,* I have endeavoured to disclose theoretically the economic and political untenability of national socialism. The theoreticians of the Comintern have kept mum about this. That is indeed the only thing left for them to do. In this book I above all restore the theory of the permanent revolution as it was formulated in 1905 with regard to the internal problems of the Russian revolution. I show wherein my position actually differed from Lenin's, and how and why it coincided with Lenin's position in every decisive situation. Finally, I endeavour to reveal the decisive significance of this question for the proletariat of the backward countries, and thereby for the Communist International as a whole.

What charges have been brought against the theory of the permanent revolution by the epigones? If we discard the innumerable contradictions of my critics, then their entire and truly vast body of writing can be reduced to the following propositions:

1. Trotsky ignored the difference between the bourgeois revolution and the socialist revolution. Already in 1905 he considered that the proletariat of Russia was directly faced with the tasks of a socialist revolution.

2. Trotsky completely forgot the agrarian question. The

---

* Included in *The Third International After Lenin*, published by Pioneer Publishers, New York.

peasantry did not exist for him. He depicted the revolution as a matter of single combat between the proletariat and Tsarism.

3. Trotsky did not believe that the world bourgeoisie would tolerate for any length of time the existence of the dictatorship of the Russian proletariat, and regarded its downfall as inevitable unless the proletariat of the West seized power within a very short period and came to our assistance. Thereby Trotsky underestimated the pressure of the Western European proletariat upon its own bourgeoisie.

4. Trotsky does not in general believe in the power of the Russian proletariat, in its ability to construct socialism independently; and that is why he has put and still puts all his hopes in the international revolution.

These motifs run through not only the numberless writings and speeches of Zinoviev, Stalin, Bukharin and others, but they are also formulated in the most authoritative resolutions of the Communist Party of the Soviet Union and the Communist International. And in spite of that, one is compelled to say that they are based upon a mixture of ignorance and dishonesty.

The first two contentions of the critics are, as will be shown later on, false to the very roots. No, I proceeded precisely from the bourgeois-democratic character of the revolution and arrived at the conclusion that the profundity of the agrarian crisis could raise the proletariat of backward Russia to power. Yes, this was precisely the idea I defended on the eve of the 1905 Revolution. This was precisely the idea that was expressed by the very designation of the revolution as a 'permanent', that is, an uninterrupted one, a revolution passing over directly from the bourgeois stage into the socialist. To express the same idea Lenin later used the excellent expression of the bourgeois revolution *growing over* into the socialist. The conception of 'growing over' was counterposed by Stalin, after the event (in 1924), to the permanent revolution, which he presented as a direct leap from the realm of autocracy into the realm of socialism. This ill-starred 'theoretician' did not even bother to ponder the question: What meaning can there be to the *permanency* of the revolution, that is, its *uninterrupted* development, if all that is involved is a mere leap?

As for the third accusation, it was dictated by the short-lived faith of the epigones in the possibility of *neutralizing* the *imperialist* bourgeoisie for an unlimited time with the aid of the 'shrewdly' organized pressure of the proletariat. In the years 1924-27, this was Stalin's central idea. The Anglo-Russian Committee was its fruit. Disappointment in the possibility of binding the world bourgeoisie hand and foot with the help of Purcell, Radic, LaFollette and Chiang Kai-shek led to an acute paroxysm of fear of an immediate war danger. The Comintern is still passing through this period.

The fourth objection to the theory of the permanent revolution simply amounts to saying that I did not in 1905 defend the standpoint of the theory of socialism in one country which Stalin first manufactured for the Soviet bureaucracy in 1924. This accusation is a sheer historical curiosity. One might actually believe that my opponents, insofar as they thought politically at all in 1905, were of the opinion then that Russia was ripe for an independent socialist revolution. As a matter of fact, in the period 1905-17 they were tireless in accusing me of utopianism because I allowed the probability that the Russian proletariat could come to power before the proletariat of Western Europe. Kamenev and Rykov accused Lenin of utopianism in April 1917, and therewith they explained to Lenin in simple language that the socialist revolution must first be achieved in Britain and in the other advanced countries before it could be Russia's turn. The same standpoint was defended by Stalin, too, up to April 4, 1917. Only gradually and with difficulty did he adopt the Leninist formula of the dictatorship of the proletariat in contradistinction to the democratic dictatorship. In the spring of 1924, Stalin was still repeating what others had said before him : taken separately, Russia is not ripe for the construction of a socialist society. In the autumn of 1924, Stalin, in his struggle against the theory of the permanent revolution, for the first time discovered the possibility of building an isolated socialism in Russia. Only then did the Red Professors collect quotations for Stalin which convicted Trotsky of having believed in 1905—how terrible!—that Russia could reach socialism only with the aid of the proletariat of the West.

Were one to take the history of the ideological struggle over a period of a quarter-century, cut it into little pieces, mix them in a mortar, and then command a blind man to stick the pieces together again, a greater theoretical and historical jumble of nonsense could hardly result than the one with which the epigones feed their readers and hearers.

To illumine the connection of yesterday's problems with today's, one must recall here, even if only very generally, what the leadership of the Comintern, that is, Stalin and Bukharin, perpetrated in China.

Under the pretext that China was faced with a national liberationist revolution, the leading role was allotted in 1924 to the Chinese bourgeoisie. The party of the national bourgeoisie, the Kuomintang, was officially recognised as the leading party. Not even the Russian Mensheviks went that far in 1905 in relation to the Cadets (the party of the liberal bourgeoisie).

But the leadership of the Comintern did not stop there. It compelled the Chinese Communist Party to enter the Kuomintang and submit to its discipline. In special telegrams from Stalin, the Chinese Communists were urged to curb the agrarian movement. The workers and peasants rising in revolt were forbidden to form their own soviets in order not to alienate Chiang Kai-shek, whom Stalin defended against the Oppositionists as a 'reliable ally' at a party meeting in Moscow at the beginning of April, 1927, that is, a few days before the counter-revolutionary coup d'etat in Shanghai.

The official subordination of the Communist Party to the bourgeois leadership, and the official prohibition of forming soviets (Stalin and Bukharin taught that the Kuomintang 'took the place' of soviets), was a grosser and more glaring betrayal of Marxism than all the deeds of the Mensheviks in the years 1905-1917.

After Chiang Kai-shek's coup d'etat in April, 1927, a Left Wing, under the leadership of Wang Ching-wei, split off temporarily from the Kuomintang. Wang Ching-wei was immediately hailed in *Pravda* as a reliable ally. In essence, Wang Ching-wei bore the same relation to Chiang Kai-shek as Kerensky to Milyukov, with this difference that in China Milyukov and Kornilov were united in the single person of Chiang Kai-shek.

After April, 1927, the Chinese party was ordered to enter the 'Left' Kuomintang and to submit to the discipline of the Chinese Kerensky instead of preparing open warfare against him. The 'reliable' Wang Ching-wei crushed the Communist Party, and together with it the workers' and peasants' movement, no less brutally than Chiang Kai-shek, whom Stalin had declared his reliable ally.

Though the Mensheviks supported Milyukov in 1905 and afterwards, they nevertheless did not enter the liberal party. Though the Mensheviks went hand in hand with Kerensky in 1917, they still retained their own organisation. Stalin's policy in China was a malicious caricature even of Menshevism. That is what the first and most important chapter looked like.

After its inevitable fruits had appeared—complete decline of the workers' and peasants' movement, demoralisation and break-up of the Communist Party—the leadership of the Comintern gave the command : "Left about turn! " and demanded immediate transition to the armed uprising of the workers and peasants. Up to yesterday the young, crushed and mutilated Communist Party still served as the fifth wheel in the wagon of Chiang Kai-shek and Wang Ching-wei, and consequently lacked the slightest independent political experience. And now suddenly this party was commanded to lead the workers and peasants—whom the Comintern had up to yesterday held back under the banner of the Kuomintang—in an armed insurrection against the same Kuomintang which had meanwhile found time to concentrate the power and the army in its hands. In the course of 24 hours a fictitious soviet was improvised in Canton. An armed insurrection, timed in advance for the opening of the Fifteenth Congress of the Communist Party of the Soviet Union, expressed simultaneously the heroism of the advanced Chinese workers and the criminality of the Comintern leaders. Lesser adventures preceded the Canton uprising and followed it. Such was the second chapter of the Chinese strategy of the Comintern. It can be characterised as the most malicious caricature of Bolshevism.

The liberal-opportunist and adventurist chapters delivered a blow to the Chinese Communist Party from which, even with a correct policy, it can only recover after a number of years.

The Sixth Congress of the Comintern drew up the balance sheet of all this work. It gave it unreserved approval. This is hardly surprising, since the Congress was convoked for this purpose. For the future, the Congress advanced the slogan 'democratic dictatorship of the proletariat and peasantry.' Wherein this dictatorship would differ from the dictatorship of the Right or Left Kuomintang, on the one side, and the dictatorship of the proletariat on the other—this was not explained to the Chinese Communists. Nor is it possible to explain it.

Proclaiming the slogan of the democratic dictatorship the Sixth Congress at the same time condemned democratic slogans as impermissible (constituent assembly, universal suffrage, freedom of speech and of the press, etc.) and thereby completely disarmed the Chinese Communist Party in the face of the dictatorship of the military oligarchy. For a long number of years, the Russian Bolsheviks had mobilized the workers and peasants around democratic slogans. Democratic slogans played a big role in 1917. Only after the Soviet power had actually come into existence and clashed politically with the Constituent Assembly, irreconcilably and in full view of the entire people, did our party liquidate the institutions and slogans of formal democracy, that is, bourgeois democracy, in favour of real soviet democracy, that is, proletarian democracy.

The Sixth Congress of the Comintern, under the leadership of Stalin and Bukharin, turned all this upside down. While on the one hand it prescribed the slogan of 'democratic' and not 'proletarian' dictatorship for the party, it simultaneously forbade it to use democratic slogans in preparing for this dictatorship. The Chinese Communist Party was not only disarmed, but stripped naked. By way of consolation it was finally permitted in the period of unlimited domination of the counter-revolution, to use the slogan of soviets, which had remained under ban throughout the upsurge of the revolution. A very popular hero of Russian folk-lore sings wedding songs at funerals and funeral hymns at weddings. He is soundly thrashed on both occasions. If what was involved was only thrashings administered to the strategists of the incumbent leadership of the Comintern, one might perhaps reconcile oneself to it. But much greater issues are at stake. Involved here is the fate of the proletariat. The tactics of the Comintern constituted an unconsciously, but all the more reliably, organized sabotage of the Chinese Revolution. This sabotage was accomplished with certainty of success, for the Right Menshevik policy of 1924-27 was clothed by the Comintern with all the authority of Bolshevism, and at the same time was protected by the Soviet power, through its mighty machine of repression, from the criticism of the Left Opposition.

As a result, we saw accomplished a finished experiment of Stalinist strategy, which proceeded from beginning to end under the flag of a struggle against the permanent revolution. It was, therefore, quite natural that the principal Stalinist theoretician of the subordination of the Chinese Communist Party to the national-bourgeois Kuomintang should have been Martynov. This same Martynov had been the principal Menshevik critic of the theory of the permanent revolution from 1905 right up to 1923, the year when he began to fulfil his historic mission in the ranks of Bolshevism.

The essential facts about the origin of the present work are dealt with in the first chapter. In Alma-Ata I was unhurriedly preparing a theoretical polemic against the epigones. The theory of the permanent revolution was to occupy a large place in this book. While at work, I received a manuscript by Radek which was devoted to counterposing the permanent revolution to the strategic line of Lenin. Radek needed to make this, so to say, unexpected sortie because he was himself submerged up to his ears in Stalin's Chinese policy : Radek (together with Zinoviev) defended the subordination of the Communist Party to the Kuomintang not only before Chiang Kai-shek's coup d'etat but even after it.

To provide a basis for the enslavement of the proletariat to the bourgeoisie, Radek naturally cited the necessity of an alliance with the peasantry and my 'underestimation' of this necessity. Following Stalin, he too defended Menshevik policy with Bolshevik phraseology. With the formula of the democratic dictatorship of the proletariat and the peasantry, Radek, following

Stalin, once again covered up the fact that the Chinese proletariat had been diverted from independent struggle for power at the head of the peasant masses. When I exposed this ideological masquerade, there arose in Radek the urgent need to prove that my struggle against opportunism disguising itself with quotations from Lenin was derived in reality from the contradiction between the theory of the permanent revolution and Leninism. Radek, speaking as attorney in defence of his own sins, converted his speech into a prosecutor's indictment of the permanent revolution. This served him only as a bridge to capitulation. I had all the more reason to suspect this since Radek, years before, had planned to write a pamphlet in defence of the permanent revolution. Still I did not hasten to write Radek off. I tried to answer his article frankly and categorically without at the same time cutting off his retreat. I print my reply to Radek just as it was written, confining myself to a few explanatory notes and stylistic corrections.

Radek's article was not published in the press, and I believe it will not be published, for in the form in which it was written in 1928 it could not pass through the sieve of the Stalinist censorship. Even for Radek himself this article would be downright fatal today, for it would give a clear picture of his ideological evolution, which very strongly recalls the 'evolution' of a man who throws himself out of a sixth-floor window.

The origin of this work explains sufficiently why Radek occupies a larger place in it than it is perhaps his right to claim. Radek did not think up a single new argument against the theory of the permanent revolution. He came forward only as an epigone of the epigones. The reader is, therefore, recommended to see in Radek not simply Radek but the representative of a certain corporation, in which he purchased an associate membership at the price of renouncing Marxism. Should Radek personally feel that too many digs have fallen to his share, then he should at his own discretion turn them over to the more appropriate addresses. That is the private affair of the firm. For my part, I raise no objections.

Various groupings of the German Communist Party have come into power or fought for it by demonstrating their qualifications for leadership by means of critical exercises against the permanent revolution. But this entire literature, emanating from Maslow, Thalheimer and the rest, is on such a sorry level that it does not even provide a pretext for a critical answer. The Thaelmanns, the Remmeles and other incumbent leaders by appointment, have taken this question even a stage lower. All these critics have succeeded merely in demonstrating that they are unable to reach even the threshold of the question. For this reason, I leave them—beyond the threshold. Anyone interested in the theoretical critiques by Maslow, Thalheimer and the rest, can, after reading this book, turn to their writings in order to convince himself of the ignorance and dishonesty of these authors. This will be, so to speak, a by-product of the work I am offering the reader.

L. TROTSKY.

Prinkipo, November 30, 1929.

INTRODUCTION TO THE GERMAN EDITION

As this book goes to press in the German language, the entire thinking section of the world working class and, in a sense, the whole of 'civilized' humanity is following with particularly keen interest the economic turn, and its reverberations, now taking place over most of the former Tsarist empire. The greatest attention in this connection is aroused by the problem of collectivizing the peasant holdings. This is hardly surprising: in this sphere the break with the past assumes a particularly sweeping character. But a correct evaluation of collectivization is unthinkable without a general conception of the socialist revolution. And here, on a much higher plane, we once again become convinced that in the field of Marxist theory there is nothing that fails to impinge on practical activity. The most remote, and it would seem, the most 'abstract' disagreements, if they are thought out to the end, will sooner or later be invariably expressed in practice, and practice does not allow a single theoretical mistake to be made with impunity.

The collectivization of peasant holdings is, of course, a most necessary and fundamental part of the socialist transformation of society. However, the scope and tempo of collectivization are not determined by the government's will alone, but, in the last analysis, by the economic factors: by the height of the country's economic level, by the inter-relationship between industry and agriculture, and consequently by the technical resources of agriculture itself.

Industrialization is the driving force of the whole of modern culture and by this token the only conceivable basis for socialism. In the conditions of the Soviet Union, industrialization means first of all the strengthening of the base of the proletariat as a ruling class. Simultaneously it creates the material and technical premises for the collectivization of agriculture. The tempos of these two processes are interdependent. The proletariat is interested in the highest possible tempos for these processes to the extent that the new society in the making is thus best protected from external danger, and at the same time a source is created for systematically improving the material level of the toiling masses.

However, the tempos that can be achieved are limited by the general material and cultural level of the country, by the relationship between the city and the village and by the most pressing needs of the masses, who are able to sacrifice their today for the sake of tomorrow *only up to a certain point*. The optimum tempos, i.e., the best and most advantageous ones, are those which not only promote the most rapid growth of industry and collectivization at a given moment, but which also secure the necessary stability of the social régime, that is, first of all strengthen the alliance of the workers and peasants, thereby preparing the possibility for future successes.

From this standpoint, of decisive significance is the general historical criterion in accordance with which the party and state leadership direct economic development by means of planning. Here two main variants are possible : (a) the course outlined above toward the economic strengthening of the proletarian dictatorship in one country until further victories of the world proletarian revolution (the viewpoint of the Russian Left Opposition); and (b) the course toward the construction of an isolated national socialist society, and this 'in the shortest possible time' (the current official position).

These are two completely different, and, in the last analysis, directly opposed conceptions of socialism. From these are derived basically different lines, strategy and tactics.

In the limits of this preface we cannot deal in detail with the question of building socialism in one country. To this we have devoted a number of writings, particularly *Criticism of the Draft Programme of the Comintern*. Here we confine ourselves to the fundamental elements of this question. Let us recall, first of all, that the theory of socialism in one country was first formulated by Stalin in the autumn of 1924, in complete contradiction not only to all the traditions of Marxism and the school of Lenin, but even to what Stalin himself had written in the spring of the same year. From the standpoint of principle, the departure from Marxism by the Stalinist 'school' on the issues of socialist construction is no less significant and drastic than, for example, the break of the German Social Democrats from Marxism on the issues of war and patriotism in the fall of 1914, exactly ten years before the Stalinist turn. This comparison is by no means accidental in character. Stalin's 'mistake', just like the 'mistake' of the German Social Democracy, is *national socialism*.

Marxism takes its point of departure from world economy, not as a sum of national parts but as a mighty and independent reality which has been created by the international division of labour and the world market, and which in our epoch imperiously dominates the national markets. The productive forces of capitalist society have long ago outgrown the national boundaries. The imperialist war (of 1914-1918) was one of the expressions of this fact. In respect of the technique of production socialist society must represent a stage higher than capitalism. To aim at building a *nationally isolated* socialist society means, in spite of all passing successes, to pull the productive forces backward even as compared with capitalism. To attempt, regardless of the geographical, cultural and historical conditions of the country's development, which constitutes a part of the world unity, to realize a shut-off proportionality of all the branches of economy within a national framework, means to pursue a reactionary utopia. If the heralds and supporters of this theory nevertheless participate in the international revolutionary struggle (with what success is a different question) it is because, as hopeless eclectics, they mechanically combine abstract internationalism with reactionary utopian national socialism. The crowning expression of this eclecticism is the programme of the Comintern adopted by the Sixth Congress.

In order to expose graphically one of the main theoretical mistakes underlying the national socialist conception we cannot do better than quote from a recently published speech of Stalin, devoted to the internal questions of American Communism.* 'It would be wrong,' says Stalin, arguing against one of the American factions, 'to ignore the specific peculiarities of American capitalism. The Communist party must take them into account in its work. But it would be still more wrong to base the activities of the Communist party on these specific features, since the foundation of the activities of every Communist party, including the American Communist Party, on which it must base itself, must be the *general features* of capitalism, which are the *same for all countries*, and not its specific features in any given country. *It is precisely on this that the internationalism of the Communist Parties rests.* The specific features are merely *supplementary* to the general features.' (*Bolshevik*, No. 1, 1930, p. 8. Our emphasis.)

These lines leave nothing to be desired in the way of clarity. Under the guise of providing an economic justification for internationalism, Stalin in reality presents a justification for national socialism. It is false that world economy is simply a sum of national parts of one and the same type. It is false that the specific features are 'merely supplementary to the general features,' like warts on a face. In reality, the national peculiarities represent an original combination of the basic features of the world process. This originality can be of decisive significance for revolutionary strategy over a span of many years. Suffice it to recall that the proletariat of a backward country has come to power many years before the proletariat of the advanced countries. This historic lesson alone shows that in spite of Stalin, it is absolutely wrong to base the activity of the Communist parties on some 'general features', that is, on an abstract type of national

* Stalin delivered this speech on May 6, 1929; it was first published early in 1930, in circumstances that cause it to acquire a sort of 'programmatic' significance.—L.T. (The speech was published in *The Communist* (U.S.A.) June, 1930. See W. Z. Foster, *History of the C.P.U.S.A.*, 1952, p. 273. It does not appear in Stalin's collected works.)

capitalism. It is utterly false to contend that 'this is what the internationalism of the Communist parties rests upon'. In reality, it rests on the insolvency of the national state, which has long ago outlived itself and which has turned into a brake upon the development of the productive forces. National capitalism cannot be even understood, let alone reconstructed, except as a part of world economy.

The economic peculiarities of different countries are in no way of a subordinate character. It is enough to compare England and India, the United States and Brazil. But the specific features of national economy, no matter how great, enter as component parts and in increasing measure into the higher reality which is called world economy and on which alone, in the last analysis, the internationalism of the Communist parties rests.

Stalin's characterization of national peculiarities as a simple 'supplement' to the general type, is in crying and therewith not accidental contradiction to Stalin's understanding (that is, his lack of understanding) of the law of uneven development of capitalism. This law, as is well known, is proclaimed by Stalin as the most fundamental, most important and universal of laws. With the help of the law of uneven development, which he has converted into an empty abstraction, Stalin tries to solve all the riddles of existence. But the astonishing thing is that he does not notice that *national peculiarity is nothing else but the most general product of the unevenness of historical development, its summary result, so to say.* It is only necessary to understand this unevenness correctly, to consider it in its full extent, and also to extend it to the pre-capitalist past. A faster or slower development of the productive forces; the expanded, or, contrariwise, the contracted character of entire historical epochs—for example, the Middle Ages, the guild system, enlightened absolutism, parliamentarism; the uneven development of different branches of economy, different classes, different social institutions, different fields of culture—all these lie at the base of these national 'peculiarities'. The peculiarity of a national social type is the crystallization of the unevenness of its formation.

The October Revolution came as the most momentous manifestation of the unevenness of the historic process. The theory of the permanent revolution gave the prognosis of the October Revolution; by this token this theory rested on the law of uneven development, not in its abstract form, but in its material crystallization in Russia's social and political peculiarity.

Stalin has dragged in the law of uneven development not in order to foresee in time the seizure of power by the proletariat of a backward country, but in order, after the fact, in 1924, to foist upon the already victorious proletariat the task of constructing a national socialist society. But it is precisely here that the law of uneven development is inapplicable, for it does not replace nor does it abolish the laws of world economy; on the contrary, it is subordinated to them.

By making a fetish of the law of uneven development, Stalin proclaims it a sufficient basis for national socialism, not as a type common to all countries, but exceptional, Messianic, purely Russian. It is possible, according to Stalin, to construct a self-sufficient socialist society only in Russia. By this alone he elevates Russia's national peculiarities not only above the 'general features' of every capitalist nation, but also above world economy as a whole. It is just here that the fatal flaw in Stalin's whole conception begins. The peculiarity of the U.S.S.R. is so potent that it makes possible the construction of its own socialism within its own borders, regardless of what happens to the rest of mankind. As regards other countries, to which the Messianic seal has not been affixed, their peculiarities are merely 'supplementary' to the general features, only a wart on the face. 'It would be wrong,' teaches Stalin, 'to base the activities of the Communist parties on these specific features'. This moral holds good for the American C.P., and the British, and the South African and the Serbian, but—not for the Russian, whose activity is based not on the 'general features' but precisely on the 'peculiarities.' From this flows the thoroughly dualistic strategy of the Comintern. While the U.S.S.R. 'liquidates the classes' and builds socialism, the proletariat of all the other countries, in complete disregard of existing national conditions, is obligated to carry on uniform activity according to the calendar (First of August, March Sixth, etc.). Messianic nationalism is supplemented by bureaucratically abstract internationalism. This dualism runs through the whole programme of the Comintern, and deprives it of any principled significance.

If we take Britain and India as polarised varieties of the capitalist type, then we are obliged to say that the internationalism of the British and Indian proletariats does not at all rest on an *identity* of conditions, tasks and methods, but on their indivisible *interdependence*. Successes for the liberation movement in India presuppose a revolutionary movement in Britain and vice versa. Neither in India, nor in England is it possible to build an *independent* socialist society. Both of them will have to enter as parts into a higher whole. Upon this and only upon this rests the unshakeable foundation of Marxist internationalism.

Recently, on March 8, 1930, *Pravda* expounded anew Stalin's ill-starred theory, in the sense that 'socialism, as a social-economic formation,' that is, as a definite system of production relations, can be fully realized 'on the national scale of the U.S.S.R.' Something else again is 'the *final victory of socialism*' in the sense of a guarantee against the intervention of capitalist encirclement—such a final victory of socialism 'actually demands the triumph of the proletarian revolution in several advanced countries.' What an abysmal decline of theoretical thought was required for such shoddy scholasticism to be expounded with a learned air in the pages of the central organ of Lenin's party! If we assume for a minute the possibility of realizing socialism as a finished social system within the isolated framework of the U.S.S.R., then that would be the 'final victory'—because in that case what talk could there be about a possible intervention? The socialist order presupposes high levels of technology and culture and solidarity of population. Since the U.S.S.R., at the moment of complete construction of socialism, will have, it must be assumed, a population of between 200,000,000 and 250,000,000, we then ask : What intervention could even be talked of then? What capitalist country, or coalition of countries, would dare think of intervention in these circumstances? The only conceivable intervention could come from the side of the U.S.S.R. But would it be needed? Hardly. The example of a backward country, which in the course of several Five-Year Plans was able to construct a mighty socialist society with its own forces, would mean a death blow to world capitalism, and would reduce to a minimum, if not to zero, the costs of the world proletarian revolution. This is why the whole Stalinist conception actually leads to the liquidation of the Communist International. And indeed, what would be its historical significance, if the fate of socialism is to be decided by the highest possible authority — the State Planning Commission of the U.S.S.R.? In that case, the task of the Comintern, along with the notorious 'Friends of the Soviet Union,' would be to protect the construction of socialism from intervention, that is, in essence, to play the role of frontier patrols.

The article mentioned attempts to prove the correctness of the Stalinist conception with the very newest and freshest economic arguments : '. . . . Precisely now,' says *Pravda*, 'when productive relations of a socialist type are taking deeper root not only in industry but also in agriculture through the growth of state farms, through the gigantic rise, quantitatively and qualitatively, of the collective-farm movement and the liquidation of the kulaks as a class on the basis of complete collectivization, precisely now what is shown clearest of all is the sorry bankruptcy of the Trotskyite-Zinovievite theory of defeat, which has meant in essence "the Menshevik denial of the legitimacy of the October Revolution" (Stalin)'. (*Pravda*, March 8, 1930.)

These are truly remarkable lines, and not merely for their glib tone which covers a complete confusion of thought. Together with Stalin, the author of *Pravda's* article accuses the 'Trotskyite' conception of 'denying the legitimacy of the October Revolution.' But it was exactly on the basis of this conception, that is, the theory of the permanent revolution, that the writer of these lines *foretold the inevitability* of the October Revolution, thirteen years before it took place. And Stalin? Even after the February Revolution, that is seven to eight months prior to the October Revolution, he came forward as a vulgar revolutionary democrat. It was necessary for Lenin to arrive in Petrograd (April 3, 1917) with his merciless struggle against the conceited 'Old Bolsheviks,' whom Lenin ridiculed so at that time, for Stalin carefully and noiselessly to glide over from the democratic position to the socialist. This inner 'growing over' of Stalin, which by the way was never completed, took place, at any rate, not earlier than 12 years after I had offered proof of the 'legitimacy' of the seizure of power by the working class of Russia before the beginning of the proletarian revolution in the West.

But, in elaborating the theoretical prognosis of the October Revolution, I did not at all believe that, by conquering state power, the Russian proletariat would exclude the former Tsarist empire from the orbit of world economy. We Marxists know the role and meaning of state power. It is not at all a passive reflection of economic processes, as the Social Democratic servants of the bourgeois state depict it. Power can have a gigantic significance, reactionary as well as progressive, depending on which class holds power in its hands. But state power is nonetheless an instrument of the superstructural order. The passing of power from the hands of Tsarism and the bourgeoisie into the hands of the proletariat abolishes neither the processes nor the laws of world economy. To be sure, for a certain time after the October Revolution, the economic ties between the Soviet Union and the world market were weakened. But it would be a monstrous mistake to make a generalization out of a phenomenon that was merely a brief stage in the dialectical process. The international division of labour and the supra-national character of modern productive forces not only retain but will increase twofold and tenfold their significance for the Soviet Union in proportion to the degree of Soviet economic ascent.

Every backward country integrated with capitalism has passed through various stages of decreasing or increasing dependence upon the other capitalist countries, but in general the tendency of capitalist development is toward a colossal growth of world ties, which is expressed in the growing volume of foreign trade, including, of course, capital export. Britain's dependence upon India naturally bears a qualitatively different character from India's dependence upon Britain. But this difference is determined, at bottom, by the difference in the respective levels of development of their productive forces, and not at all by the degree of their economic self-sufficiency. India is a colony; Britain, a metropolis. But if Britain were subjected today to an economic blockade, it would perish sooner than would India under a similar blockade. This, by the way, is one of the convincing illustrations of the reality of world economy.

Capitalist development—not in the abstract formulas of the second volume of *Capital*, which retain all their significance as *a stage in analysis*, but in historical reality—took place and could only take place by a systematic expansion of its base. In the process of its development, and consequently in the struggle with its internal contradictions, every national capitalism turns in an ever-increasing degree to the reserves of the 'external market,' that is, the reserves of world economy. The uncontrollable expansion growing out of the permanent internal crises of capitalism constitutes a progressive force up to the time when it turns into a force fatal to capitalism.

Over and above the internal contradictions of capitalism, the October Revolution inherited from old Russia the contradictions, no less profound, between capitalism as a whole and the pre-capitalist forms of production. These contradictions possessed, as they still do, a material character, that is, they are embodied in the material relations between town and country, they are lodged in the particular proportions or disproportions between the various branches of industry and in the national economy as a whole, etc. Some of the roots of these contradictions lie directly in the geographical and demographical conditions of the country, that is, they are nurtured by the abundance or scarcity of one or another natural resource, the historically-created distribution of the masses of the population, and so on. The strength of Soviet economy lies in the nationalization of the means of production and their planned direction. The weakness of Soviet economy, in addition to the backwardness inherited from the past, lies in its present post-revolutionary isolation, that is, in its inability to gain access to the resources of world economy, not only on a socialist but even on a capitalist basis, that is, in the shape of normal international credits and 'financing' in general, which plays so decisive a role for backward countries. Meanwhile, the contradictions of the Soviet Union's capitalist and pre-capitalist past not only do not disappear of themselves, but on the contrary rise up from the recovery from the years of decline and destruction; they revive and are aggravated with the growth of Soviet economy, and in order to be overcome or even mitigated they demand at every step that access to the resources of the world market be achieved.

To understand what is happening now in the vast territory which the October Revolution awakened to new life, it is necessary to take clearly into account that to the old contradictions recently revived by the economic successes there has been added a new and most powerful contradiction between the concentrated character of Soviet industry, which opens up the possibility of unexampled tempos of development, and the isolation of Soviet economy, which excludes the possibility of a normal utilization of the reserves of world economy. The new contradiction, pressing down upon the old ones, leads to this, that alongside of tremendous successes, painful difficulties arise. These find their most immediate and onerous expression, felt daily by every worker and peasant, in the fact that the conditions of the toiling masses do not keep step with the general rise of the economy, but are even growing worse at present as a result of the food difficulties. The sharp crises of Soviet economy are a reminder that the productive forces created by capitalism are not adapted to national markets, and can be socialistically co-ordinated and harmonized only on an international scale. To put it differently, the crises of Soviet economy are not merely maladies of growth, a sort of infantile sickness, but something far more significant—namely, they are the harsh curbings of the world market, the very one 'to which,' in Lenin's words, 'we are subordinated, with which we are bound up, and from which we cannot escape.' (Speech at the Eleventh Party Congress, March 27, 1922).

From the foregoing, however, there in no way follows a denial of the historical 'legitimacy' of the October Revolution, a conclusion which reeks of shameful philistinism. The seizure of power by the international proletariat cannot be a single, simultaneous act. The political superstructure—and a revolution is part of the ' superstructure '—has its own dialectic, which intervenes imperiously in the process of world economy, but does not abolish its deep-going laws. The October Revolution is 'legitimate' as the *first stage of the world revolution* which unavoidably extends over decades. The interval between the first and the second stage has turned out to be considerably longer than we had expected. Nevertheless it remains an interval, and it is by no means converted into a self-sufficient epoch of the building of a national socialist society.

Out of the two conceptions of the revolution there stem two guiding lines on (Soviet) economic questions. The first swift economic successes, which were completely unexpected by Stalin, inspired him in the fall of 1924 with the theory of socialism in one country as the culmination of the practical prospect of an isolated national economy. It was precisely in this period that Bukharin advanced his famous formula that by protecting ourselves from world economy by means of the monopoly of foreign trade, we should be in a position to build socialism 'although at a tortoise pace.' This was the common formula of the bloc of the Centrists (Stalin) with the Rights (Bukharin). Already at that time, Stalin tirelessly propounded the idea that the tempo of our industrialization is our 'own affair,' having no relation whatever to world economy. Such a national smugness naturally could not last long, for it reflected the first, very brief stage of economic revival, which necessarily revived our dependence on the world market. The first shocks of international dependence, unexpected by the national socialists, created an alarm, which in the next stage turned into panic. We must gain economic 'independence' as speedily as possible with the aid of the speediest possible tempos of industrialization and collectivization!—this is the transformation that has taken place in the economic policy of national socialism in the past two years. Creeping and penny-pinching was replaced all along the line by adventurism. The theoretical base under both remains the same : the national socialist conception.

The basic difficulties, as has been shown above, derive from the objective situation, primarily from the isolation of the Soviet Union. We shall not pause here to consider to what extent this objective situation is itself a product of the subjective mistakes of the leadership (the false policy in Germany in 1923, in Bulgaria and Estonia in 1924, in Britain and Poland in 1926, in China in 1925-27; the current false strategy of the 'Third Period,' etc., etc.). But the sharpest convulsions in the U.S.S.R. are created by the fact that the incumbent leadership tries to make a virtue out of necessity, and out of the political isolation of the workers' state constructs a programme of an economically-isolated socialist society. This has given rise to the attempt at complete socialist collectivization of peasant holdings on the basis of a pre-capitalist inventory—a most dangerous adventure which threatens to undermine the very possibility of collaboration between the proletariat and the peasantry.

Remarkably, just at the moment when this has become deline-ated in all its sharpness, Bukharin, yesterday's theoretician of the 'tortoise pace,' has composed a pathetic hymn to the present-day 'furious gallop' of industrialization and collectivization. It is to be feared that this hymn, too, will presently be declared the greatest heresy. For there are already new melodies in the air. Under the influence of the resistance of economic reality, Stalin has been compelled to beat a retreat. Now the danger is that yesterday's adventuristic offensive, dictated by panic, may turn into a panic-stricken retreat. Such alternation of stages results inexorably from the nature of national socialism.

A realistic programme for an isolated workers' state cannot set itself the goal of achieving 'independence' from world economy, much less of constructing a national socialist society 'in the shortest time.' The task is not to attain the abstract maximum tempo, but the optimum tempo, that is, the best, that which fol-lows from both internal and world economic conditions, strengthens the position of the proletariat, prepares the national elements of the future international socialist society, and at the same time, and above all, systematically improves the living stand-ards of the proletariat and strengthens its alliance with the non-exploiting masses of the countryside. This prospect must remain in force for the whole preparatory period, that is, until the vic-torious revolution in the advanced countries liberates the Soviet Union from its present isolated position.

Some of the thoughts expressed here are developed in greater detail in other works by the author, particularly in the 'Criticism of the Draft Programme of the Comintern.' In the near future I hope to publish a pamphlet specially devoted to an evaluation of the present stage of economic development of the USSR. To these

works I am obliged to direct the reader who seeks a closer acqaint-
ance with the way in which the problem of the permanent
revolution is posed *today*. But the considerations brought out
above are sufficient, let me hope, to reveal the full significance of
the struggle over principles which was carried on in recent years,
and is being carried on right now in the shape of two contrasting
theories: *socialism in one country* versus *the permanent revolution*.
Only this topical significance of the question justifies the fact that
we present here to foreign readers a book that is largely devoted to
a critical reproduction of the pre-revolutionary prognoses and
theoretical disputes among the Russian Marxists A different form
of exposition of the questions that interest us might, of course,
have been selected. But this form was never created by the author,
and was not selected by him of his own accord. It was imposed
upon him partly by the opponent's will and partly by the very
course of political development. Even the truths of mathematics,
the most abstract of the sciences, can best be learned in connection
with the history of their discovery. This applies with even greater
force to the more concrete, i.e. historically-conditioned truths of
Marxist politics. The history of the origin and development of the
prognoses of the revolution under the conditions of pre-revolutionary Russia will, I think, bring the reader much closer and far more
concretely to the essence of the revolutionary tasks of the world
proletariat than a scholastic and pedantic exposition of these
political ideas, torn out of the conditions of struggle which gave
them birth.

March 29, 1930.

THE PERMANENT REVOLUTION

1. THE ENFORCED NATURE OF THIS WORK, AND ITS AIM

THE demand for theory in the party under the leadership of the Right-Centrist bloc has been met for six successive years by anti-Trotskyism, this being the one and only product available in unlimited quantities and for free distribution. Stalin engaged in theory for the first time in 1924, with the immortal articles against the permanent revolution. Even Molotov was baptised as a 'leader' in this font. Falsification is in full swing. A few days ago I happened upon an announcement of the publication in German of Lenin's writings of 1917. This is an invaluable gift to the advanced German working class. One can, however, picture in advance what a lot of falsifications there will be in the text and more especially in the notes. It is enough to point out that first place in the table of contents is given to Lenin's letters to Kollontai in New York. Why? Merely because these letters contain harsh remarks about me, based on *completely false* information from Kollontai, who had given her organic Menshevism an inoculation of hysterical ultra-leftism in those days. In the Russian edition the epigones were compelled to indicate, even if only ambiguously, that Lenin had been misinformed. But it may be assumed that the German edition will not present even this evasive reservation. We might also add that in the same letters of Lenin to Kollontai there are furious assaults upon Bukharin, with whom Kollontai was then in solidarity. This aspect of the letters has been suppressed, however, for the time being. It will be made public only when an open

campaign against Bukharin is launched. We shall not have to wait
very long for that.* On the other hand a number of very valuable
documents, articles and speeches of Lenin's, as well as minutes,
letters, etc., remain concealed only because they are directed
against Stalin and Co. and undermine the legend of 'Trotskyism.'
Of the history of the three Russian revolutions, as well as the
history of the party, literally not a single shred has been left intact:
theory, facts, traditions, the heritage of Lenin, all these have been
sacrificed to the struggle against 'Trotskyism,' which was invented
and organized, after Lenin was taken ill, as a personal struggle
against Trotsky, and which later developed into a struggle against
Marxism.

It has again been confirmed that what might appear as the most
useless raking up of long-extinct disputes usually satisfies some unconscious social requirement of the day, a requirement which, in
itself, does not follow the line of old disputes. The campaign
against 'the old Trotskyism' was in a reality a campaign against the
October traditions, which had become more and more cramping and
unbearable for the new bureaucracy. They began to characterize
as 'Trotskyism' everything they wanted to get rid of. Thus the
struggle against Trotskyism gradually became the expression of
the theoretical and political *reaction* among broad non-proletarian
and partly also among proletarian circles, and the reflection of
this reaction inside the party. In particular, the caricatured and
historically distorted counterposition of the permanent revolution
to Lenin's line of 'alliance with the *muzhik*' sprang full-grown in
1923. It arose along with the period of social, political and party
reaction, as its most graphic expression, as the organic antagonism
of the bureaucrat and the property-owner to world revolution with
its 'permanent' disturbances, and the yearning of the petty-bourgeoisie and officialdom for tranquillity and order. The vicious
baiting of the permanent revolution served, in turn, only to clear
the ground for the theory of socialism in one country, that is, for
the latest variety of national socialism. In themselves, of course,
these new social roots of the struggle against 'Trotskyism' do not
prove anything either for or against the correctness of the theory of

---

* This prediction has in the meantime been fulfilled.—L.T.

the permanent revolution. Yet, without an understanding of these hidden roots, the controversy must inevitably bear a barren academic character.

In recent years I have not found it possible to tear myself away from the new problems and return to old questions which are bound up with the period of the 1905 Revolution, in so far as these questions are primarily concerned with my past and have been artificially used against it. To give an analysis of the old differences of opinion and particularly of my old mistakes, against the background of the situation in which they arose—an analysis so thorough that these controversies and mistakes would become comprehensible to the young generation, not to speak of the old-timers who have fallen into political second childhood—this would require a whole volume to itself. It seemed monstrous to me to waste my own and others' time upon it, when constantly new questions of enormous importance were being placed on the order of the day: the tasks of the German Revolution, the question of the future fate of Britain, the question of the interrelationship of America and Europe, the problems broached by the strikes of the British proletariat, the tasks of the Chinese Revolution and, lastly and mainly, our own internal economic and socio-political contradictions and tasks—all this, I believe, amply justified my continual putting-off of my historico-polemical work on the permanent revolution. But social consciousness abhors a vacuum. In recent years this theoretical vacuum has been, as I have said, filled up with the rubbish of anti-Trotskyism. The epigones, the philosophers and the brokers of party reaction slipped down ever lower, went to school under the dull-witted Menshevik Martynov, trampled Lenin underfoot, floundered around in the swamp, and called all this the struggle against Trotskyism. In all these years they have not managed to produce a single work serious or important enough to be mentioned out loud without a feeling of shame; they did not bring forth a single political appraisal that has retained its validity, not a single prognosis that has been confirmed, not a single independent slogan that has advanced us ideologically. Nothing but trash and hack-work everywhere.

Stalin's *Problems of Leninism* constitutes a codification of this ideological garbage, an official manual of narrow-mindedness, an anthology of enumerated banalities (I am doing my best to find the most moderate designations possible). *Leninism* by Zinoviev is . . . Zinovievist Leninism, and nothing more or less. Zinoviev acts almost on Luther's principle. But whereas Luther said, 'Here I stand; I cannot do otherwise.' Zinoviev says, 'Here I stand . . . but I can do otherwise, too.' To occupy oneself in either case with these theoretical products of epigonism is equally unbearable, with this difference: that in reading Zinoviev's *Leninism* one experiences the sensation of choking on loose cotton-wool, while Stalin's *Problems* evokes the sensation of finely-chopped bristles. These two books are, each in its own way, the image and crown of the epoch of ideological reaction.

Fitting and adjusting all questions, whether from the right or the left, from above or below, from before or behind—to Trotskyism, the epigones have finally contrived to make every world event directly or indirectly dependent upon how the permanent revolution looked to Trotsky in 1905. The legend of Trotskyism, chock-full of falsifications, has become to a certain extent a factor in contemporary history. And while the right-centrist line of recent years has compromised itself in every continent by bankruptcies of historic dimensions, the struggle against the centrist ideology in the Comintern is today already unthinkable, or at least made very difficult, without an evaluation of the old disputes and prognosis that originated at the beginning of 1905

The resurrection of Marxist, and consequently Leninist, thought in the party is unthinkable without a polemical *auto-da-fé* of the scribblings of the epigones, without a merciless theoretical execution of the Party-machine ushers.* It is really not difficult to write such a book. All its ingredients are to hand. But it is also hard to write such a book, precisely because in doing so one must, in the words of the great satirist Saltykov, descend into the domain of 'ABC effluvia' [i.e., laboriously-composed trash—Trans.] and dwell for a considerable time in this scarcely ambrosial atmosphere. Nevertheless, the work has become absolutely unpostponable, for it is precisely upon the struggle against the permanent revolution that the defence of the opportunist line in the problems of

---

* An untranslatable pun on the Russian word *ekzekutor,* meaning an usher.

the East, that is, the larger half of humanity, is directly constructed.

I was already on the point of entering into this hardly alluring task of theoretical polemic with Zinoviev and Stalin, putting aside our Russian classics for my recreation hours (even divers must rise to the surface now and then to breathe a draught of fresh air) when, quite unexpected by me, an article by Radek appeared and began to circulate, devoted to the 'more profound' counterposition of the theory of the permanent revolution to Lenin's views on this subject. At first I wanted to put Radek's work aside, lest I be distracted from the combination of loose cotton-wool and finely-chopped bristles intended for me by fate. But a number of letters from friends induced me to read Radek's work more attentively, and I came to the following conclusion: for a smaller circle of persons who are capable of thinking independently and not upon command, and are conscientiously studying Marxism, Radek's work is more dangerous than the official literature— just as opportunism in politics is all the more dangerous the more camouflaged it is and the greater the personal reputation that covers it. Radek is one of my closest political friends. This has been amply witnessed by the events of the latest period. In recent months, however, various comrades have followed with misgivings the evolution of Radek, who has moved all the way over from the extreme Left Wing of the Opposition to its Right Wing. All of us who are Radek's intimate friends know that his brilliant political and literary gifts, which are combined with an exceptional impulsiveness and impressionability, are qualities which constitute a valuable source of initiative and criticism under conditions of collective work, but which can produce entirely different fruits under conditions of isolation. Radek's latest work—in connection with a number of his actions preceding it—leads to the opinion that Radek has lost his compass, or that his compass is under the influence of a steady magnetic disturbance. Radek's work is in no sense an episodic excursion into the past. No, it is an insufficiently-thought-out but no less harmful contribution in support of the official course, with all its theoretical mythology.

The above-characterized political function of the present struggle against 'Trotskyism' naturally does not in any way signify that within the Opposition, which took shape as the Marxist buttress against the ideological and political reaction, internal criticism is inadmissable, in particular criticism of my old differences of opinion with Lenin. On the contrary such a work of self-clarific-ation could only be fruitful. But here, at all events, a scrupulous preservation of historical perspective, a serious investigation of original sources and an illumination of the past differences in the light of the present struggle, would be absolutely necessary. There is not a trace of all this in Radek. As if unaware of what he is doing, he simply falls into step with the struggle against 'Trotsky-ism,' utilizing not only the one-sidedly selected quotations, but also the utterly false official interpretations of them. Where he seem-ingly separates himself from the official campaign, he does it in so ambiguous a manner that he really supplies it with the twofold support of an 'important' witness. As always happens in a case of ideological backsliding, the latest work of Radek does not con-tain a single trace of his political perspicacity and his literary skill. It is a work without perspective, without depth, a work solely on the plane of quotations, and precisely for this reason—*flat*.

Out of what political needs was it born? Out of the differences of opinion that arose between Radek and the overwhelming majority of the Opposition on the questions of the Chinese Revolu-tion. A few objections are heard, it is true, to the effect that the differences of opinion on China are 'not relevant today' (Preobrazhensky). But these objections do not merit serious con-sideration. The whole of Bolshevism grew and definitely took shape in the criticism and the assimilation of the experiences of 1905, in all their freshness, while these experiences were still an *immediate experience* of the first generation of Bolsheviks. How could it be otherwise? And what other event could the new generation of proletarian revolutionists learn from today if not from the fresh, still uncongealed experiences of the Chinese Revolution, still reeking with blood? Only lifeless pedants are capable of 'postponing' the questions of the Chinese Revolution, in order to study them later on at leisure and in 'tranquillity'. It becomes Bolshevik-Leninists all the less, since the revolutions in the countries of the East have in no sense been removed from the order of the day and their dates are not known to anybody.

Adopting a false position on the problems of the Chinese Revolution, Radek attempts to justify this position retrospectively by a one-sided and distorted presentation of my old differences of opinion with Lenin. And this is where Radek is compelled to borrow weapons from another's arsenal and to navigate without a compass in another's channel.

Radek is my friend, but the truth is dearer to me. I am compelled once again to set aside the more extensive work on the problems of revolution in order to refute Radek. Questions have been raised that are far too important to ignore, and they have been raised point-blank. I have a threefold difficulty to overcome here: the multiplicity and variety of errors in Radek's work; the profusion of literary and historical facts over twenty-three years (1905-28) that refute Radek; and thirdly, the short time that I can devote to this work, for the economic problems of the USSR are pressing to the foreground.

All these circumstances determine the character of the present work. This work does not exhaust the question. There is much that remains unsaid—in part, incidentally, because it is a sequel to other works, primarily the *Criticism of the Draft Programme of the Communist International*. Mountains of factual material which I have assembled on this question must remain unused—pending the writing of my contemplated book against the epigones, that is, against the official ideology of the era of reaction.

Radek's work on the permanent revolution rests on the conclusion:

'The new section of the party (The Opposition) is threatened with the danger of the rise of tendencies which will tear the development of the proletarian revolution away from its ally—the peasantry.'

One is first of all astonished by the fact that this conclusion concerning a 'new' section of the party is adduced during the second half of the year 1928 as a *new* conclusion. We have already heard it reiterated constantly since the autumn of 1923. But how does Radek justify his going-over to the main official thesis? Again, not in a new way: He turns back to the theory of the permanent revolution. In 1924-25, Radek more than once intended to write a pamphlet dedicated to proving the idea that the theory of the permanent revolution and Lenin's slogan of the democratic dictatorship of the proletariat and peasantry, taken on an historical scale—that is, in the light of the experience of our three revolutions—could in no case be counterposed to each other but were, on the contrary, essentially the same. Now, after having thoroughly examined the question 'anew'—as he writes to one of his friends—Radek has reached the conclusion that the old theory of the permanent revolution threatens the 'new' section of the party with nothing more or less than the danger of a breach with the peasantry.

But how did Radek 'thoroughly examine' this question? He gives us some information on this point:

'We do not have at hand the formulations which Trotsky presented in 1904 in a preface to Marx's *Civil War in France* and in 1905 in *Our Revolution*.'

The years are not correctly stated here, but it is not worthwhile to dwell upon this. The whole point is that the only work in which I presented my views more or less systematically on the development of the revolution is a rather extensive article, *Results and Prospects* (in *Our Revolution*, Petersburg, 1906, pages 224-86). The article in the Polish organ of Rosa Luxemburg and Tyszko (1909), to which Radek refers, but unfortunately interprets in Kamenev's way, lays no claim to completeness or comprehensiveness. Theoretically this work is based upon the above-mentioned book *Our Revolution*. Nobody is obliged to read this book now, Since that time such great events have taken place and we have learned so much from these events that, to tell the truth, I feel an aversion to the epigones' present manner of considering new historical problems not in the light of the living experience of the revolutions already carried out by us, but mainly in the light of quotations that relate only to our forecasts regarding what were then *future* revolutions. Naturally, by this I do not want to deprive Radek of the right to take up the question from the historico-literary side also. But in that case, it must be done properly. Radek undertakes to illuminate the fate of the theory of the permanent revolution in the course of almost a quarter of a century, and remarks in passing that he 'has not at hand' precisely those documents in which I set down this theory.

I want to point out right here that Lenin, as has become particularly clear to me now in reading his old articles, never read my basic work mentioned above. This is probably to be explained not only by the fact that *Our Revolution*, which appeared in 1986, was soon confiscated and that all of us shortly went into emigration, but also perhaps by the fact that two-thirds of the book consisted of reprints of old articles. I heard later from many comrades that they had not read this book because they thought it consisted exclusively of reprints of old works. In any case, the few scattered polemical remarks of Lenin against the permanent revolution are based almost exclusively upon the foreword by Parvus to my pamphlet *Before the Ninth of January*; upon Parvus's proclamation *No Tsar!* which remained completely unknown to me; and upon internal disputes of Lenin's with Bukharin and others. Never did Lenin anywhere analyse or quote, even in passing, *Results and Prospects*, and certain objections of Lenin to the permanent revolution, which obviously have no reference to me, directly prove that he did not read this work.*

* In 1909, Lenin did indeed quote my *Results and Prospects* in an article polemicizing against Martov. It would not, however, be difficult to prove that Lenin took over the quotations at second-hand, that is, from Martov himself. This is the only way that certain of his objections directed at me, which are based upon obvious misunderstandings, can be explained.

In 1919, the State Publishing House issued my *Results and Prospects* as a pamphlet. The annotation to the complete edition of Lenin's works, to the effect that the theory of the permanent revoluion is especially noteworthy 'now', after the October Revolution, dates back to approximately the same time. Did Lenin read my *Results and Prospects* in 1919, or merely glance through it? On this I cannot say anything definite. I was then constantly travelling, came to Moscow only for short stays, and during my meetings with Lenin in that period—at the height of the civil war—factional theoretical reminiscences never entered our minds. But A. A. Joffe did have a conversation with Lenin, just at that time, on the theory of the permanent revolution. Joffe reported this conversation in the farewell letter he wrote me before his death. (See *My Life*, New York, pages 535, 537.)* Can A. A. Joffe's assertions be construed as meaning that Lenin in 1919 became acquainted *for the first time* with *Results and Prospects* and recognised the correctness of the historical prognosis contained in it? On this matter I can only express psychological conjectures. The power of conviction of these conjectures depends upon the evaluation of the kernel of the disputed question itself. A. A. Joffe's words, that Lenin had confirmed my prognosis as correct, must appear incomprehensible to a man who has been raised upon the theoretical margarine of the post-Leninist epoch. On the other hand, whoever

* London edition, pp. 456, 458.

It would be rash to suppose, however, that this is just what Lenin's 'Leninism' consists of. But this seems to be Radek's opinion. In any case, Radek's article which I have to examine here shows not only that he did 'not have at hand' my fundamental works, but also that he had never even read them. If he did, then it was long ago, before the October Revolution. In any case he did not retain much of it in his memory.

But the matter does not end there. It was admissible and even unavoidable in 1905 or 1909 to polemicize with each other over individual articles that were topical then and even over single sentences in isolated articles—especially under the conditions of the split. But today it is impermissible for a revolutionary Marxist, should he want to review retrospectively this tremendous historical period, not to ask himself the question: How were the formulas under discussion applied in practice? How were they interpreted and construed in action? What tactics were applied? Had Radek taken the trouble to glance through merely the two books of *Our First Revolution* (volume II of my *Collected Works*), he would not have ventured to write his present work; at all events, he would have struck out a whole series of his sweeping contentions. At least, I should like to hope he would.

reflects upon the evolution of Lenin's ideas in connection with the development of the revolution itself will understand that Lenin, in 1919, had to make—could not have failed to make—a new evaluation of the theory of the permanent revolution, different from the ones he had pronounced desultorily, in passing, and often manifestly self-contradictory, at various times before the October Revolution, on the basis of isolated quotations, without even once examining my position as a whole.

In order to confirm my prognosis as correct in 1919, Lenin did not need to counterpose my position to his. It sufficed to consider both positions in their historical development. It is not necessary to repeat here that the concrete content which Lenin always gave to his formula of 'democratic dictatorship', and which flowed less from a hypothetical formula than from the analysis of the actual changes in class relationships—that this tactical and organisational content has passed once and for all into the inventory of history as a classic model of revolutionary realism. In almost all the cases, at any rate in all the most important cases, where I placed myself in contradiction to Lenin tactically or organizationally, right was on his side. That is just why it did not interest me to come forward in favour of my old historical prognosis, so long as it might appear that it was only a matter of historical reminiscences. I found myself compelled to return to this question only at the moment when the epigones' criticism of the theory of the permanent revolution not only began to nurture theoretical reaction in the whole International, but also became converted into a means of direct sabotage of the Chinese Revolution.—L.T.

From these two books Radek would have learned, in the first place, that in my political activity the permanent revolution in no case signified for me a jumping-over of the democratic stage of the revolution or any of its specific steps. He would have convinced himself that, though I lived in Russia illegally throughout 1905 without any connection with the emigrants, I formulated the tasks of the successive stages of the revolution in exactly the same manner as Lenin; he would have learned that the fundamental appeals to the peasants that were issued by the central press of the Bolsheviks in 1905 were written by me; that the *Novaya Zhizn* (*New Life*), edited by Lenin, in an editorial note resolutely defended my article on the permanent revolution which appeared in *Nachalo* (*The Beginning*); that Lenin's *Novaya Zhizn*, and on occasion Lenin personally, supported and defended invariably those political decisions of the Soviets of Deputies which were written by me and on which I acted as reporter nine times out of ten; that, after the December defeat, I wrote while in prison a pamphlet on tactics in which I pointed out that the combination of the proletarian offensive with the agrarian revolution of the peasants was the central strategical problem; that Lenin had this pamphlet published by the Bolshevik publishing house *Novaya Volna* (*New Wave*) and informed me through Knunyants of his hearty approval; that Lenin spoke at the London Congress in 1907 of my 'solidarity' with Bolshevism in my views on the peasantry and the liberal bourgeoisie. None of this exists for Radek; evidently he did not have this 'at hand' either.

How does the matter stand with Radek in relation to the works of Lenin? No better, or not much better. Radek confines himself to those quotations which Lenin did direct against me but quite often intended for others (for example, Bukharin and Radek; an open reference to this is found in Radek himself). Radek was unable to adduce a single new quotation against me; he simply made use of the ready-made quotation material that almost every citizen of the USSR has 'at hand' nowadays. Radek only added a few quotations in which Lenin elucidated elementary truths to the anarchists and Socialist-Revolutionaries on the difference between a bourgeois republic and socialism—and thereupon Radek depicts matters as if these quotations too had been directed against me. Hardly credible, but it is true!

Radek entirely avoids those old declarations in which Lenin, very cautiously and very sparingly but with all the greater weight, recognised my solidarity with Bolshevism on the basic questions of the revolution. Here it must not be forgotten for an instant that Lenin did this at a time when I did not belong to the Bolshevik faction and when Lenin was attacking me mercilessly (and quite rightly so) for my conciliationism—not for the permanent revolution, where he confined himself to occasional objections, but for my conciliationism, for my readiness to hope for an evolution of the Mensheviks to the left. Lenin was much more concerned with the struggle against conciliationism than with the 'justice' of isolated polemical blows against the ' conciliator ' Trotsky.

In 1924, defending against me Zinoviev's conduct in October, 1917, Stalin wrote :

'Comrade Trotsky fails to understand Lenin's letters (on Zinoviev—L.T.), their significance and their purpose. Lenin sometimes deliberately ran ahead, pushing into the forefront mistakes that might possibly be committed, and criticizing them in advance with the object of warning the party and of safeguarding it against mistakes. Sometimes he would even magnify a "trifle" and "make a mountain out of a molehill" for the same pedagogical purpose. . . . But to infer from such letters of Lenin's (and he wrote quite a number of such letters) the existence of "tragic" disagreements and to trumpet them forth means not to understand Lenin's letters, means not to know Lenin.' (J. Stalin, *Trotskyism or Leninism*, 1924).*

The idea is here formulated crudely—'the style is the man'—but the essence of the idea is correct, even though it applies least of all to the disputes during the October period, which bore no resemblance to 'molehills.' But if Lenin used to resort to 'pedagogical' exaggerations and preventive polemics in relation to the closest members of his own faction, then he did so all the more in relation to an individual who was at the time outside

* Stalın, *Works*, Eng. ed., VI. 355.

the Bolshevik faction and preached conciliationism. It never occurred to Radek to introduce this necessary corrective co-efficient into the old quotations.

In the 1922 foreword of my book *The Year* 1905, I wrote that my forecast of the possibility and probability of establishing the dictatorship of the proletariat in Russia before it was achieved in the advanced countries was verified in reality 12 years later. Radek, following not very attractive examples, represents matters as though I had *counterposed* this prognosis to Lenin's strategical line. From the foreword, however, it can be clearly seen that I dealt with the prognosis of the permanent revolution from the standpoint of those basic features which *coincide* with the *strategic* line of Bolshevism. When I speak in a footnote of the 'rearming' of the party at the beginning of 1917, then it is certainly not in the sense that Lenin recognized the previous road of the party as 'erroneous' but rather that Lenin came to Russia—even though delayed, yet opportunely enough for the success of the revolution—to teach the party to *reject the outlived slogan* of the 'democratic dictatorship' to which the Stalins, Kamenevs, Rykovs, Molotovs and others were still clinging. When the Kamenevs grow indignant at the mention of the 'rearming,' this is comprehensible, for it was undertaken against them. But Radek? He first began to grow indignant only in 1928, that is, only after he himself had begun to fight against the necessary 'rearming' of the Chinese Communist Party.

Let me remind Radek that my books *The Year* 1905 (with the criminal foreword) and *The October Revolution* played the role, while Lenin was alive, of fundamental historical textbooks on both revolutions. At that time, they went through innumerable editions in Russian as well as in foreign languages. Never did anybody tell me that my books contained a counterposing of two lines, because at that time, before the revisionist volte-face by the epigones, no sound-thinking party member subordinated the October experience to old quotations, but instead viewed old quotations in the light of the October Revolution.

In connection with this there is one other subject which Radek misuses in an impermissible manner : Trotsky did acknowledge—he says—that Lenin was right against him. Of course I did.

And in this acknowledgment there was not one iota of diplomacy. I had in mind the whole historical road of Lenin, his whole theoretical position, his strategy, his building of the party. This acknowledgment certainly does not, however, apply to every single one of the polemical quotations—which are, moreover, misused today for purposes hostile to Leninism. In 1926, in the period of the bloc with Zinoviev, Radek warned me that Zinoviev needed my declaration that Lenin was right, as against me, in order to screen somewhat the fact that he, Zinoviev, was wrong as against me. Naturally, I understood this very well. And that is why I said at the Seventh Plenum of the Executive Committee of the Communist International that I meant the historical rightness of Lenin and his party, but in no case the rightness of my present critics, who strive to cover themselves with quotations plucked from Lenin. Today I am unfortunately compelled to extend these words to Radek.

With regard to the permanent revolution, I spoke only of the *defects* of the theory, which were inevitable insofar as it was a question of *prediction*. At the Seventh Plenum of the E.C.C.I., Bukharin rightly emphasized that Trotsky did not renounce the conception as a whole. On the 'defects' I shall speak in another, more extensive work, in which I shall endeavour to present the experiences of the three revolutions and their application to the further course of the Comintern, especially in the East. But in order to leave no room for misunderstandings, I wish to say here briefly : Despite all its defects, the theory of the permanent revolution, even as presented in my earliest works, primarily *Results and Prospects* (1906), is immeasurably more permeated with the spirit of Marxism and consequently far closer to the historical line of Lenin and the Bolshevik Party, than not only the present Stalinist and Bukharinist retrospective wisdom but also the latest work of Radek.

By this I do not at all want to say that my conception of the revolution follows, in all my writings, one and the same unswerving line. I did not occupy myself with collecting old quotations— I am forced to do so now only by the period of party reaction and epigonism—but I tried, for better or for worse, to analyse the real processes of life. In the 12 years (1905-17) of my revolutionary journalistic activity, there are also articles in which the episodic circumstances and even the episodic polemical exaggerations inevitable in struggle protrude into the foreground in violation of the strategic line. Thus, for example, articles can be found in which I expressed doubts about the future revolutionary role of the peasantry *as a whole, as an estate,* and in connection with this refused to designate, especially during the imperialist war, the future Russian revolution as 'national,' for I felt this designation to be ambiguous. But it must not be forgotten here that the historical processes that interest us, including the processes in the peasantry, are far more obvious now that they have been accomplished than they were in those days when they were only developing. Let me also remark that Lenin—who never for a moment lost sight of the peasant question in all its gigantic historical magnitude and from whom we all learned this—considered it uncertain even after the February Revolution whether we should succeed in tearing the peasantry away from the bourgeoisie and drawing it after the proletariat. I will say quite in general to my harsh critics that it is far easier to dig out in one hour the formal contradictions of another person's newspaper articles over a quarter of a century, than it is to preserve, oneself, if only for a year, unity of fundamental line.

There remains only to mention in these introductory lines one other completely ritualistic consideration : had the theory of the permanent revolution been incorrect—says Radek—Trotsky would have assembled a large faction on that basis. But that did not happen. Therefore it follows . . . that the theory was false.

This argument of Radek's, *taken as a general proposition,* does not contain a trace of dialectics. One could conclude from it that the standpoint of the Opposition on the Chinese Revolution or the position of Marx on British affairs, was false; that the position of the Comintern with regard to the reformists in America, in Austria and—if you wish—in all countries, is false.

If Radek's argument is taken not in its general 'historico-philosophical' form, but only as applied to the question under discussion, then it hits Radek himself. The argument might have a shade of sense had I been of the opinion or, what is still more important, had events shown, that the line of the permanent revolution *contradicts* the strategic line of Bolshevism, *stands in conflict* with it, and *diverges* from it more and more. Only then would there have been grounds for two factions. But that is just what Radek wants to prove. I show, on the contrary, that in spite of all the factional polemical exaggerations and conjectural accentuations of the question, the basic strategical line was one and the same. Where, then, should a second faction have come from? In reality, it turned out that I worked hand in hand with the Bolsheviks in the first revolution and later defended this joint work in the international press against the Menshevik renegades' criticism. In the 1917 Revolution I fought together with Lenin against the democratic opportunism of those 'old Bolsheviks' who have today been elevated by the reactionary wave and whose sole armament consists of their baiting of the permanent revolution.

Finally, I never endeavoured to create a grouping on the basis of the ideas of the permanent revolution. My inner-party stand was a *conciliationist* one, and when at certain moments I strove for the formation of groupings, then it was precisely on this basis. My conciliationism flowed from a sort of social-revolutionary fatalism. I believed that the logic of the class struggle would compel both factions to pursue the same revolutionary line. The great historical significance of Lenin's policy was still unclear to me at that time, his policy of irreconcilable ideological demarcation and, when necessary, split, for the purpose of welding and tempering the core of the truly revolutionary party. In 1911, Lenin wrote on this subject :

'Conciliationism is the sum total of moods, strivings and views which are indissolubly bound up with the very essence of the historical task set before the Russian Social Democratic Party during the period of the counter-revolution of 1908-11. That is why, during that period, a number of Social Democrats, *starting from quite different premises,* fell into conciliationism. Trotsky expressed conciliationism more consistently than anyone else. He was probably the only one who attempted to give this tendency a theoretical foundation.' (XI, part 2, page 371).*

By striving for unity at all costs, I involuntarily and unavoidably idealized centrist tendencies in Menshevism. Despite my thrice-

---

* 'The New Faction of Conciliators or the Virtuous', 4th edition, XVI, 227 : *Selected Works,* Eng. edn., IV, 93.

repeated episodic attempts, I arrived at no common task with the Mensheviks, and I could not arrive at it. Simultaneously, however, the conciliationist line brought me into still sharper conflict with Bolshevism, since Lenin, in contrast to the Mensheviks, relentlessly rejected conciliationism, and could not but do this. It is obvious that no faction could be created on the platform of conciliationism.   •

Hence the lesson: It is impermissible and fatal to break or weaken a political line for purposes of vulgar conciliationism; it is impermissible to paint up centrism when it zig-zags to the left; it is impermissible, in the hunt after the will-o'-the-wisps of centrism, to exaggerate and inflate differences of opinion with genuine revolutionary co-thinkers. These are the real lessons of Trotsky's real mistakes. These lessons are very important. They preserve their full force even today, and it is precisely Radek who should meditate upon them.

With the ideological cynicism characteristic of him, Stalin once said:

' Trotsky cannot but know that Lenin fought against the theory of the permanent revolution to the end of his life. But that does not worry Trotsky.' (*Pravda*, No. 262, November 12, 1926).*

This is a crude and disloyal, that is, a purely Stalinist caricature of the reality. In one of his communications to foreign Communists, Lenin explained that differences of opinion among Communists are something quite different from differences of opinion with the Social Democrats. Such differences of opinion, he wrote, Bolshevism had also gone through in the past. But '. . . at the moment when it seized power and created the Soviet Republic, Bolshevism proved united *and drew to itself all the best of the currents of socialist thought that were nearest to it. . . .*' (XVI, page 333).†

What nearest currents of socialist thought did Lenin have in mind when he wrote these lines? Martynov or Kuusinen? Or Cachin, Thaelmann and Smeral? Did they perhaps appear to him as the 'best of the nearest currents'? What other tendency

---

* Stalin, *Works*, Eng. edn., VIII, 350.

† 'Greetings to the Italian, French and German Communists', 4th edition, **XXX, 37.**

was nearer to Bolshevism than the one which I represented on all fundamental questions, including the peasant question? Even Rosa Luxemburg shrank back at first from the agrarian policy of the Bolshevik government. For me, however, there was no doubt about this at all. I was together with Lenin at the table when, pencil in hand, he drafted his agrarian law. And our interchange of opinions hardly consisted of more than a dozen brief remarks, the sense of which was about the following: The step is a contradictory one, but historically it is absolutely unavoidable; under the régime of the proletarian dictatorship and on the scale of world revolution, the contradictions will be adjusted —we only need time. If a basic antagonism existed on the peasant question between the theory of the permanent revolution and Lenin's dialectic how then does Radek explain the fact that without renouncing my basic views on the course of development of the revolution, I did not stumble in the slightest over the peasant question in 1917, as did the majority of the Bolshevik leadership of that time? How does Radek explain the fact that after the February Revolution the present theoreticians and politicians of anti-Trotskyism—Zinoviev, Kamenev, Stalin, Rykov, Molotov, etc., etc.—adopted, to the last man, the vulgar-democratic and not the proletarian position? And once again : Of what and of whom could Lenin have spoken when he referred to the merging of Bolshevism and the best elements of the Marxist currents nearest to it? And does not this evaluation in which Lenin *drew the balance sheet* of the past differences of opinion show that in any case he saw no two irreconcilable strategic lines?

Still more noteworthy in this respect is Lenin's speech at the November 1 (14), 1917, session of the Petrograd Committee.* There the question was discussed, whether to make an agreement with the Mensheviks and the Socialist-Revolutionaries. The supporters of a coalition endeavoured even there—very timidly, to be sure—to hint at 'Trotskyism'. What did Lenin reply?

'Agreement? I cannot even speak seriously about that. Trotsky has long ago said that unity is impossible. Trotsky under-

---

* As is known, the voluminous minutes of this historic session were torn out of the *Jubilee Book* by special command of Stalin and to this day are kept concealed from the party.—L.T.

stood this—and since then there has been no better Bolshevik.'

Not the permanent revolution but conciliationism was what separated me, in Lenin's opinion, from Bolshevism. In order to become the 'best Bolshevik', I only needed, as we see, to understand the impossibility of an agreement with Menshevism.

But how is the abrupt character of Radek's turn precisely on the question of the permanent revolution to be explained? I believe I have one element of explanation. In 1916, as we learn from his article, Radek was in agreement with 'permanent revolution'; but his agreement was with Bukharin's interpretation of it, according to which the bourgeois revolution in Russia had been completed—not only the revolutionary role of the bourgeoisie, and not even only the historical role of the slogan of the democratic dictatorship, but the bourgeois revolution as such— and the proletariat must therefore proceed to the capture of power under a purely socialist banner. Radek manifestly interpreted my position at that time also in the Bukharinist manner; otherwise he could not have declared his solidarity with Bukharin and me at one and the same time. This also explains why Lenin polemized against Bukharin and Radek, with whom he collaborated, having them appear under the pseudonym of Trotsky. (Radek admits this also in his article.) I remember also that M. N. Pokrovsky, a co-thinker of Bukharin's and a tireless constructor of historical schemas which he very skilfully painted up as Marxism, alarmed me in conversations I had with him in Paris with his dubious 'solidarity' on this question. In politics, Pokrovsky was and remains an anti-Cadet, which he honestly believes to constitute Bolshevism.

In 1924-25, Radek apparently still lived upon ideological recollections of the Bukharinist position of 1916, which he continued to identify with mine. Rightly disillusioned with this hopeless position, Radek—on the basis of a fleeting study of Lenin's writings—as frequently happens in such cases, described an arc of 180 degrees right over my head. This is quite probable, because it is typical. Thus, Bukharin, who in 1923-25 turned himself inside out, that is, transformed himself from an ultra-left into an opportunist, constantly attributes to me his own ideological past, which he palms off as ' Trotskyism'. In the first period of the campaign against me, when I still forced myself occasionally to read Bukharin's articles, I would frequently ask myself: Where did he get this from?—but I soon guessed that he had glanced into his diary of yesterday. And now I wonder if the same psychological foundation does not lie at the bottom of Radek's conversion from a Paul of the permanent revolution into its Saul. I do not presume to insist upon this hypothesis. But I can find no other explanation.

Anyway, as the French saying goes: the wine is drawn, it must be drunk. We are compelled to undertake a lengthy excursion into the realm of old quotations. I have reduced their number as much as was feasible. Yet there are still many of them. Let it serve as my justification, that I strive throughout to find in my enforced rummaging among these old quotations the threads that connect up with the burning questions of the present time.

2. THE PERMANENT REVOLUTION IS NOT A 'LEAP' BY THE PROLETARIAT, BUT THE RECONSTRUCTION OF THE NATION UNDER THE LEADERSHIP OF THE PROLETARIAT

Radek writes:

'The essential feature that distinguishes the train of thought which is called the theory and tactic (observe: *tactic*, too.—L.T.) of the "permanent revolution" from Lenin's theory lies in *mixing up the stage of the bourgeois revolution with the stage of the socialist revolution.*'

Connected with this fundamental accusation, or resulting from it, there are other no less serious accusations: Trotsky did not understand that 'under Russian conditions, a socialist revolution which does not grow out of the democratic revolution is impossible'; and from this followed 'skipping the stage of the democratic dictatorship'. Trotsky 'denied' the role of the peasantry, which is where 'the community of views of Trotsky and the Mensheviks' lay. As already said, all this is intended to prove, by means of circumstantial evidence, the incorrectness of my position on the fundamental questions of the Chinese Revolution.

To be sure, so far as the formal literary side is concerned, Radek can refer here and there to Lenin. And he does that; everybody has 'at hand' *this* section of the quotations. But as I shall presently demonstrate, these contentions of Lenin in regard to me had a purely episodic character and were incorrect, that is, in no sense did they characterize what my real position was, even in 1905. In Lenin's own writings there are quite different, directly contrary and far better grounded remarks on my attitude on the basic questions of the revolution. Radek did not even make the attempt to unite the various and directly contradictory remarks of Lenin, and to elucidate these polemical contradictions by a comparison with my actual views.*

In 1906, Lenin published, with his own foreword, an article by Kautsky on the driving forces of the Russian Revolution. Without knowing anything about this, I also translated Kautsky's article in prison, provided it with a foreword and included it in my book *In Defence of the Party*. Both Lenin and I expressed our thorough accord with Kautsky's analysis. To Plekhanov's question : Is our revolution bourgeois or socialist? Kautsky had answered that it is no longer bourgeois, but not yet socialist, that is, it represents the transitional form from the one to the other. In this connection, Lenin wrote in his foreword :

'Is our revolution bourgeois or socialist in its general character? That is the old schema, says Kautsky. That is not how the question should be put, that is not the Marxist way. The revolution in Russia is not bourgeois, for the bourgeoisie is not one of the driving forces of the present revolutionary movement in Russia. But neither is the revolution in Russia socialist.' (VIII, 82).†

Yet not a few passages can be found in Lenin, written both before and after this foreword, where he categorically calls the Russian Revolution bourgeois. Is this a contradiction? If Lenin is approached with the methods of the present critics of 'Trotskyism', then dozens and hundreds of such contradictions can be found without difficulty, which are clarified for the serious and conscientious reader by the difference in the approach to the question at different times, which in no way violates the fundamental unity of Lenin's conception.

---

* I recollect that when Bukharin at the Eighth Plenum of the Executive Committee of the Communist International cited the same quotations, I called to him : 'But there are also directly contrary quotations in Lenin.' After a brief moment of perplexity, Bukharin retorted : 'I know that, I know that, bu: I am taking what I need, not what you need.' There is the presence of mind of this theoretician for you!—L.T.

† Preface to Kautsky's pamphlet 'The Driving Forces and Prospects of the Russian Revolution', Dec., 1906; 4th edn., XI, 372.

On the other hand, I never denied the *bourgeois* character of the revolution in the sense of its immediate historical tasks, but only in the sense of its driving forces and its perspectives. My fundamental work of those days (1905-06) on the permanent revolution begins with the following sentences :

'The Russian Revolution came unexpectedly to everybody but the Social Democrats. Marxism long ago predicted the inevitability of the Russian Revolution, which was bound to break out as a result of the conflict between capitalist development and the forces of ossified absolutism . . . In calling it a bourgeois revolution, Marxism thereby pointed out that the *immediate objective* tasks of the revolution consisted in the creation of "normal conditions for the development of bourgeois society as a whole". Marxism has proved to be right, and this is now past the need for discussion or proof. The Marxists are now confronted by a task of quite another kind: to discover the "possibilities" of the developing revolution by means of an analysis of its internal mechanism . . . The Russian Revolution has a quite peculiar character, which is the result of the peculiar trend of our whole social and historical development, and which in its turn opens before us quite new historical prospects.' (*Our Revolution*, 1906, article ' Results and Prospects', page 224).*

'The general sociological term *bourgeois revolution* by no means solves the politico-tactical problems, contradictions and difficuties which the mechanics of a *given* bourgeois revolution throw up.' (Ibid., page 249).†

Thus I did not deny the bourgeois character of the revolution that stood on the order of the day, and I did not mix up democracy and socialism. But I endeavoured to show that in our country the class dialectics of the bourgeois revolution would bring the proletariat to power and that without its dictatorship not even democratic tasks could be solved.

In the same article (1905-06) I wrote :

'The proletariat grows and becomes stronger with the growth of capitalism. In this sense, the development of capitalism is also the development of the proletariat toward dictatorship. But

---

* See page 36 of the present volume.
† See page 67 of the present volume.

the day and the hour when power will pass into the hands of the working class depends *directly* not upon the level attained by the productive forces but upon the relations in the class struggle, upon the international situation and finally, upon a number of subjective factors: the traditions, the initiative, readiness to fight of the workers.

'It is possible for the workers to come to power in an economically backward country sooner than in an advanced country . . . To imagine that the dictatorship of the proletariat is in some way dependent upon the technical development and resources of a country is a prejudice of "economic" materialism simplified to absurdity. This point of view has nothing in common with Marxism.

'In our view, the Russian Revolution will create conditions in which power can pass into the hands of the workers—and in the event of the victory of the revolution it must do so—*before* the politicians of bourgeois liberalism get the chance to display to the full their ability to govern.' (Ibid., page 245).*

These lines contain a polemic against the vulgar 'Marxism' which not only prevailed in 1905-06, but also set the tone of the March, 1917, conference of the Bolsheviks before Lenin's arrival, and found its crassest expression in Rykov's speech at the April conference. At the Sixth Congress of the Comintern, this pseudo-Marxism, that is, philistine 'common sense' debauched by scholasticism, constituted the 'scientific' basis of the speeches of Kuusinen and many, many others. And this, ten years after the October Revolution!

Since I have not the possibility of setting out here the whole train of thought of 'Results and Prospects', I should like to adduce one more summary quotation from my article in *Nachalo* (1905):

'Our liberal bourgeoisie comes forward as a counter-revolutionary force even before the revolutionary climax. At each critical moment, our intellectual democrats only demonstrate their impotence. The peasantry as a whole represents an elemental force in rebellion. It can be put at the service of the revolution only by a force that takes state power into its hands. The vanguard position of the working class in the revolution, the

---

* See pages 62-63 of the present volume.

direct connection established between it and the revolutionary countryside, the attraction by which it brings the army under its influence—all this impels it inevitably to power. The complete victory of the revolution means the victory of the proletariat. This in turn means the further uninterrupted character of the revolution.' (*Our Revolution*, page 172).

The prospect of the dictatorship of the proletariat consequently grows here precisely out of the bourgeois-democratic revolution—in contradiction to all that Radek writes. That is just why the revolution is called permanent (uninterrupted). But the dictatorship of the proletariat does not come *after* the completion of the democratic revolution, as Radek would have it. If that were the case it would simply be impossible in Russia, for in a backward country the numerically weak proletariat could not attain power if the tasks of the peasantry had been solved during the preceding stage. No, the dictatorship of the proletariat appeared probable and even inevitable on the basis of the bourgeois revolution precisely because there was no other power and no other way to solve the tasks of the agrarian revolution. But exactly this opens up the prospect of a democratic revolution growing over into the socialist revolution.

' The very fact of the proletariat's representatives entering the government, not as powerless hostages, but as the leading force, destroys the border line between maximum and minimum programme; that is to say, it *places collectivism on the order of the day*. The point at which the proletariat will be held up in its advance in this direction depends upon the relation of forces, but in no way upon the original intentions of the proletarian party

'For this reason there can be no talk of any sort of *special* form of proletarian dictatorship in the bourgeois revolution, of *democratic* proletarian dictatorship (or dictatorship of proletariat and peasantry). The working class cannot preserve the democratic character of its dictatorship without overstepping the limits of its democratic programme . . .

'The proletariat, once having taken power, will fight for it to the very end. While one of the weapons in this struggle for the maintenance and the consolidation of power will be agitation and organization, especially in the countryside, another will be a policy of collectivism. Collectivism will become not only the inevitable way forward from the position in which the party in power will find itself, but will also be a means of preserving this position with the support of the proletariat.' ('Results and Prospects', page 258.)*

Let us go further

'We know a classic example (I wrote in 1908 against the Menshevik Cherevanin) of a revolution in which the conditions for the rule of the capitalist bourgeoisie were prepared by the terrorist dictatorship of the victorious *sans-culottes*. That was in an epoch when the bulk of the urban population was composed of petty-bourgeoisie of the artisan and tradesman type. It followed the leadership of the Jacobins. The bulk of the urban population in Russia is composed today of the industrial proletariat. This analogy alone points to the possibility of a historical situation in which the victory of the "bourgeois" revolution will prove possible only through the conquest of revolutionary power by the proletariat. Does the revolution thereby cease to be bourgeois? Yes and no. This does not depend upon the formal designation but upon the further development of events. If the proletariat is overthrown by a coalition of bourgeois classes, among them also the peasantry it has liberated, then the revolution will retain its limited bourgeois character. Should the proletariat, however, prove able and find it possible to set in motion all the means of its political rule in order to break through the national framework of the Russian revolution, then the latter can become the prologue to the world socialist cataclysm. The question: what *stage* will the Russian Revolution attain? permits naturally only a conditional reply. Only one thing is absolutely and indubitably correct: the mere characterization of the Russian revolution as bourgeois tells us nothing about the type of its internal development and in no case signifies that the proletariat must adapt its tactics to the conduct of bourgeois democracy as the sole legal claimant to state power.' (L. Trotsky, *The Year* 1905, page 263.)

From the same article:

---

* See page 80 of the present volume.

'Our revolution, which is a bourgeois revolution with regard to the immediate tasks it grew out of, knows, as a consequence of the extreme class differentiation of the industrial population, of no bourgeois class capable of placing itself at the head of the popular masses by combining its own social weight and political experience with their revolutionary energy. The oppressed worker and peasant masses, left to their own resources, must take it upon themselves to create, in the hard school of implacable conflicts and cruel defeats, the necessary political and organizational pre-conditions for their triumph. No other road is open to them.' (L. Trotsky, *The Year* 1905, pages 267-8.)

One more quotation from *Results and Prospects* must be adduced on the most violently assailed point—on the peasantry. In a special chapter, ' The Proletariat in Power and the Peasantry', the following is said:

' The proletriat, in order to consolidate its power, cannot but widen the base of the revolution. Many sections of the working masses, particularly in the countryside, will be drawn into the revolution and become politically organized only after the advance-guard of the revolution, the urban proletariat, stands at the helm of state. Revolutionary agitation and organization will then be conducted with the help of state resources. The legislative power itself will become a powerful instrument for revolutionizing the masses . . .

' The fate of the most elementary revolutionary interests of the peasantry—even the peasantry as a whole, as an *estate*, is bound up with the fate of the revolution, i.e., with the fate of the proletariat.

' *The proletariat in power will stand before the peasantry as the class which has emancipated it.* The domination of the proletariat will mean not only democratic equality, free self-government, the transference of the whole burden of taxation to the rich classes, the dissolution of the standing army in the armed people, and the abolition of compulsory church imposts, but also recognition of all revolutionary changes (expropriations) in land relationships carried out by the peasants. The proletariat will make these changes the starting point for further state measures in agriculture. Under such conditions, the Russian peasantry in the first and most difficult period of the revolution, will be interested in the maintenance of a proletarian régime ("workers' democracy") at all events not less than was the French peasantry in the maintenance of the military régime of Napoleon Bonaparte, which guaranteed to the new property owners, by the force of its bayonets, the inviolability of their holdings . . .

' But is it not possible that the peasantry may push the proletariat aside and take its place? This is impossible. All historical experience protests against this assumption. Historical experience shows that the peasantry are absolutely incapable of taking up an *independent* political role.' (Page 251.)*

All this was written not in 1929, nor yet in 1924, but in 1905. Does this look like 'ignoring the peasantry', I should like to know? Where is the 'jumping over' of the agrarian question here? Is it not time, friends, to be somewhat more scrupulous?

Now let us see how 'scrupulous' Stalin is on this question. Referring to my New York articles on the February, 1917, Revolution, which agree in every essential with Lenin's Geneva articles, this theoretician of party reaction writes:

'. . . Trotsky's letters "do not in the least resemble" Lenin's letters either in spirit or in conclusions, for they wholly and entirely reflect Trotsky's anti-Bolshevik slogan of "no Tsar, but a workers' government", a slogan which implies a revolution *without* the peasantry.' (Speech to the Party fraction in the All-Union Central Committee of the Trade Unions, November 19, 1924.)†

Remarkable is the sound of these words on the 'anti-Bolshevik slogan' (allegedly Trotsky's): ' No Tsar—but a workers' government.' According to Stalin, the Bolshevik slogan should have read: ' No workers' government, but a Tsar.' We will speak later of this alleged 'slogan' of Trotsky's. But first let us hear from another would-be master of contemporary thought, less illiterate perhaps, but one who has taken leave forever of any theoretical scruples—I speak of Lunacharsky :

'In 1905, Lev Davidovich Trotsky inclined to the idea : *the proletariat must remain isolated* (!) and must not support the bourgeoisie, for that would be opportunism; for the proletariat

---

* See pages 70-72 of the present volume.
† Stalin, **Works**, Eng. edn., VI, 349.

alone, however, it would be very difficult to carry through the revolution, because the proletariat at that time amounted to only seven to eight per cent of the total population and victory could not be won with so small a cadre. Thus, Lev Davidovich decided that the proletariat must maintain a permanent revolution in Russia that is, fight for the greatest possible results until the fiery sparks of this conflagration should blow up the entire world powder-magazine.' (*Vlast Sovyetov* [*The Power of the Soviets*], No. 7, 1927, ' On the Characterization of the October Revolution', by A Lunacharsky, page 10.)

The proletariat 'must remain isolated' until the fiery sparks blow up the powder magazines . . . How well many People's Commis-sars write who are for the moment not yet 'isolated' in spite of the threatened position of their own little heads.* But we do not want to be too hard on Lunacharsky; from each according to his abilities. In the last analysis, his slovenly absurdities are no more senseless than those of many others.

But how, according to Trotsky, must 'the proletariat remain isolated' ? Let us adduce one quotation from my pamphlet against Struve (1906). At that time, by the way, Lunarcharsky praised this work immoderately. In the chapter that deals with the Soviet of Deputies, it is stated that while the bourgeois parties 'remained completely on the sidelines', away from the awakening masses, 'political life became concentrated around the workers' Soviet. The attitude of the petty-bourgeois city masses toward the Soviet (in 1905) was manifestly sympathetic, even if not very conscious. All the oppressed and aggrieved sought its protection. The popularity of the Soviet spread far beyond the confines of the city. It received "petitions" from peasants who suffered injustices, peasants' resolutions poured into the Soviet, delegations from village communities came to it. Here, right here, is where were concentrated the thoughts and sympathies of the nation, of the real and not the falsified democratic nations'. (*Our Revolution,* page 199.)

In all these quotations—their number can easily be increased two—, three—, and tenfold—the permanent revolution is described

---

* The Russian word rendered in the preceding passage as 'sparks' also means 'little heads.'

as a revolution which welds together the oppressed masses of town and country around the proletariat organised in soviets; as a national revolution that raises the proletariat to power and thereby opens up the possibility of a democratic revolution growing over into the socialist revolution.

The permanent revolution is no isolated leap of the proletariat; rather it is the rebuilding of the whole nation under the leadership of the proletariat. That is how I conceived and interpreted the prospect of the permanent revolution, beginning with 1905.

Radek is also wrong with regard to Parvus*—whose views on the Russian Revolution in 1905 bordered closely on mine, without however being identical with them—when he repeats the stereotyped phrase about Parvus's 'leap' from a Tsarist Government to a Social Democratic one. Radek actually refutes himself when, in another part of his article, he indicates, in passing but quite correctly, wherein my views on the revolution actually differed from those of Parvus. Parvus was not of the opinion that a workers' Government in Russia could move in the direction of the socialist revolution, that is, that in the process of fulfilling the democratic tasks it could grow over into the socialist dictatorship. As is proved by the 1905 quotation adduced by Radek himself, Parvus confined the tasks of the workers' government to the *democratic* tasks. Then where, in that case, is the leap to *socialism*? What Parvus had in mind even at that time was the establishment of a workers' regime after the 'Australian' model, as a consequence of the revolution. Parvus also juxtaposed Russia and Australia after the October Revolution, by which time he himself had already long since taken his stand at the extreme right of social reformism. Bukharin asserted in this connection that Parvus had 'thought up' Australia after the fact, in order to cover up his old aims with regard to the permanent revolution. But that is not so. In 1905, too, Parvus saw in the conquest of power by the proletariat the road to democracy and not to socialism, that is, he assigned to the proletariat only that role which it actually played in Russia in the first eight to ten months of the October Revolution. In further perspective, Parvus even then pointed to

---

* It should be remembered that at that time Parvus stood at the extreme left of international Marxism.—L.T.

the Australian democracy of that time, that is, to a regime in which the workers' party does indeed govern but does not rule, and carries out its reformist demands only as a supplement to the programme of the bourgeoisie. By an irony of fate the fundamental tendency of the Right-Centrist bloc of 1923-28 consisted precisely in drawing the dictatorship of the proletariat closer to a workers' democracy of the Australian model, that is, in drawing closer to the prognosis of Parvus. This becomes all the clearer when it is recalled that the Russian petty-bourgeois 'socialists' of two or three decades ago continually depicted Australia in the Russian press as a workers' and peasants' country which, shut off from the outer world by high tariffs, was developing 'socialist' legislation and in that way was building socialism in one country. Radek would have acted correctly had he pushed *this* side of the question to the foreground instead of repeating fairy tales about my fantastic leap over democracy.

3. THREE ELEMENTS OF THE 'DEMOCRATIC DICTATORSHIP': CLASSES, TASKS AND POLITICAL MECHANICS

The difference between the 'permanent' and the Leninist standpoints expressed itself politically in the counterposing of the slogan of the dictatorship of the *proletariat* relying on the peasantry to the slogan of the *democratic* dictatorship of the proletariat and the peasantry. The dispute was not concerned with whether the bourgeois-democratic stage could be skipped and whether an alliance between the workers and the peasants was necessary—it concerned the *political mechanics* of the collaboration of the proletariat and the peasantry in the democratic revolution.

Far too presumptuous, not to say light-minded, is Radek's contention that only people 'who have not thought through to the end the complex method of Marxism and Leninism' could raise the question of the *party-political expression* of the democratic dictatorship, whereas Lenin allegedly reduced the whole question to the collaboration of the two classes in the objective historical tasks. No, that is not so.

If in the given question we abstract ourselves from the subjective factor of the revolution: parties and their programmes—the political and organizational form of the collaboration of proletariat and peasantry—then there will also vanish all the differences of opinion, not only between Lenin and me, which marked two shades of the same revolutionary wing, but what is much worse, also the differences of opinion between Bolshevism and Menshevism, and finally, the differences between the Russian Revolution of 1905 and the Revolutions of 1848 and even of 1789, insofar as the proletariat can at all be spoken of in relation to the latter. *All* bourgeois revolutions were based on the collaboration of the oppressed masses of town and country. That is just what invested the revolutions to a lesser or greater degree with a national character, that is, one embracing the whole people.

The theoretical as well as the political dispute among us was not over the collaboration of the workers and peasants as such, but over the programme of this collaboration, its party forms and political methods. In the old revolutions, workers and peasants 'collaborated' under the leadership of the liberal bourgeoisie or its petty-bourgeois democratic wing. The Communist International repeated the experience of the *old* revolutions in a new historical situation by doing everything it could to subject the Chinese workers and peasants to the political leadership of the national liberal Chiang Kai-shek and later of the 'democrat' Wang Ching-wei. Lenin raised the question of an alliance of the workers and peasants irreconcilably opposed to the liberal bourgeoisie. Such an alliance had never before existed in history. It was a matter, so far as its method went, of a new experiment in the collaboration of the oppressed classes of town and country. Thereby the question of the political forms of collaboration was posed anew. Radek has simply overlooked this. That is why he leads us not only back from the formula of the permanent revolution, but also back from Lenin's 'democratic dictatorship'—into an empty historical abstraction.

Yes, Lenin refused for a number of years *to prejudge* the question of what the party-political and state organisation of the democratic dictatorship of the proletariat and the peasantry would look like, and he pushed into the foreground the collaboration of these two classes as against a coalition with the liberal bourgeoisie. Lenin said: At a certain historical stage, there inevitably results from the whole objective situation the revolutionary alliance of the working class with the peasantry for the solution of the tasks of the democratic revolution. Will the peasantry be able to create an independent party and will it succeed in doing this? Will this party be in the majority or the minority in the government of the dictatorship?   What will be the specific weight of the proletarian representatives in the revolutionary government?   None of these questions permits of an *a priori* answer.   'Experience will show!' Insofar as the formula of the democratic dictatorship left half-open the question of the political mechanics of the alliance of workers and peasants, it thereby remained up to a certain point—without in any way becoming transformed into Radek's barren abstraction— an algebraic formula, allowing of extremely divergent political interpretations in the future.

In addition, Lenin himself was in no way of the opinion that the question would be exhausted by the class basis of the dictatorship and its objective historical aims.   The significance of the subjective factor—the aims, the conscious method, the party—Lenin well understood and taught this to all of us.   And that is why Lenin in his commentaries on his slogan did not renounce at all an approximate, hypothetical prejudgment of the question of what political forms might be assumed by the first independent alliance of workers and peasants in history.   However, Lenin's approach to this question at different times was far from being one and the same.   Lenin's thought must not be taken dogmatically but historically.   Lenin brought no finished commandments from Mt Sinai, but hammered out ideas and slogans to fit reality, making them concrete and precise, and at different times filled them with different content.   But *this side* of the question, which later gained a decisive character and brought the Bolshevik Party to the verge of a split at the beginning of 1917, has not been studied by Radek at all.   He has simply ignored it.

It is, however, a fact that Lenin did not always characterize the possible party-political expression and governmental form of the alliance of the two classes in the same way, refraining, however, from binding the party by these hypothetical interpretations.   What are the reasons for this caution?   The reasons are to be sought in the fact that this algebraic formula contains a quantity, gigantic in significance, but politically extremely indeterminate: *the peasantry*.

I want to quote only a few examples of Lenin's interpretation of the democratic dictatorship, with the reservation that a rounded presentation of the *evolution* of Lenin's thought on this question would require a separate work.

Developing the idea that the proletariat and the peasantry would be the basis of the dictatorship, Lenin wrote in March, 1905 :

'And such a composition of the social basis of the probable and desirable revolutionary-democratic dictatorship will, of course, find its reflection in the composition of the revolutionary government. *With such a composition the participation or even the predominance of the most diversified representatives of revolutionary democracy in such a government will be inevitable.*' (VI, 132, My emphasis)*

In these words, Lenin indicates not only the class basis of, but also sketches out a specific governmental form of the dictatorship with a possible predominance of the representatives of petty-bourgeois democracy.

In 1907, Lenin wrote:

'In order to be victorious, the "peasant agrarian revolution" of which you gentlemen speak must, as such, as a peasant revolution, take over the central power throughout the whole state.' (IX, 539.)†

This formula goes even further. It can be understood in the sense that the revolutionary power must be directly concentrated in the hands of the peasantry. But this formula also embraces, in the more far-reaching interpretation introduced into it by the very course of development, the October Revolution which brought the proletariat to power as the 'agent' of the peasant revolution. Such is the amplitude of the possible interpretations of the formula of the democratic dictatorship of the proletariat and the peasantry. We may grant that, up to a certain point, its strong side lay in this algebraic character, but its dangers also lay there, manifesting themselves among us graphically enough after February, and in China leading to catastrophe.

In July 1905, Lenin wrote:

'Nobody speaks of the seizure of power by the party—we speak

---

* 'Social Democracy and the Revolutionary Provisional Government', 4th edition, VIII, 262-263. *Selected Works,* Eng. edn., III, 35.

† ' Political and Tactical Considerations in Questions of the Agrarian Programme' (chapter 4 of 'The Agrarian Programme of the Social-Democrats in the Russian Revolution of 1905-07 '), 4th edition, XIII, 304. *Selected Works,* Eng. edn., III, 243.

only of participation, *as far as possible* a leading participation in the revolution . . . .' (VI, 278)*

In December, 1906, Lenin considered it possible to agree with Kautsky on the question of seizure of power by the party:

'Kautsky considers it not only "as very probable" that "victory will fall to the Social Democratic Party in the course of the revolution," but declares it the duty of the Social Democrats "to instil in their adherents the certainty of victory, for one cannot fight successfully if victory is renounced beforehand".' (VIII, 58)†

The distance between these two interpretations given by Lenin himself is no smaller than between Lenin's formulations and mine. We shall see this even more plainly later on. Here we want to raise the question: What is the meaning of these contradictions in Lenin? They reflect the one and the same 'great unknown' in the political formula of the revolution: *the peasantry*. Not for nothing did the radical thinkers occasionally refer to the peasant as the Sphinx of Russian history. The question of the nature of the revolutionary dictatorship—whether Radek wishes it or not— is inseparably bound up with the question of the possibility of a revolutionary peasant party hostile to the liberal bourgeoisie and independent of the proletariat. The decisive meaning of the latter question is not hard to grasp. Were the peasantry capable of creating their own independent party in the epoch of the democratic revolution, then the democratic dictatorship could be realized in its truest and most direct sense, and the question of the participation of the proletarian minority in the revolutionary government would have an important, it is true, but subordinate significance. The case is entirely otherwise if we proceed from the fact that the peasantry, because of its intermediate position and the heterogeneity of its social composition, can have neither an independent policy nor an independent party, but is compelled, in the revolutionary epoch, to choose between the policy of the bourgeoisie and the policy of the proletariat. Only this evaluation of the political

---

* 'The Paris Commune and The Tasks of the Democratic Dictatorship'. 4th ed., IX, 120, gives only the concluding section of this article, which does not include the passage quoted, on the grounds that the manuscript is not in Lenin's handwriting, though extensively corrected by him.

† 'The Proletariat and its Ally in the Russian Revolution', 4th ed., XI, 337.

nature of the peasantry opens up the prospect of the dictatorship of the proletariat growing directly out of the democratic
revolution. In this, naturally, there lies no 'denial', 'ignoring'
or 'underestimation' of the peasantry. Without the decisive significance of the agrarian question for the life of the whole of society
and without the great depth and gigantic sweep of the peasant
revolution there could not even be any talk of the proletarian
dictatorship in Russia. But the fact that the *agrarian* revolution
created the conditions for the dictatorship *of the proletariat* grew
out of the inability of the peasantry to solve its own historical
problem with its own forces and under its own leadership. Under
present conditions in bourgeois countries, even in the backward
ones, insofar as they have already entered the epoch of capitalist
industry and are bound into a unit by railroads and telegraphs—
this applies not only to Russia but to China and India as well—
the peasantry is even less capable of a leading or even only an
independent political role than in the epoch of the old bourgeois
revolutions. The fact that I invariably and persistently stressed
this idea, which forms one of the most important features of the
theory of the permanent revolution, also provided a quite inadequate and, in essence, absolutely unfounded pretext for accusing
me of underestimating the peasantry.

What were Lenin's views on the question of a peasant party?
To reply to this question, a comprehensive review would be
required of the evolution of Lenin's views on the Russian revolution in the period of 1905-17. I shall confine myself here to
two quotations :

In 1907, Lenin wrote:

'It is possible . . . that the objective difficulties of a political
unification of the petty bourgeoïsie will check the formation of
such a party and leave the peasant democracy for a long time in
the present state of a spongy, shapeless, pulpy, Trudovik-like*
mass.' (VIII, 494).†

In 1909, Lenin expressed himself on the same theme in a different
way:

---

* The Trudoviks were representatives of the peasants in the four Dumas,
constantly vacillating between the Cadets (Liberals) and the Social Democrats.—L.T.

† 'Revolution and Counter-Revolution', 4th ed., XIII, 104.

'There is not the slightest doubt that a revolution which reaches ... so high a degree of development as the revolutionary dictatorship will create a more firmly-formed and more powerful revolutionary peasant party. To judge the matter otherwise would mean to assume that in a grown-up man, the size, form and degree of development of certain essential organs could remain in a childish state.' (XI, Part 1, 230.)*

Was this assumption confirmed? No, it was not. But that is just what induced Lenin, *up to the moment of the complete verification by history*, to give an algebraic answer to the question of the revolutionary government. Naturally, Lenin never put his hypothetical formula above the reality. The struggle for the independent political party of the proletariat constituted the main content of his life. The woeful epigones, however, in their hunt after a peasant party, ended up with the subordination of the Chinese workers to the Kuomintang, the strangulation of communism in India in the name of the 'Workers' and Peasants' Party', the dangerous fiction of the Peasants' International, the masquerade of the League Against Imperialism, and so on.

Prevailing official thought makes no effort to dwell on the contradictions in Lenin adduced above, which are in part external and apparent, in part real, but which always stem from the problem itself. Now that there have arisen among us a special species of 'Red' professors who are frequently distinguished from the old reactionary professors not by a firmer backbone but only by a profounder ignorance, Lenin is professorially trimmed and purged of all contradictions, that is, of the dynamics of his thought; standard quotations are threaded on separate threads, and then one 'series' or another set in circulation, according to the requirements of the 'current moment'.

It must not be forgotten for a moment that the problems of the revolution in a politically 'virgin' country became acute after a great historical interval, after a lengthy reactionary epoch in Europe and in the whole world, and for that reason alone contained many unknowns. Through the formula of the democratic dictatorship of the workers and peasants, Lenin expressed the peculiarity

---

* 'The Aim of the Struggle of the Proletariat in Our Revolution', 4th ed., XV, 345.

of Russian social conditions. He gave different interpretations to this formula, but did not reject it until he had probed to the end the peculiar conditions of the Russian revolution. Wherein lay this peculiarity?

The gigantic role of the agrarian question and the peasant question in general, as the soil or the subsoil of all other problems, and the great number of the peasant intellectuals and those who sympathised with the peasants, with their Narodnik ideology, with their 'anti-capitalist' traditions and their revolutionary tempering— all this in its entirety signified that *if an anti-bourgeois revolutionary peasant party was at all possible anywhere, then it was possible precisely and primarily in Russia.*

And as a matter of fact, in the endeavours to create a peasant party, or a workers' and peasants' party—as distinct from a liberal or a proletarian party—every possible political variant was attempted in Russia, illegal and parliamentary as well as a combination of the two: *Zemlya i Volya* (Land and Freedom), *Narodnaya Volya* (People's Will), *Cherny Peredel* (Black Redistribution), the legal *Narodnichestvo* (Populists), 'Socialist-Revolutionaries', 'People's Socialists', 'Trudoviks', 'Left Socialist-Revolutionaries', etc., etc. For half a century we had, as it were, a huge laboratory for the creation of an 'anti-capitalist' peasant party with an independent position toward the proletarian party. The largest scope was attained, as is well known, by the experiment of the S.R. Party which, for a time in 1917, actually constituted the party of the overwhelming majority of the peasantry. But what happened? This party used its position only to betray the peasants completely to the liberal bourgeoisie. The S.R.s entered into a coalition with the imperialists of the Entente and together with them conducted an armed struggle against the Russian proletariat.

This truly classic experiment shows that petty-bourgeois parties based on the peasantry are still able to retain a semblance of independent policy during the humdrum periods of history when secondary questions are on the agenda; but when the revolutionary crisis of society puts the fundamental questions of property on the order of the day, the petty-bourgeois 'peasant' party automatically becomes a tool in the hands of the bourgeoisie against the proletariat.

If my old differences of opinion with Lenin are analysed not on the plane of quotations indiscriminately torn out of this and that year, month and day, but in their correct historical perspective, then it becomes quite clear that the dispute, at least on my part, was not over whether an alliance of the proletariat with the peasants was required for the solution of the democratic tasks, but over what party-political and state form the revolutionary co-operation of the proletariat and the peasantry could assume, and what consequences could result from it for the further development of the revolution. I speak of course of my position in this dispute, not of the position of Bukharin and Radek at that time, for which they themselves must answer.

How close the formula of the 'permanent revolution' approximated to Lenin's formula is graphically illustrated by the following comparison. In the summer of 1905, that is, before the October general strike and before the December uprising in Moscow, I wrote in the foreword to one of Lassalle's speeches:

'It is self-evident that the proletariat, as in its time the bourgeoisie, fulfils its mission supported by the peasantry and the urban petty bourgeoisie. The proletariat leads the countryside, draws it into the movement, gives it an interest in the success of its plans. The proletariat, however, unavoidably remains the leader. This is not "the dictatorship of the peasantry and proletariat" but *the dictatorship of the proletariat supported by the peasantry*'.* (L. Trotsky, *The Year* 1905, page 281.)

Now compare these words, written in 1905 and quoted by me in the Polish article of 1909, with the following words of Lenin written likewise in 1909, just after the party conference, under the pressure of Rosa Luxemburg, had adopted the formula 'dictatorship of the proletariat supported by the peasantry' instead of the old Bolshevik formula. To the Mensheviks, who spoke of the radical change of Lenin's position, the latter replied:

'. . . The formula which the Bolsheviks have here chosen for

---

* This quotation, among a hundred others, shows in passing that I did have an inkling of the existence of the peasantry and the importance of the agrarian question as far back as the eve of the 1905 Revolution, that is, some time before the significance of the peasantry was explained to me by Maslov, Thalheimer, Thaelmann, Remmele, Cachin, Monmousseau, Bela Kun, Pepper, Kuusinen and other Marxist sociologists.—L.T.

themselves reads : *"the proletariat which leads the peasantry behind it."**

'. . . Isn't it obvious that the idea of all these formulations is one and the same? Isn't it obvious that this idea expresses precisely the dictatorship of the proletariat and peasantry—that the *"formula" of the proletariat supported by the peasantry, remains entirely within the bounds of that very same dictatorship of the proletariat and peasantry?'* (XI, Part I, pp. 219 and 224. My emphasis.)†

Thus Lenin puts a construction on the 'algebraic' formula here which excludes the idea of an *independent* peasant party and even more its dominant role in the revolutionary government: the proletariat leads the peasantry, the proletariat *is supported* by the peasantry, consequently the revolutionary power is concentrated in the hands of the party of the proletariat. But this is precisely the central point of the theory of the permanent revolution.

Today, that is, *after* the historical test has taken place, the utmost that can be said about the old differences of opinion on the question of the dictatorship is the following :

While Lenin, always proceeding from the leading role of the proletariat, emphasized and developed in every way the necessity of the revolutionary democratic collaboration of the workers and peasants—teaching this to all of us—I, invariably proceeding from this collaboration, emphasized in every way the necessity of proletarian leadership, not only in the bloc but also in the government which would be called upon to head this bloc. No other differences can be read into the matter.

In connexion with the foregoing, let us take two quotations: one out of ' Results and Prospects ', which Stalin and Zinoviev utilized to prove the antagonism between my views and Lenin's, the other out of a polemical article by Lenin against me, which Radek employs for the same purpose.

Here is the first quotation :

---

* At the 1909 Conference, Lenin proposed the formula of 'the proletariat which leads the peasantry behind it,' but in the end he associated himself with the formula of the Polish Social Democrats, which won the majority at the conference against the Mensheviks.—L.T.

† 'The Aim of the Struggle of the Proletariat in Our Revolution', 4th edn., XV, 333 and 339.

'The participation of the proletariat in a government is also objectively most probable, and permissible on principle, only as a *dominating and leading participation.* One may, of course, describe such a government as the dictatorship of the proletariat and peasantry, a dictatorship of the proletariat, peasantry and intelligentsia, or even a coalition government of the working class and the petty bourgeoisie, but the question nevertheless remains: who is to wield the hegemony in the government itself, and through it, in the country? And when we speak of a workers' government, by this we reply that the hegemony should belong to the working class.' (*Our Revolution,* 1906, page 250.)*

Zinoviev (in 1925!) raised a hue and cry because I (in 1905!) had placed the peasantry and the intelligentsia on the same plane. He got nothing else from the above-cited lines. The reference to the intelligentsia resulted from the conditions of that period, during which the intelligentsia played politically an entirely different role from that which it plays today. Only exclusively intellectual organizations spoke at that time in the name of the peasantry; the Socialist-Revolutionaries officially built their party on the 'triad': proletariat, peasantry, intelligentsia; the Mensheviks, as I wrote at that time, clutched at the heels of every radical intellectual in order to prove the blossoming of bourgeois democracy. I expressed myself hundreds of times in those days on the impotence of the intellectuals as an 'independent' social group and on the decisive significance of the revolutionary peasantry.

But after all, we are certainly not discussing here a single polemical phrase, which I have no intention at all of defending. The essence of the quotation is this : that I completely accept the Leninist content of the democratic dictatorship and only demand a more precise definition of its political mechanism, that is, the exclusion of the sort of coalition in which the proletariat would only be a hostage amid a petty-bourgeois majority.

Now let us examine Lenin's 1916 article which, as Radek himself points out, was directed '*formally* against Trotsky, but *in reality* against Bukharin, Pyatakov, the writer of these lines (that is, Radek) and a number of other comrades'. This is a very

---

* See page 70 of the present volume.

valuable admission, which entirely confirms my impression of
that time that Lenin was directing the polemic against me only
in appearance, for the content, as I shall demonstrate forthwith,
did not in reality at all refer to me.   This article contains (in two
lines) that very accusation concerning my alleged 'denial of the
peasantry' which later became the main capital of the epigones
and their disciples.   The 'nub' of this article—as Radek puts it—
is the following passage :

'Trotsky has not taken into consideration,' says Lenin, quoting
my own words, 'that if the proletariat draws behind it the non-
proletarian masses of the village to confiscate the landlords'
estates and overthrow the monarchy, then this will constitute the
consummation of the "national bourgeois revolution", and that in
Russia this is just what *the revolutionary democratic dictatorship
of the proletariat and the peasantry will be.'   (XIII, 214.)*

That Lenin did not direct to the 'right address' this reproach of
my 'denial' of the peasantry, but really meant Bukharin and
Radek, who actually did skip over the democratic stage of the
revolution is clear not only from everything that has been said
above, but also from the quotation adduced by Radek himself,
which he rightly calls the 'nub' of Lenin's article.   In point of
fact, *Lenin directly quotes the words of my article to the effect
that only an independent and bold policy of the proletariat can
'draw behind it the non-proletarian masses of the village to con-
fiscates the landlords' estates and overthrow the monarchy* ', etc.—
and then Lenin adds : 'Trotsky has not taken into consideration
that . . . this is just what the revolutionary democratic dictatorship will be.'   In other words, Lenin confirms here and, so to
speak, certifies that Trotsky in reality accepts the whole actual
content of the Bolshevik formula (the collaboration of the workers
and peasants and the democratic tasks of this collaboration), but
refuses to recognise that this is just what the democratic dictatorship, the consummation of the national revolution, will be.   It
therefore follows that the dispute in this apparently 'sharp' polemical article involves not the programme of the next stage of the
revolution and its driving class forces, but precisely the *political*

---

* 'About the Two Lines of the Revolution.'   4th edn., XXI, 382.

*correlation of these forces, the political and party character of the
dictatorship.* While, as a result in part of the unclarity at that
time of the processes themselves and in part of factional exaggerations, polemical misunderstandings were comprehensible and unavoidable in *those* days, it is completely incomprehensible how
Radek contrived to introduce such confusion into the question
after the event.

My polemic with Lenin was waged in essence over the possibility
of the independence (and the degree of the independence) of the
peasantry in the revolution, particularly over the possibility of an
independent peasants' party. In this polemic, I accused Lenin
of overestimating the *independent* role of the peasantry. Lenin
accused me of underestimating the *revolutionary* role of the peasantry. This flowed from the logic of the polemic itself. But is
it not contemptible for anyone today, two decades later, to use
these old quotations, tearing them out of the context of the party
relationships of that time and investing each polemical exaggeration or episodic error with an absolute meaning, instead of laying
bare in the light of the very great revolutionary experience we
have had what the actual axis of the differences was and what
was the real and not verbal scope of these differences?

Compelled to limit myself in the selection of quotations, I shall
refer here only to the summary theses of Lenin on the stages of
the revolution, which were written at the end of 1905 but only
published for the first time in 1926 in the fifth volume of *Lenin
Miscellanies* (page 451).* I recall that all the Oppositionists,
Radek included, regarded the publication of these theses as the
handsomest of gifts to the Opposition, for Lenin turned out in
these theses to be guilty of 'Trotskyism' in accordance with all the
articles of the Stalinist code. The most important points of the
resolution of the Seventh Plenum of the E.C.C.I. which condemns
Trotskyism seem to be avowedly and deliberately directed against
the fundamental theses of Lenin. The Stalinists gnashed their
teeth in rage at their publication. The Editor of this volume of
the *Miscellanies*, Kamenev, told me flatly with the not very bash-

---

* The Stages, Direction and Prospects of the Revolution', 4th edn.,
X, 73-74. *Little Lenin Library*, Eng. edn., Vol. VI, ' The Revolution of
1905' (1931), pp. 54-55.

ful 'good nature' that is characteristic of him that if a bloc between us were not being prepared he would never under any circumstances have allowed the publication of this document. Finally, in an article by Kostrzewa in *Bolshevik*, these theses were fraudulently falsified precisely to spare Lenin from being charged with Trotskyism in his attitude toward the peasantry as a whole and the middle peasant in particular.

In addition I quote here Lenin's own evaluation of his differences of opinion with me, which he made in 1909 :

'Comrade Trotsky himself, in this instance, grants "the participation of the representatives of the democratic population" in the "workers' government," that is, *he grants a government of representatives of the proletariat and the peasantry.* Under what conditions the participation of the proletariat in the revolutionary government is permissible is a separate question, and on this question, the Bolsheviks will most likely fail to see eye to eye not only with Trotsky but also with the Polish Social Democrats. The question of the dictatorship of the revolutionary classes, however, is in no case reducible to the question of the "majority" in this or that revolutionary government, or to the conditions under which the participation of the Social Democrats in this or that government is permissible.' (XI, Part I, page 229. My emphasis.)*

In this quotation from Lenin, it is again confirmed that Trotsky accepts a government of representatives of the proletariat and the peasantry, and therefore does not 'skip over' the latter. Lenin furthermore emphasizes that the question of the dictatorship is not reducible to the question of the majority of the government. This is altogether beyond dispute. What is involved here, first and foremost, is the joint struggle of the proletariat and peasantry and consequently the struggle of the proletarian vanguard against the liberal or national bourgeoisie for influence over the peasants. But while the question of the revolutionary dictatorship of the workers and peasants is *not reducible* to the question of this or that majority in the government, nevertheless, upon the victory of the revolution, this question inescapably *arises* as the decisive

---

* 'The Aim of the Struggle of the Proletariat in Our Revolution.' 4th edn., XV, 344.

one. As we have seen, Lenin makes a cautious reservation (against all eventualities) to the effect that should matters reach the point of participation by the party in the revolutionary government, then perhaps differences might arise with Trotsky and the Polish comrades *over the conditions* of this participation. It was a matter therefore of *possible* difference of opinion, insofar as Lenin considered theoretically permissible the participation of the representatives of the proletariat as a minority in a democratic government. Events, however, showed that no differences arose between us. In November, 1917, a bitter struggle flared up in the top leadership of the party over the question of the coalition government with the Socialist-Revolutionaries and the Mensheviks. Lenin, without objecting in principle to a coalition on the basis of the soviets, categorically demanded that the Bolshevik majority be firmly safeguarded. I stood shoulder to shoulder with Lenin.

Now let us hear from Radek. To just what does he reduce the whole question of the democratic dictatorship of the proletariat and the peasantry?

'Wherein,' he asks, 'did the old Bolshevik theory of 1905 prove to be fundamentally correct? In the fact that the joint action of the Petrograd workers and peasants (the soldiers of the Petrograd garrison) overthrew Tsarism (in 1917—L.T.). After all, the 1905 formula foresees in its fundamentals only the correlation of classes, and not a concrete political institution.'

Just a minute, please! By designating the old Leninist formula as 'algebraic,' I do not imply that it is permissible to reduce it to an empty commonplace, as Radek does so thoughtlessly. 'The fundamental thing was realized : the proletariat and the peasantry jointly overthrew Tsarism.' But this 'fundamental thing' was realized without exception in all victorious or semi-victorious revolutions. Tsars, feudal lords, and priests were always and everywhere beaten with the fists of the proletarians or the precursors of the proletarians, the plebeians and peasants. This happened as early as the 16th century in Germany and even earlier. In China it was also workers and peasants who beat down the 'militarists.' What has this to do with the democratic dictatorship? Such a dictatorship never arose in the old revolutions, nor did it arise in the Chinese revolution. Why not? Be-

cause astride the backs of the workers and peasants, who did the
rough work of the revolution, sat the bourgeoisie. Radek has
abstracted himself so violently from 'political institutions' that he
has forgotten the 'most fundamental thing' in a revolution, namely,
who leads it and who seizes power. A revolution, however, is a
struggle for power. It is a political struggle which the classes
wage *not* with bare hands but through the medium of 'political
institutions' (parties, etc.).

'People who have not thought out to the end the complexity of
the method of Marxism and Leninism', Radek thunders against
us sinners, entertain the following conception: ' The whole thing
must invariably end in a joint government of workers and
peasants; and some even think that this must invariably be a
coalition government of workers' and peasants' parties.'

What blockheads these 'some' are! And what does Radek himself think? Does he think that a victorious revolution is not
bound to reflect and set its seal upon a specific correlation of
revolutionary classes? Radek has deepened the 'sociological'
problem to the point where nothing remains of it but a verbalistic
shell.

How impermissible it is to abstract oneself from the question
of the political forms of the collaboration of the workers and
peasants will best be shown to us by the following words from
an address by the same Radek to the Communist Academy in
March, 1927 :

'A year ago, I wrote an article in *Pravda* on this (Canton)
government designating it as a *peasants' and workers' government*.
A comrade of the editorial board assumed that it was an oversight
on my part and changed it to *workers' and peasants' government*.
I did not protest against this and let it stand : workers' and
peasants' government.'

Thus, in March, 1927 (not in 1905), Radek was of the opinion
that there could be a peasants' and workers' government in contradistinction to a workers' and peasants' government. This was
beyond the editor of *Pravda*. I confess that for the life of me I
can't understand it either. We know well what a workers' and
peasants' government is. But what is a peasants' and workers'
government, in contrast and as opposed to a workers' and peasants'

government? Please be so kind as to explain this mysterious transposition of adjectives. Here we touch the very heart of the question. In 1926, Radek believed the Canton government of Chiang Kai-shek was a peasants' and workers' government. In 1927 he repeated this formula. In reality, however, it proved to be a *bourgeois* government, exploiting the revolutionary struggle of the workers and peasants and then drowning them in blood. How is this error to be explained? Did Radek simply misjudge? From far away it is easy to misjudge. Then why not say it: I did not understand, could not see, I made a mistake. But no, this is no factual error due to lack of information, but rather, as is now clear, a profound mistake in principle. The peasants' and workers' government, as opposed to the workers' and peasants' government, is nothing else but the Kuomintang. It can mean nothing else. If the peasantry does not follow the proletariat, it follows the bourgeoisie. I believe that this question has been sufficiently clarified in my criticism of the factional Stalinist idea of a 'two-class, worker-peasant party' (see *The Draft Programme of the Communist International; A Criticism of Fundamentals*). The Canton 'peasants' and workers' government', in contrast to a workers' and peasants' government, is also the only conceivable expression, in the language of present-day Chinese politics, of the 'democratic dictatorship' as opposed to the proletarian dictatorship; in other words, the embodiment of the Stalinist Kuomintang policy as opposed to the Bolshevik policy which the Communist International labels 'Trotskyist'.

4. WHAT DID THE THEORY OF THE PERMANENT REVOLUTION LOOK LIKE IN PRACTICE?

In his criticism of our theory, Radek adds to it, as we have seen, also the *'tactic derived from it'*. This is a very important addition. The official Stalinist criticism of 'Trotskyism' on this question prudently limited itself to theory . . . For Radek, however, this does not suffice. He is conducting a struggle against a definite (Bolshevik) tactical line in China. He seeks to discredit this line by the theory of the permanent revolution, and to do this he must show, or pretend that somebody else has already shown, that a false tactical line has in the past flowed from this theory. Here Radek is directly misleading his readers. It is possible that he himself in unfamiliar with the history of the revolution, in which he never took a direct part. But apparently he has not made the slightest effort to examine the question through documents. Yet the most important of these are contained in the second volume of my *Collected Works*. They can be checked by anyone who can read. And so, let me inform Radek that virtually throughout all the stages of the first revolution I was in complete solidarity with Lenin in evaluating the forces of the revolution and its successive tasks, in spite of the fact that I spent the whole of 1905 living illegally in Russia, and 1906 in prison. I am compelled to confine myself here to a minimum of proofs and documentation.

In an article written in February and printed in March, 1905,

that is, two or three months before the first Bolshevik Congress
(which is recorded in history as the Third Party Congress), I
wrote :

'The bitter struggle between the people and the Tsar, which
knows no other thought than victory; the all-national insurrection as the culminating point of this struggle; the provisional
government as the revolutionary culmination of the victory of the
people over their age-old foe; the disarming of the Tsarist reaction
and the arming of the people by the provisional government; the
convocation of the constituent assembly on the basis of universal,
equal, direct and secret suffrage—these are the objectively indicated stages of the revolution.' (*Collected Works*, Volume II,
Part I, page 232.)

It is enough to compare these words with the resolutions of
the Bolshevik Congress of May, 1905, in order to recognize in
the formulation my complete solidarity with the Bolsheviks on
the fundamental problems.

Nor is this all. In harmony with this article, I formulated in
Petersburg, in agreement with Krassin, the theses on the provisional government which appeared illegally at that time. Krassin
defended them at the Bolshevik Congress. The following words
of Lenin show how much he approved of them :

'I share entirely the views of Comrade Krassin. It is natural
that, as a writer, I gave attention to the literary formulation of
the question. *The importance of the aim* of the struggle has
been shown very correctly by Comrade Krassin, and *I am with
him completely*. One cannot engage in struggle without reckoning on capturing the position for which one is fighting. . . .'
(VI, 180.)*

The major part of Krassin's extensive amendment, to which
I refer the reader, was embodied in the Congress resolution. That
I was the author of this amendment is proved by a note from
Krassin, which I still possess. This whole episode in the history
of the Party is well known to Kamenev and others.

The problem of the peasantry, the problem of drawing the

---

* Speech at Third Congress of R.S.D.L.P., on Amendments to Resolution
on Revolutionary Provisional Government. 4th edn., VIII, 366: Lenin
actually used Krassin's party name, Zimin.

peasantry close to the workers' soviets, of co-ordinating work with the Peasants' League, engaged the attention of the Petersburg Soviet more and more every day. Is Radek perhaps aware that the leadership of the Soviet devolved upon me? Here is one of the hundreds of formulations I wrote at that time on the tactical tasks of the revolution :

'The proletariat creates city-wide "soviets" which direct the fighting actions of the urban masses, and puts upon the order of the day the fighting alliance with the army and the peasantry.' (*Nachalo*, No. 4, November 17 [new style, November 30], 1905.)

It is boring, and even embarrassing, let me confess, to cite quotations proving that I never even talked of a 'leap' from autocracy into Socialism. But it can't be helped. I wrote the following, for example, in February, 1906, on the tasks of the Constituent Assembly, without in any way counterposing the latter to the soviets. as Radek, following Stalin, now hastens to do in regard to China in order to sweep away with an ultra-leftist broom all traces of yesterday's opportunist policy :

'The liberated people will convoke the Constituent Assembly by its own power. The tasks of the Constituent Assembly will be gigantic. It will have to reconstruct the State upon democratic principles, that is, upon the principles of the absolute sovereignty of the people. Its duty will be to organize a people's militia, carry through a vast agrarian (land) reform, and introduce the eight-hour day and a graduated income tax.' (*Collected Works*, Volume II, Part I, page 349.)

And here is what I wrote, in 1905, in an agitational leaflet, specifically on the question of the 'immediate' introduction of socialism :

'Is it thinkable to introduce socialism in Russia immediately? No, our countryside is far too benighted and unconscious. There are still too few real socialists among the peasants. We must first overthrow the autocracy, which keeps the masses of the people in darkness. The rural poor must be freed of all taxation; the graduated progressive income tax, universal compulsory education, must be introduced; finally, the rural proletariat and semi-proletariat must be fused with the town proletariat into a single social democratic army. Only this army can accomplish the great socialist revolution.' (*Collected Works*, Volume II, Part 1, page 228.)

It therefore follows that I did differentiate somewhat between the democratic and socialist stages of the revolution, long before Radek, tailing after Stalin and Thaelmann, began lecturing me on this subject. Twenty-two years ago, I wrote:

' When the idea of uninterrupted revolution was formulated in the socialist press — an idea which connected the liquidation of absolutism and feudalism with a socialist revolution, along with growing social conflicts, uprisings of new sections of the masses, unceasing attacks by the proletariat upon economic and political privileges of the ruling classes—our "progressive" press raised a unanimous howl of indignation.' (*Our Revolution*, 1906, p. 258.)*

First of all, I should like to call attention to the definition of the uninterrupted revolution contained in these words: it connects the liquidation of mediaevalism with the socialist revolution through a number of sharpening social clashes. Where then is the leap? Where is the ignoring of the democratic stage? And after all, isn't this what actually happened in 1917?

It is noteworthy, by the way, that the howl raised by the 'progressive' press in 1905 over the uninterrupted revolution can in no wise be compared with the hardly progressive howling of the present-day hacks who have intervened in the affair after a brief delay of a quarter of a century.

What was the attitude of the then leading organ of the Bolshevik faction, *Novaya Zhizn*, published under the vigilant editorship of Lenin, when I raised the question of the permanent revolution in the press? Surely, this point is not devoid of interest. To an article of the 'radical' bourgeois newspaper *Nasha Zhizn* (*Our Life*), which endeavoured to set up the 'more rational' views of Lenin against the 'permanent revolution' of Trotsky, the Bolshevik *Novaya Zhizn* replied (on November 27, 1905) as follows :

'This gratituous assumption is of course sheer nonsense. Comrade Trotsky said that the proletarian revolution can, without halting at the first stage, continue on its road, elbowing the exploiters aside; Lenin, on the other hand, pointed out that the

---

* See page 81 of the present volume.

political revolution is only the first step. The publicist of *Nasha Zhizn* would like to see a contradiction here. . . . The whole misunderstanding comes, first, from the fear with which the name alone of the social revolution fills *Nasha Zhizn*; secondly, out of the desire of this paper to discover some sort of sharp and piquant difference of opinion among the Social Democrats; and thirdly, in the figure of speech used by Comrade Trotsky: "at a single blow." In No. 10 of *Nachalo*, Comrade Trotsky explains his idea quite unambiguously:

"The complete victory of the revolution signifies the victory of the proletariat", writes Comrade Trotsky. "But this victory in turn implies the uninterruptedness of the revolution in the future. The proletariat realizes in life the fundamental democratic tasks, and the very logic of its immediate struggle to consolidate its political rule poses before the proletariat, at a certain moment, purely socialist problems. Between the minimum and the maximum programme (of the Social Democrats) a revolutionary continuity is established. It is not a question of a single 'blow', or of a single day or month, but of a whole historical epoch. It would be absurd to try to fix its duration in advance." '

This one reference in a way exhausts the subject of the present pamphlet. What refutation of the entire subsequent criticism by the epigones could be more clear, precise and incontrovertible than this refutation contained in my newspaper article so approvingly quoted by Lenin's *Novaya Zhizn*? My article explained that the victorious proletariat, in the process of carrying out the democratic tasks, would by the logic of its position inevitably be confronted at a certain stage by purely socialist problems. That is just where the *continuity* lies between the minimum and the maximum programmes, which grows inevitably out of the dictatorship of the proletariat. This is not a single blow, it is not a leap—I explained to my critics in the camp of the petty bourgeoisie of that time—it is a whole historical epoch. And Lenin's *Novaya Zhizn* associated itself completely with this prospect. Even more important, I hope, is the fact that it was verified by the actual course of development and in 1917 was decisively confirmed as correct.

Apart from the petty-bourgeois democrats of *Nasha Zhizn*, it was mainly the Mensheviks who in 1905, and particularly in 1906 after the defeat of the revolution had begun, spoke of the fantastic 'leap' over democracy to socialism. Among the Mensheviks it was especially Martynov and the late Yordansky who distinguished themselves in this field. Both of them, be it said in passing later became stalwart Stalinists. To the Menshevik writers who sought to hang the 'leap to socialism' on me, I expounded, in a special article written in 1906, in detail and in popular style, not only the error but also the stupidity of such a contention.   I could reprint this article today, almost unabridged, against the criticism of the epigones. But it will perhaps suffice to say that the conclusion of this article was summed up in the following words :

'I understand perfectly—let me assure my reviewer (Yordansky) —that to leap, in a newspaper article, over a political obstacle is far from the same as surmounting it in practice.' (*Collected Works*, Volume II, Part 1, page 454.)

Perhaps this will suffice? If not, I can continue, so that critics like Radek will not be able to say that they did not have 'at hand' the material on which they pass judgment so cavalierly.

Our Tactics, a small pamphlet which I wrote in prison in 1906, and which was immediately published by Lenin, contains the following characteristic conclusion :

'The proletariat will be able to support itself upon the uprising of the village, and in the towns, the centres of political life, it will be able to carry through to a victorious conclusion the cause which it has been able to initiate. Supporting itself upon the elemental forces of the peasantry, and leading the latter, the proletariat will not only deal reaction the final triumphant blow, but it will also know how to secure the victory of the revolution.' (*Collected Works*, Volume II, Part 1, page 448.)

Does this smack of ignoring the peasantry? In the same pamphlet, by the way, the following idea also is developed :

'Our tactics, calculated upon the irresistible development of the revolution, must not of course ignore the inevitable or the possible or even only the probable phases and stages of the revolutionary movement.' (*Collected Works*, Volume II, Part 1, page 436.)

Does this look like a fantastic leap?

In my article, *The Lessons of the First Soviet* (1906), I depict the prospects for the further development of the revolution (or, as it turned out in reality, for the new revolution) in the following manner :

'History does not repeat itself—and the new Soviet will not have once more to go through the events of the fifty days (October to December 1905); instead, it will be able to borrow its programme of action completely from this period. This programme is perfectly clear. Revolutionary co-operation with the army, the peasantry, and the lowest plebeian strata of the urban petty bourgeoisie. Abolition of the autocracy. Destruction of its material organization: in part through reorganization and in part through the immediate dissolution of the army; destruction of the bureaucratic police apparatus. Eight-hour day. Arming of the population, above all of the proletariat. Transformation of the soviets into organs of revolutionary urban self-administration. Creation of soviets of peasants' deputies (peasant committees) as organs of the agrarian revolution in the localities. Organization of elections to the Constituent Assembly, and electoral struggle on the basis of a definite programme of action for the people's representatives.' (*Collected Works*, Volume II, Part 2, page 206.)

Does this look like skipping over the agrarian revolution, or underestimation of the peasant question as a whole? Does this look as though I was blind to the democratic tasks of the revolution? No, it does not. But what then does the political picture drawn by Radek look like? Nothing at all.

Magnanimously, but very ambiguously, Radek draws a line between my 1905 position, which he distorts, and the position of the Mensheviks, without suspecting that he is himself repeating three-fourths of the Menshevik criticism; even though Trotsky, to be sure, employed the same methods as the Mensheviks, Radek explains jesuitically, his aim was nevertheless different. By this subjective formula, Radek completely discredits his own approach to the question. Even Lassalle knew that the end depends upon the means and in the final analysis is conditioned by it. He even wrote a play on this subject (*Franz Von Sickingen*). But what is it that renders my means and that of the Mensheviks one and the same? The attitude towards the peasantry. As evidence, Radek adduces three polemical lines from the above-cited 1916 article by Lenin, observing in passing, however, that here Lenin, although he names Trotsky, was in reality polemicizing against Bukharin and against Radek himself. Besides this quotation from Lenin which, as we have already seen, is refuted by the whole content of Lenin's article, Radek makes reference to Trotsky himself. Exposing the emptiness of the Menshevik conception, I asked in my 1916 article: If it is not the liberal bourgeoisie that will lead, then who will? After all, you Mensheviks do not in any case believe in the *independent* political role of the peasantry. So then, Radek has caught me red-handed: Trotsky 'agreed' with the Mensheviks about the role of the peasantry. The Mensheviks held it impermissible to 'repulse' the liberal bourgeoisie for the sake of a dubious and unreliable alliance with the peasantry. This was the 'method' of the Mensheviks; while mine consisted of brushing aside the liberal bourgeoisie and fighting for the leadership of the revolutionary peasantry. On this fundamental question I had no differences with Lenin. And when I said to the Mensheviks in the course of the struggle against them: 'You are in any case not inclined to assign a *leading* role to the peasantry,' then this was not an agreement with the method of the Mensheviks as Radek tries to insinuate, but only the clear posing of an alternative: *either* the dictatorship of the liberal plutocracy *or* the dictatorship of the proletariat.

The same completely correct argument put forward by me in 1916 against the Mensheviks, which Radek now disloyally tries to utilize against me also, had been used by me nine years earlier, at the London Congress of 1907, when I defended the theses of the Bolsheviks on the attitude toward non-proletarian parties. I quote here the essential part of my London speech which, in the first years of the revolution, was often reprinted in anthologies and textbooks as the expression of the Bolshevik attitude toward classes and parties in the revolution. Here is what I said in this speech, which contains a succinct formulation of the theory of the permanent revolution.

'To the Menshevik comrades, their own views appear extremely complex. I have repeatedly heard accusations from them that my conception of the course of the Russian revolution is oversimplified. And yet, despite their extreme amorphousness, which is one of the forms of complexity,—and perhaps just because of this amorphousness—the views of the Mensheviks fall into a very simple pattern comprehensible even to Mr. Milyukov.

'In a postscript to the recent published book, *How Did The Elections To The Second State Duma Turn Out?* the ideological leader of the Cadet Party writes: "As to the left groups in the narrower sense of the word, that is, the socialist and revolutionary groups, an agreement with them will be more difficult. But even here again, there are, if no definite positive reasons, then at least some very weighty negative ones which can to a certain extent facilitate an agreement between us. Their aim is to criticize and to discredit us; for that reason alone it is necessary that we be present and act. As we know, to the socialists, not only in Russia but throughout the world, the revolution now taking place is a bourgeois and not a socialist revolution. It is a revolution which is to be accomplished by bourgeois democracy. To supersede this democracy . . . is something no socialists in the whole world are ready to do, and if the country has sent them into the Duma in such great numbers, then it was certainly not for the purpose of realizing socialism now or in order to carry through the preparatory 'bourgeois' reforms with their own hands . . . It will be far more advantageous for them to leave the role of parliamentarians to us than to compromise themselves in this role."

'As we see, Milyukov brings us straight to the heart of the question. The quotation cited gives all the most important elements of the Menshevik attitude toward the revolution and the relationship between bourgeois and socialist democracy.

' "The revolution that is taking place is a bourgeois and not a socialist revolution"—that's the first and most important point. The bourgeois revolution "must be accomplished by the bourgeois democracy"—that's the second point. The socialist democracy cannot carry through bourgeois reforms with its own hands, its role remains purely oppositional: "Criticize and discredit." This is the third point. And finally—as the fourth point—in order to enable the socialists to remain in the opposition, "it is necessary that we (that is, the bourgeois democracy) be present and act."

'But what if "we" are not present? And what if there is no bourgeois democracy capable of marching at the head of the bourgeois revolution? Then it must be invented. This is just the conclusion to which Menshevism arrives. It produces bourgeois democracy, its attributes and history, out of its own imagination.

'As materialists, we must first of all pose the question of the social bases of bourgeois democracy: upon what strata or classes can it rest?

'As a revolutionary force the big bourgeoisie can be dismissed— we all agree on this. Even at the time of the Great French Revolution, which was a national revolution in the broadest sense, certain Lyons industrialists played a counter-revolutionary role. But we are told of the middle bourgeoisie, and also and primarily of the petty bourgeoisie, as being the leading force of the bour- geois revolution. But what does this petty bourgeoisie represent?

'The Jacobins based themselves upon the urban democracy, which had grown out of the craft guilds. Small masters, journey- men, and the town population closely bound up with them, constituted the army of the revolutionary *sansculottes*, the prop of the leading party of the Montagnards. It was precisely this compact mass of the city population, which had gone through the long historical school of the craft guilds, that bore upon its shoulders the whole burden of the revolution. The objective result of the revolution was the creation of 'normal' conditions of capitalist exploitation. The social mechanics of the historical process, however, produced this result, that the conditions for bourgeois domination were created by the 'mob', the democracy of the streets, the *sansculottes*. Their terrorist dictatorship purged bourgeois society of the old rubbish and then, after it had over- thrown the dictatorship of the petty-bourgeois democracy, the bourgeoisie came to power.

'Now I ask—alas, not for the first time! —what social class in our country will raise up revolutionary bourgeois democracy, put it in power, and make it possible for it to carry out gigantic tasks, if the proletariat remains in opposition? This is the central question, and I again put it to the Mensheviks.

'It is true, in our country there are huge masses of the revolu- tionary peasantry. But the Menshevik comrades know just as well as I do that the peasantry, regardless of how revolutionary it may be, is incapable of playing an *independent*, much less a *leading*

political role. The peasantry can undoubtedly prove to be a
tremendous force in the service of the revolution; but it would be
unworthy of a Marxist to believe that a peasant party is capable
of placing itself at the head of a bourgeois revolution and, upon
its own initiative, liberating the nation's productive forces from
the archaic fetters that weigh upon them. The town is the
hegemon in modern society and only the town is capable of
assuming the role of hegemon in the bourgeois revolution.*

'Now, where is the urban democracy in our country capable of
leading the nation behind it? Comrade Martynov has already
sought it repeatedly, magnifying-glass in hand. He discovered
Saratov teachers, Petersburg lawyers, and Moscow statisticians.
Like all his co-thinkers, the only thing that he refused to notice
was that in the Russian revolution the industrial proletariat has
conquered the very same ground as was occupied by the semi-
proletarian artisan democracy of the *sansculottes* at the end of the
eighteenth century. I call your attention, Comrades, to this fundamental fact.

'Our large-scale industry did not grow organically out of the
crafts. The economic history of our towns knows absolutely
nothing of any period of guilds. Capitalist industry arose in our
country under the direct and immediate pressure of European
capital. It took possession of a soil essentially virginal, primitive,
without encountering any resistance from craft culture. Foreign
capital flowed into our country through the channels of state loans
and through the pipe-lines of private initiative. It gathered around
itself the army of the industrial proletariat and prevented the rise
and development of crafts. As a result of this process there
appeared among us as the main force in the towns, at the moment
of the bourgeois revolution, an industrial proletariat of an extremely highly developed social type. This is a fact. It cannot be
disputed, and must be taken as the basis of our revolutionary
tactical conclusions.

'If the Menshevik comrades believe in the victory of the revolution, or even if they only recognize the possibility of such a victory,

---

* Do the belated critics of the permanent revolution agree with this?
Are they prepared to extend this elementary proposition to the countries
of the East, China, India, etc.? Yes or no?—L.T.

they cannot dispute the fact that in our country there is no historical claimant to revolutionary power other than the proletariat. As the petty bourgeois urban democracy in the Great French Revolution placed itself at the head of the revolutionary nation, in just the same way the proletariat, which is the one and only revolutionary democracy of our cities, must find a support in the peasant masses and place itself in power—if the revolution has any prospect of victory at all.

'*A government resting directly upon the proletariat, and through it upon the revolutionary peasantry, does not yet signify the socialist dictatorship.* I shall not here deal with the further prospects before a proletarian government. It may be that the proletariat is destined to fall, as did the Jacobin democracy, in order to clear the road for the rule of the bourgeoisie. I want to establish only one point: if the revolutionary movement in our country, as Plekhanov foretold, triumphs as a workers' movement, then the victory of the revolution is possible only as the revolutionary victory of the proletariat—otherwise it is altogether impossible.

'I insist upon this conclusion, most emphatically. If it is assumed that the social antagonisms between the proletariat and the peasant masses will prevent the proletariat from placing itself at the head of the latter, and that the proletariat by itself is not strong enough to gain victory—then one must necessarily draw the conclusion that there is no victory at all in store for our revolution. Under such circumstances, an agreement between the liberal bourgeoisie and the old authorities is bound to be the natural outcome of the revolution. This is a variant the possibility of which can by no means be denied. But clearly this variant lies along the path of the revolution's defeat, and is conditioned by its internal weakness. In essence *the entire analysis of the Mensheviks—above all, their evaluation of the proletariat and its possible relations with the peasantry—leads them inexorably to the path of revolutionary pessimism.*

'But they persistently turn aside from this path and generate revolutionary optimism on the basis of—bourgeois democracy.

'From this is derived their attitude to the Cadets. For them the Cadets are the symbol of bourgeois democracy, while bourgeois democracy is the natural claimant to revolutionary power . . .

'Upon what then do you base your belief that the Cadets will still rise and stand erect? Upon facts of political development? No, upon your own schema. In order "to carry the revolution through to the end" you need the bourgeois urban democracy, you search for it eagerly, and find nothing but Cadets. And you generate in relation to them amazing optimism, you dress them up, you want to force them to play a creative role, a role which they do not want to play, cannot play and will not play. To my basic question—I have put it repeatedly—I have heard no response. You have no prognosis of the revolution. Your policy lacks any large prospects.

'And in connection with this, your attitude to bourgeois parties is formulated in words which the congress should keep in its memory: "as the occasion may require." The proletariat is not supposed to carry on a systematic struggle for influence over the masses of the people, it is not supposed to determine its tactical steps in accordance with a single guiding idea, namely, to unite around itself all the toilers and the downtrodden and to become their herald and leader.' (*Minutes and Resolutions of the Fifth Party Congress*, pages 180-5.)

This speech, which succinctly sums up all my articles, speeches and acts of 1905 and 1906, was completely approved by the Bolsheviks, not to mention Rosa Luxemburg and Tyszko (on the basis of this speech, we entered upon more intimate relations which led to my collaboration in the Polish journal). Lenin, who did not forgive me my conciliatory attitude toward the Mensheviks—and he was right—expressed himself upon my speech with a deliberately emphasized reserve. Here is what he said:

'I merely wish to observe that Trotsky, in his little book *In Defence of the Party* publicly expressed his solidarity with Kautsky, who wrote of the economic community of interests of the proletariat and the peasantry in the present revolution in Russia. Trotsky recognized the admissibility and expediency of a left bloc against the liberal bourgeoisie. These facts are enough for me to recognize that Trotsky is drawing closer to our conceptions. *Independently of the question of the "uninterrupted revolution"*, there is solidarity here between us on the fundamental points of

the question concerning the relationship to the bourgeois parties.'
(VIII, 400)*

Lenin did not devote himself in his speech to a general evaluation
of the theory of the permanent revolution, since I too, in my
speech, did not develop the further prospects for the dictatorship
of the proletariat. He had obviously not read my fundamental
work on this question, otherwise he would not have spoken of my
'drawing closer' to the conceptions of the Bolsheviks as of something new, for my London speech was only a condensed restate-
ment of my works of 1905-06. Lenin expressed himself very
reservedly, because I did stand outside the Bolshevik faction. In
spite of that, or more correctly, precisely because of that, his words
leave no room for false interpretations. Lenin established 'solidarity between us on the fundamental points of the question'
concerning the attitude toward the peasantry and the liberal
bourgeoisie. This solidarity applies not to my *aims*, as Radek
preposterously represents it, but precisely to *method*. As to the
prospect of the democratic revolution growing into the socialist
revolution, it is right here that Lenin makes the reservation,
'independently of the question of the "uninterrupted revolution".'
What is the meaning of this reservation? It is clear that Lenin in
no way identified the permanent revolution with ignoring the
peasantry or skipping over the agrarian revolution, as is the rule
with the ignorant and unscrupulous epigones. Lenin's idea is as
follows: How far our revolution will go, whether the proletariat
can come to power in our country sooner than in Europe and what
prospects this opens up for socialism—this question I do not touch
upon; however, on the fundamental question of the attitude of the
proletariat toward the peasantry and the liberal bourgeoisie 'there
is solidarity here between us.'

We have seen above how the Bolshevik *Novaya Zhizn* responded
to the theory of the permanent revolution virtually at its birth, that
is, as far back as in 1905. Let us also recall how the editors of
Lenin's *Collected Works* expressed themselves on this theory after
1917. In the notes† to Volume XIV, Part 2, page 481, it is stated:

---

* 'London Congress of the R.S.D.L.P.: Concluding Remarks on the
Question of Attitude to Bourgeois Parties,' 4th edn., XII, 423.
† Note 79.

' Even before the 1905 Revolution he (Trotsky) advanced the original and *now especially noteworthy* theory of the permanent revolution, in which he asserted that *the bourgeois revolution of 1905 would pass directly over into a socialist revolution*, constituting the first in a series of national revolutions.'

I grant that this is not at all an acknowledgement of the correctness of all that I have written on the permanent revolution. But in any case it is an acknowledgement of the incorrectness of what Radek writes about it. 'The *bourgeois* revolution will pass directly over into a socialist revolution'—but this is precisely the theory of *growing into* and not of *skipping over*; from this flows a realistic, and not an adventuristic tactic. And what is the meaning of the words '*now especially noteworthy* theory of the permanent revolution'? They mean that the October revolution has shed a new light on those aspects of the theory which had formerly remained in obscurity for many or had simply appeared 'improbable'. The second part of Volume XIV of Lenin's *Collected Works* appeared while the author was alive. Thousands and tens of thousands of party members read this note. And nobody declared it to be false until the year 1924. And it occured to Radek to do this only in the year 1928.

But insofar as Radek speaks not only of theory but also of tactics, the most important argument against him still remains the character of my practical participation in the revolutions of 1905 and 1917. My work in the Petersburg Soviet of 1905 coincided with the definitive elaboration of those of my views on the nature of the revolution which the epigones now subject to uninterrupted fire. How could such allegedly erroneous views fail to be reflected in any way in my political activity, which was carried on before the eyes of everyone and recorded daily in the press? But if it is assumed that such a false theory was mirrored in my politics, then why did those who are now the consuls remain silent at that time? And what is rather more important, why did Lenin at that time most energetically defend the line of the Petersburg Soviet, at the highest point of the revolution as well as after its defeat?

The very same questions, only in a perhaps sharper form, apply to the 1917 revolution. In a number of articles which I wrote in New York, I evaluated the February Revolution from the point of view of the theory of the permanent revolution. All these articles have now been reprinted. My tactical conclusions coincided completely with the conclusions which Lenin drew at the same time in Geneva, and consequently were in the same irreconcilable contradiction to the conclusions of Kamenev, Stalin and the other epigones. When I arrived in Petrograd, nobody asked me if I renounced my 'errors' of the permanent revolution. Nor was there anyone to ask. Stalin slunk around in embarrassment from one corner to another and had only one desire, that the party should forget as quickly as possible the policy which he had advocated up to Lenin's arrival. Yaroslavsky was not yet the inspirer of the Control Commission; together with Mensheviks, together with Ordzhonikidze and others, he was publishing a trivial semi-liberal sheet in Yakutsk. Kamenev accused Lenin of Trotskyism and declared when he met me: 'Now you have the laugh on us.' On the eve of the October Revolution, I wrote in the central organ of the Bolsheviks on the prospect of the permanent revolution. It never occurred to anyone to come out against me. My solidarity with Lenin turned out to be complete and unconditional. What then, do my critics, among them Radek, wish to say? That I myself completely failed to understand the theory which I advocated, and that in the most critical historical periods I acted directly counter to this theory, and quite correctly? Is it not simpler to assume that my critics failed to understand the permanent revolution, like so many other things? For if it is assumed that these belated critics are so well able to analyse not only their own ideas but those of others, then how explain that all of them without exception adopted such a wretched position in the 1917 Revolution, and forever covered themselves with shame in the Chinese Revolution?

But after all, some reader may suddenly recall : What about your most important tactical slogan; ' No Tsar—but a workers' government'?

In certain circles this argument is deemed decisive. Trotsky's horrid slogan, ' No Tsar! ' runs through all the writings of all the critics of the permanent revolution; with some it emerges as the final, most important and decisive argument; with others, as the ready harbour for weary minds.

This criticism naturally reaches its greatest profundity in the 'Master' of ignorance and disloyalty, when he says in his incomparable *Problems of Leninism* :

' We shall not dwell at length (No indeed! —L.T.) on Comrade Trotsky's attitude in 1905, when he 'simply' forgot all about the peasantry as a revolutionary force, and advanced the slogan of " No Tsar, but a workers' government", that is, the slogan of revolution without the peasantry.' (Stalin, *Problems of Leninism*, pages 174-175.)*

Despite my almost hopeless position in face of this annihilating criticism, which does not want to 'dwell', I should nevertheless like to refer to some mitigating circumstances. There are some. I beg a hearing.

Even if one of my 1905 articles contained an isolated, ambiguous or inappropriate slogan which might be open to misunderstanding, then today, i.e., 23 years later, it should not be taken by itself but rather placed in context with my other writings on the same subject, and, what is most important, in context with my political participation in the events. It is impermissible merely to provide readers with the bare title of a work unknown to them (as well as to the critics) and then to invest this title with a meaning which is diametrically opposed to everything I wrote and did.

But it may not be superfluous to add—O my critics!—that at no time and in no place did I ever write or utter or propose such a slogan as ' No Tsar—but a workers' government! ' At the basis of the main argument of my judges there lies, aside from everything else, a shameful factual error. The fact of the matter is that a proclamation entitled ' No Tsar—but a workers' government' was written and published abroad in the summer of 1905 by Parvus. I had already been living illegally for a long time in Petersburg at that period, and had nothing at all to do with this leaflet either in ideas or in actions. I learned of it much later from polemical articles. I never had the occasion or opportunity to express myself on it. As for the proclamation I (as

---

* Stalin, *Works,* Eng. edn., VI, 382.

also, moreover, all my critics) neither saw it nor read it. This is the factual side of this extraordinary affair. I am sorry that I must deprive all the Thaelmanns and Semards of this easily portable and convincing argument. But facts are stronger than my humane feelings.

Nor is this all. Accident providentially brought events together, so that, at the same time that Parvus was publishing abroad the circular, unknown to me, ' No Tsar—but a workers' government', a proclamation written by me appeared illegally in Petersburg with the title: *Neither Tsar nor Zemtsi,* but the People!* This title, which is frequently repeated in the text of the leaflet as a slogan embracing the workers and peasants, might have been conceived in order to refute in a popular form the later contentions about skipping the democratic stage of the revolution. The appeal is reprinted in my *Collected Works* (Volume II, Part 1, page 256). There also are my proclamations, published by the Bolshevik Central Committee, to that peasantry, which, in the ingenious expression of Stalin, I 'simply forgot'.

But even this is not yet all. Only a short time ago, the worthy Rafes, a theoretician and leader of the Chinese Revolution, wrote in the theoretical organ of the Central Committee of the Communist Party of the Soviet Union about the same horrid slogan which Trotsky raised *in the year* 1917. Not in 1905, but in 1917! For the Menshevik Rafes, at any rate, there is some excuse— almost up till 1920 he was a 'minister' of Petlyura's, and how could he, weighed down by the cares of state of the struggle against the Bolsheviks, pay any heed there to what was going on in the camp of the October Revolution! Well, but the editorial board of the organ of the Central Commitee? Here's a wonder. One idiocy more or less. . . .

' But how is that possible? ' a conscientious reader raised on the trash of recent years exclaims. ' Weren't we taught in hundreds and thousands of books and articles . . .? '

' Yes, friends, taught; and that is just why you will have to

---

* i.e., members of the local self-governing authorities, the *zemstva*, set up in the last period of Tsarist rule, with restricted powers and dominated by the liberal nobility.

learn anew. These are the overhead expenses of the period of reaction. Nothing can be done about it. History does not proceed in a straight line. It has temporarily run into Stalin's blind alleys.'

5. WAS THE 'DEMOCRATIC DICTATORSHIP' REALIZED IN OUR COUNTRY ? IF SO, WHEN ?

Appealing to Lenin, Radek contends that the democratic dictatorship was realized in the form of the dual power. Yes, *occasionally*—and furthermore, conditionally—Lenin did put the question this way ; that I admit. ' Occasionally ?' Radek becomes indignant and accuses me of assailing one of the most fundamental ideas of Lenin. But Radek is angry only because he is wrong. In *Lessons of October,* which Radek likewise submits to criticism after a delay of about four years, I interpreted Lenin's words on the ' realization ' of the democratic dictatorship in the following manner :

'A democratic workers' and peasants' coalition could only take shape as an immature form of power incapable of attaining real power — it could take shape only as a tendency and not as a concrete fact.' (*Collected Works,* Vol. III, part 1, p. XXI.)*

With regard to this interpretation, Radek writes : ' Such an interpretation of the content of one of the most outstanding theoretical chapters in the work of Lenin *is worth absolutely nothing.*' These words are followed by a pathetic appeal to the traditions of Bolshevism, and finally, the conclusion : ' These questions are too important for it to be possible to reply to them with a reference to what Lenin *occasionally* said.'

Lessons of October, U.S. ed., 1937, p. 37. The version given in the English edition of *Lessons of October*, 1925, p. 35, is inadequate.

By this, Radek wants to evoke the image of my treating carelessly ' one of the most outstanding ' of Lenin's ideas. But Radek is wasting indignation and pathos for nothing. A little understanding would be more in place here. My presentation in *Lessons of October,* even though very condensed, does not rest upon a sudden inspiration on the basis of quotations taken at second hand, but upon a genuine thorough study of Lenin's writings. It reproduces the essence of Lenin's idea on this question, while the verbose presentation of Radek, despite the abundance of quotations, does not retain a single living passage of Lenin's thought.

Why did I make use of the qualifying word ' occasionally '? Because that is how the matter really stood. References to the fact that the democratic dictatorship was ' realized ' in the form of the dual power (' in a certain form and up to a certain point ') were made by Lenin only in the period between April and October 1917, that is, *before the actual carrying out of the democratic revolution.* Radek neither noticed, understood, nor evaluated this. In the struggle against the present epigones, Lenin spoke extremely conditionally of the ' realization ' of the democratic dictatorship. He did so not to give a historical characterization of the period of the dual power—in this form it would be plain nonsense—but to argue against those who expected a second, improved edition of the independent democratic dictatorship. Lenin's words only meant that there is not and will not be any democratic dictatorship outside of the miserable miscarriage of the dual power, and that for this reason it was necessary to ' rearm ' the party, i.e., change the slogan. To contend that the coalition of the Mensheviks and the Socialist-Revolutionaries with the bourgeoisie, which refused the peasants the land and hounded the Bolsheviks, constituted the ' realization ' of the Bolshevik slogan—this means either deliberately to pass off black as white or else to have lost one's head entirely.

With regard to the Mensheviks, an argument could be presented which would to a certain point be analogous to Lenin's argument against Kamenev : ' You are waiting for the bourgeoisie to fulfil a " progressive " mission in the revolution ? This mission has already been realized : the political rôle of Rodzianko, Guchkov and Milyukov is the maximum that the bourgeoisie is able to give, just as Kerenskyism is the maximum of democratic revolution that could be realized as an independent stage.'

Unmistakable anatomical features—rudiments—show that our ancestors had a tail. These features suffice to confirm the genetic unity of the animal world. But, to put it quite candidly, man has no tail. Lenin demonstrated to Kamenev the rudiments of the democratic dictatorship in the regime of the dual power, warning him that no new organ should be hoped for out of these rudiments. And we did not have an independent democratic dictatorship, even though we completed the democratic revolution more deeply, more resolutely, more purely than had ever been done anywhere else.

Radek should reflect upon the fact that if in the period from February to April the democratic dictatorship had *actually* been realized, even Molotov would have recognized it. The party and the class understood the democratic dictatorship as a régime which would mercilessly destroy the old state apparatus of the monarchy and completely liquidate manorial landed property. But there was not a trace of this in the Kerensky period. For the Bolshevik Party, however, it was a question of *the actual realization of the revolutionary tasks,* and not of the the the revelation of certain sociological and historical 'rudiments'. Lenin, in order to enlighten his adversaries theoretically, illuminated splendidly these features which did not attain development—and that is all he did in this connexion. Radek, however, endeavours in all seriousness to convince us that in the period of the dual power, that is, of powerlessness, the ' dictatorship ' did exist and the democratic revolution was realized. Only, you see, it was such a ' democratic revolution ' that all Lenin's genius was required to recognize it. But this is just the thing that signifies that it was not realized. The real democratic revolution is something that every illiterate peasant in Russia or in China would easily recognize. But so far as the morphological features are concerned, it is a more difficult thing. For example, despite the lesson provided by Kamenev in Russia, it is impossible to get Radek to finally take note of the fact that in China too the democratic dictatorship was likewise ' realized ' in Lenin's sense (through the Kuomintang); and that it was realized more completely and in a more finished form than was the case in our country through the institution of dual power. Only hopeless simpletons can expect a second and improved edition of 'democracy' in China.

If the democratic dictatorship had only been realized in our country in the form of Kerenskyism, which played the rôle of errand boy to Lloyd George and Clemenceau, then we would have to say that history indulged in cruel mockery of the strategic slogan of Bolshevism. Fortunately, it is not so. The Bolshevik slogan was realized in fact—not as a morphological trait but as a very great historical reality. Only, it was realized *not before, but after October*. The peasant war, in the words of Marx, supported the dictatorship of the proletariat. The collaboration of the two classes was realized through October on a gigantic scale. At that time every ignorant peasant grasped and felt, even without Lenin's commentaries, that the Bolshevik slogan had been given life. And Lenin himself estimated the October Revolution—its first stage— as the *true* realization of the democratic revolution, and by that also as the true, even if changed, embodiment of the strategic slogan of the Bolsheviks. The *whole* of Lenin must be considered. And above all, the Lenin of after October, when he surveyed and evaluated events from a higher vantage point. Finally, Lenin must be considered in a Leninist way, and not in that of the epigones.

The question of the class character of the revolution and its 'growing over' was submitted by Lenin (after October) to an analysis in his book against Kautsky. Here is one of the passages over which Radek should reflect a bit.

'Yes, our revolution (the October Revolution—L.T.) is a bourgeois revolution *so long* as we march with the peasantry *as a whole*. This has been clear as clear can be to us; we have said it hundreds and thousands of times since 1905, and we have never attempted to skip this necessary stage of the historical process or abolish it by decrees.'

And further on :

'Things have turned out just as we said they would. The course taken by the revolution has confirmed the correctness of our reasoning. *First*, with the "whole" of the peasantry against the monarchy, the landlords, the mediaeval regime (and to that extent, the revolution remains bourgeois, bourgeois-democratic). Then, with the poorest peasants, with the semi-proletarians, with all the exploited, *against capitalism,* including the rural rich, the kulaks, the profiteers, and to that extent the revolution becomes a *socialist* one.' (XV, 508.)*

That is how Lenin spoke—not ' occasionally ' but always, or, more accurately, *invariably*—when he gave a finished and generalized and perfected evaluation of the revolution, including October. ' Things have turned out just as we said they would.' The bourgeois-democratic revolution was realized as a coalition of the workers and peasants. During the Kerensky period ? No, *during the first period after October.* Is that right ? It is. But, as we now know, it was not realized in the form of a democratic dictatorship, but in the form of the dictatorship of the proletariat. With that there also disappeared the necessity for the old algebraic formula.

If the conditional argument of Lenin against Kamenev in 1917 and the rounded-out Leninist characterization of the October Revolution in the subsequent years are uncritically juxtaposed, then it follows that two democratic revolutions were ' realized ' in Russia. This is too much, all the more since the second is separated from the first by an armed uprising of the proletariat.

Now contrast the quotation just made from Lenin's book, *The Proletarian Revolution and the Renegade Kautsky,* with the passage from my *Results and Prospects* where, in the chapter on ' The Proletarian Regime', the first stage of the dictatorship and the prospects of its further development are outlined:

' The abolition of feudalism will meet with support from the *entire* peasantry as the burden-bearing estate. A progressive income tax will also be supported by the great majority of the peasantry. But any legislation carried through for the purpose of protecting the agricultural proletariat will not only not receive the active sympathy of the majority, but will even meet with the active opposition of a minority of the peasantry.

' The proletariat will find itself compelled to carry the class struggle into the villages and in this manner destroy the community of interest which is undoubtedly to be found among all peasants, although within comparatively narrow limits. From

---

*' The Proletarian Revolution and the Renegade Kautsky,' 1918, 4th ed., XXVIII, 276. *Selected Works,* Eng. ed., VII, 190 and 191.

the very first moment after its taking power, the proletariat will
have to find support in the antagonisms between the village poor
and the village rich, between the agricultural proletariat and the
agricultural bourgeoisie.' (*Our Revolution*, page 255, 1906.)*

How little all this resembles an ' ignoring ' of the peasantry on
my part, and the complete ' antagonism ' between the two lines,
Lenin's and mine !

The quotation from Lenin adduced above does not stand alone
in his works. On the contrary, as is always the case with Lenin,
the new formula, which illuminates events more penetratingly,
becomes for him the axis of his speeches and his articles for a
whole period. In March 1919, Lenin said :

' In October 1917 we seized power *together with the peasantry
as a whole*. This was a bourgeois revolution, inasmuch as the class
struggle in the rural districts had not yet developed.' (XVI, 143)†

The following was said by Lenin at the party congress in
March 1919 :

' In a country where the proletariat was obliged to assume power
with the aid of the peasantry, where it fell to the lot of the proletariat to serve as the agent of a petty-bourgeois revolution, until
the organisation of the Committees of Poor Peasants, i.e., down
to the summer and even the autumn of 1918, our revolution was
to a large extent a *bourgeois* revolution.' (XVI, 105)‡

These words were frequently repeated by Lenin in different
variations and on divers occasions. Radek, however, simply avoids
this cardinal idea of Lenin's, which is decisive in the controversy.

The proletariat took power together with the peasantry in
October, says Lenin. By that alone, the revolution was a bourgeois
revolution. Is that right ? In a certain sense, yes. But this means
that the *true* democratic dictatorship of the proletariat and the
peasantry, that is, the one which actually destroyed the regime of
autocracy and serfdom and snatched the land from the feudalists,
was accomplished not *before* October but only *after* October ; it
was accomplished, to use Marx's words, in the form of the *dictator-*

---

* See page **76** of the present volume.
† ' 8th Congress of the R.C.P., Report on Work in the Countryside.' 4th
ed., XXIX, 180. *Selected Works*, Eng. ed., VIII, 171.
‡ ' 8th Congress of the R.C.P., Report of the Central Committee.' 4th ed.,
XXIX, 137. *Selected Works*, Eng. ed., VIII, 37.

ship of the proletariat supported by the peasant war—and then, a few months later, began growing into a socialist dictatorship. Is *this* really hard to understand ? Can differences of opinion prevail on this point *today?*

According to Radek, the ' permanent ' theory sins by mixing up the bourgeois stage with the socialist. In reality, however, the class dynamics so thoroughly 'mixed up', that is, *combined* these two stages, that our unfortunate metaphysician is no longer in a position even to find the threads.

Certainly, many gaps and many incorrect contentions can be found in *Results and Prospects*. But after all, this work was written not in 1928, but considerably before October—before the October of 1905. The question of the gaps in the theory of the permanent revolution, or, more correctly, in my basic arguments for this theory at that time, is not even touched upon by Radek ; for, following his teachers—the epigones—he attacks not the gaps but the strong sides of the theory, those which the course of historical development confirmed, attacks them in the name of the utterly false conclusions which he deduces from Lenin's formulation—which Radek has not thoroughly studied or thought out to the very end.

Juggling with old quotations is in general practised by the whole school of epigones on a quite special plane which nowhere intersects the real historical process. But when the opponents of ' Trotskyism ' have to occupy themselves with the analysis of the real development of the October Revolution, and occupy themselves with it seriously and conscientiously—which happens to some of them from time to time—then they inevitably arrive at formulations in the spirit of the theory which they reject. We find the clearest proof of this in the works of A. Yakovlev which are devoted to the history of the October Revolution. The class relationships of old Russia are formulated by this author, today a prop of the ruling faction* and undoubtedly more literate than the other Stalinists, and particularly than Stalin himself, as follows :

' We see a twofold limitedness in the peasants' uprising (March to October 1917). Raising itself to the level of a peasant war, the

---

*Yakovlev was recently appointed People's Commissar of Agriculture of the USSR.—L.T.

uprising did not overcome its limitedness, did not burst asunder the confines of its immediate task of destroying the neighbouring landowner ; did not transform itself into an organized revolutionary movement ; did not surmount the character of an elemental outbreak that distinguishes a peasant movement.

' The peasant uprising taken by itself—an elemental uprising, limited in its aim to the extermination of the neighbouring landowner—could not triumph, could not destroy the state power hostile to the peasantry, which supported the landowner. That is why the agrarian movement is capable of winning only if it is led by the corresponding urban class . . . This is the reason why the fate of the agrarian revolution, in the final analysis, was decided not in the tens of thousands of villages, but in the hundreds of towns. Only the working class, which was dealing the bourgeoisie a mortal blow in the centres of the country, could bring the peasant uprising to victory ; only the victory of the working class in the city could tear the peasant movement out of the confines of an elemental clash of tens of millions of peasants with tens of thousands of landowners ; only the victory of the working class, finally, could lay the foundations for a new type of peasant organisation which united the poor and middle peasantry not with the bourgeoisie but with the working class. The problem of the victory of the peasant uprising was a problem of the victory of the working class in the towns.

' When the workers dealt the government of the bourgeoisie a decisive blow in October, they thereby solved in passing the problem of the victory of the peasant uprising.'

And further on :

' . . . The whole essence of the matter is this, that by virtue of the historically given conditions, bourgeois Russia in 1917 entered into an alliance with the landowners. Even the most left factions of the bourgeoisie, like the Mensheviks and the Socialist-Revolutionaries, did not go beyond arranging a deal favourable to the landowners. Therein lies the most important difference between the conditions of the Russian Revolution and the French Revolution which took place more than a hundred years earlier . . . The peasant revolution could not triumph as a bourgeois revolution in 1917. (Exactly ! —L.T.) Two roads were open to it. *Either defeat*

*under the blows of the bourgeoisie and the landowners or—victory
as a movement accompanying and auxiliary to the proletarian
revolution. By taking over the mission of the bourgeoisie in the
Great French Revolution, by taking over the task of leading the
agrarian democratic revolution, the working class of Russia
obtained the possibility of carrying out a victorious proletarian
revolution.' (The Peasant Movement in* 1917, pages x-xi, xi-xii,
State Publishing House, 1927).

What are the fundamental elements of Yakovlev's arguments ?
The incapacity of the peasantry to play an *independent* political
rôle ; the resultant inevitability of the leading rôle of an urban
class ; the inaccessibility for the Russian bourgeoisie of the rôle of
leader in the agrarian revolution ; the resultant inevitability of the
leading rôle of the proletariat ; its seizure of power as leader of
the agrarian revolution ; finally, the dictatorship of the proletariat
which supports itself upon the peasant war and opens up the
epoch of socialist revolution. This destroys to the roots the
metaphysical posing of the question concerning the ' bourgeois '
or the ' socialist ' character of the revolution. The gist of the
matter lay in the fact that the agrarian question, which constituted
the basis of the bourgeois revolution, could not be solved under
the rule of the bourgeoisie. The dictatorship of the proletariat
appeared on the scene not *after* the completion of the agrarian
democratic revolution but as the necessary *prerequisite* for its
accomplishment.   In a word, in this retrospective schema of
Yakovlev's, we have all the fundamental elements of the theory
of the permanent revolution as formulated by me in 1905. With
me, it was a question of a historical prognosis ; Yakovlev, relying
upon the preliminary studies of a whole staff of young research
workers, draws the balance sheet of the events of the three revolutions twenty-two years after the first revolution and ten years after
the October Revolution. And then ? Yakovlev repeats almost
literally my formulations of 1905.

What is Yakovlev's attitude, however, to the theory of the
permanent revolution ? It is an attitude that befits every Stalinist
functionary who wants to retain his post and even to climb to a
higher one. But how does Yakovlev, in this case, reconcile his
appraisal of the driving forces of the October Revolution with the

struggle against 'Trotskyism'? Very simply: he does not give a
thought to such a reconciliation. Like some liberal Tsarist officials,
who acknowledged Darwin's theory but at the same time appeared
regularly at communion, Yakovlev too buys the right to express
Marxist ideas from time to time at the price of participating in
the ritualistic baiting of the permanent revolution. Similar examples
can be adduced by the dozen.

It still remains to add that Yakovlev did not execute the above-
quoted work on the history of the October Revolution on his own
initiative, but on the basis of a decision of the Central Committee,
which at the same time charged me with the editing of Yakovlev's
work.* At that time, Lenin's recovery was still expected, and it
never occurred to any of the epigones to kindle an artificial dispute
around the permanent revolution. At any rate, in my capacity as
the former, or, more correctly, as the proposed editor of the official
history of the October Revolution, I can establish with complete
satisfaction that the author, in all disputed questions, consciously
or unconsciously employed the literal formulations of my pro-
scribed and heretical work on the permanent revolution (*Results
and Prospects*).

The rounded-out evaluation of the historical fate of the Bolshevik
slogan which Lenin himself gave shows with certainty that the
difference of the two lines, the ' permanent ' and Lenin's, had a
secondary and subordinate significance ; what united them, however, was most fundamental. And this foundation of both lines,
which were completely fused by the October Revolution, is in
irreconcilable antagonism not only to the February-March line of
Stalin and the April-October line of Kamenev, Rykov and
Zinoviev, not only to the whole China policy of Stalin, Bukharin
and Martynov, but also to the present ' China ' line of Radek.

And when Radek, who changed his judgment of values so
radically between 1925 and the second half of 1928, seeks to
convict me of not understanding ' the complexity of Marxism and
Leninism', then I can reply: The *fundamental* train of thought
which I developed twenty-three years ago in *Results and Prospects*,

---

*Excerpt from the minutes of the session of the Organization Bureau
of the Central Committee of May 22, 1922, No. 21 : ' To instruct Comrade
Yakovlev . . . to compile a textbook on the history of the October Revolution under the editorial supervision of Comrade Trotsky.'—L.T.

I consider confirmed by events as completely correct, and, precisely because of that, in agreement with the strategical line of Bolshevism.

In particular I fail to see the slightest reason for withdrawing anything of what I said in 1922 on the permanent revolution in the foreword to my book *The Year 1905*, which the whole party read and studied in innumerable editions and reprints while Lenin was alive, and which ' disturbed ' Kamenev only in the autumn of 1924 and Radek for the first time in the autumn of 1928.

' Precisely in the period between January 9 and the October strike ' (it says in this foreword) ' the author formed those opinions which later received the name : " theory of the permanent revolution". This somewhat unusual name expressed the idea that the Russian revolution, directly confronted by bourgeois tasks, could in no case halt at them. *The revolution would not be able to solve its immediate bourgeois tasks except by putting the proletariat in power . . .*

' This appraisal was confirmed as completely correct, though after a lapse of twelve years. The Russian revolution could not terminate with a bourgeois-democratic regime. It had to transfer power to the working class. *If the working class was still too weak for the capture of power in 1905, it had to mature and grow strong not in the bourgeois-democratic republic but in the illegality of Third-of-June Tsarism.*'* (L. Trotsky *The Year 1905*, foreword, pages 4-5).

I want to quote in addition one of the sharpest polemical judgments which I passed on the slogan of the 'democratic dictatorship'. In 1909, I wrote in the Polish organ of Rosa Luxemburg :

' While the Mensheviks, proceeding from the abstraction that "our revolution is bourgeois", arrive at the idea of adapting the whole tactic of the proletariat to the conduct of the liberal bourgeoisie, right up to the capture of state power, the Bolsheviks, proceeding from the same bare abstraction : " democratic, not socialist dictatorship", arrive at the idea of the bourgeois-democratic self-limitation of the proletariat with power in its hands. The difference between them on this question is certainly quite important : while the anti-revolutionary sides of Menshevism are

---

* On June 3 (16), 1907 the **coup d'etat** was completed which **formally** inaugurated the period of triumphant counter-revolution.

already expressed in full force today, the anti-revolutionary features of Bolshevism threaten to become a great danger only in the event of the victory of the revolution.'

To this passage in the article, which is reprinted in the Russian edition of my book *The Year 1905*, I made the following annotation in January 1922 :

'As is known, this did not take place, for Bolshevism under the leadership of Lenin (though not without internal struggle), accomplished its ideological rearmament on this most important question in the spring of 1917, that is, before the seizure of power.'

These two quotations have been subjected since 1924 to a furious barrage of criticism. Now, after a delay of four years, Radek has also joined in with this criticism. Yet, if one reflects conscientiously upon the quoted lines, it must be admitted that they contained an important prognosis and a no less important warning. The fact does remain that at the moment of the February Revolution the whole so-called ' old guard ' of the Bolsheviks held the position of the bald counterposing of the democratic dictatorship to the socialist dictatorship. Out of Lenin's ' algebraic ' formula his closest disciples made a purely metaphysical construction and directed it against the real development of the revolution. At a most important historical turning point, the top leadership of the Bolsheviks in Russia adopted a reactionary position, and had Lenin not arrived so opportunely they could have knifed the October Revolution under the banner of the struggle against Trotskyism, as they later knifed the Chinese Revolution. Very piously, Radek describes the false position of the whole leading party stratum as a sort of 'accident'. But that has little value as a Marxist explanation of the vulgar democratic position of Kamenev, Zinoviev, Stalin, Molotov, Rykov, Kalinin, Nogin, Milyutin, Krestinsky, Frunze, Yaroslavsky, Ordjonikidze, Preobrazhensky, Smilga and a dozen other 'old Bolsheviks'. Would it not be more correct to acknowledge that the old, algebraic Bolshevik formula contained certain dangers within it ? Political development filled it—as always happens with an ambiguous revolutionary formula—with a content hostile to the proletarian revolution. It is self-evident that if Lenin had lived in Russia and had observed the development of the party, day by day, especially during the war, he would have

given the necessary correctives and clarifications in time. Luckily
for the revolution, he arrived soon enough, even though delayed,
to undertake the necessary ideological rearmament. The class
instinct of the proletariat and the revolutionary pressure of the
party rank and file, prepared by the entire preceding work of
Bolshevism, made it possible for Lenin, in struggle with the top
leadership and despite their resistance, to switch the policy of the
party to a new track in ample time.

Does it really follow from this that today we must accept for
China, India and other countries Lenin's formula of 1905 in its
algebraic form, i.e., in all its ambiguity ; and that we must leave
it to the Chinese and Indian Stalins and Rykovs (Tang Ping-shan,
Roy and others) to fill the formula with a petty-bourgeois national-
democratic content—and then wait for the timely appearance of a
Lenin who will undertake the necessary correctives of April 4 ?
But is such a corrective assured for China and India ? Wouldn't
it be more appropriate to introduce into this formula those specific
corrections the necessity for which has been demonstrated by
historical experience both in Russia and in China ?

Does the foregoing mean that the slogan of the democratic
dictatorship of the proletariat and peasantry should be understood
simply as a 'mistake'? Nowadays, as we know, all ideas and
actions of man are divided into two categories : absolutely correct
ones, that is, those that comprise the 'general line', and absolutely
false ones, that is, deviations from this line. This, of course, does
not prevent what is absolutely correct today from being declared
absolutely false tomorrow. But the real development of ideas knew
also, before the emergence of the 'general line', the method of
successive approximations to the truth. Even in simple division in
arithmetic it is necessary to experiment in the selection of digits ;
one starts with larger or smaller digits, and then rejects all but one
in the process of testing. In ranging the target in artillery fire, the
method of successive approximations is known as 'bracketing'.
There is absolutely no avoiding the method of approximation in
politics as well. The whole point is to understand in time that a
miss is a miss, and to introduce the necessary corrections without
delay.

The great historic significance of Lenin's formula lay in the fact

that, under the conditions of a new historical epoch, it probed to
the end one of the most important theoretical and political questions, namely the question of the degree of political independence
attainable by the various petty-bourgeois groupings, above all, the
peasantry. Thanks to its completeness, the Bolshevik experience of
1905-17 firmly bolted the door against the ' democratic dictatorship'. With his own hand, Lenin wrote the inscription over this
door : No Entrance—No Exit. He formulated it in these words :
The peasant must go either with the bourgeois or with the worker.
The epigones, however, completely ignore this conclusion to which
the old formula of Bolshevism led, and contrary to this conclusion
they canonise a provisional hypothesis by inserting it into the
programme. It is really in this, generally speaking, that the essence
of epigonism lies.

6. ON THE SKIPPING OF HISTORICAL STAGES

Radek does not simply repeat a few of the official critical exercises of recent years, he also sometimes simplifies them, if that be possible. From what he writes, it follows that I make no distinction at all between the bourgeois and the socialist revolutions, between the East and the West, either in 1905 or today. Following Stalin, Radek too enlightens me on the impermissibility of skipping historical stages.

The question must be put first and foremost : If in 1905 it was for me simply a matter of the ' socialist revolution ' then why did I believe that it could begin in backward Russia sooner than in advanced Europe ? Out of patriotism ? Out of national pride ? And yet, somehow, that is what did happen. Does Radek understand that if the democratic revolution had been realised in Russia as an *independent* stage, we should not have had today the dictatorship of the proletariat ? If this came earlier here than in the West, then it was precisely and only because history combined the main content of the bourgeois revolution with the first stage of the proletarian revolution—did not mix them up but combined them organically.

To distinguish between the bourgeois and the proletarian revolution is political A.B.C. But after the A.B.C. come syllables, that is, combinations of letters. History accomplished just such a combination of the most important letters of the bourgeois alphabet with the first letters of the socialist alphabet. Radek, however, would like to drag us back from the already accomplished syllables to the alphabet. This is sad, but true.

It is nonsense to say that stages cannot in general be skipped. The living historical process always makes leaps over isolated ' stages ' which derive from theoretical breakdown into its component parts of the process of development in its entirety, that is, taken in its fullest scope. The same is demanded of revolutionary policy at critical moments. It may be said that the first distinction between a revolutionist and a vulgar evolutionist lies in the capacity to recognize and exploit such moments.

Marx's breakdown of the development of industry into handicraft, manufacture and factory is part of the A.B.C. of political economy, or more precisely, of historico-economic theory. In Russia, however, the factory came by skipping over the epoch of manufacture and of urban handicrafts. This is already among the syllables of history. An analogous process took place in our country in class relationships and in politics. The modern history of Russia cannot be comprehended unless the Marxist schema of the three stages is known : handicraft, manufacture, factory. But if one knows *only* this, one still comprehends nothing. For the fact is that the history of Russia—Stalin should not take this personally—skipped a few stages. The theoretical distinction of the stages, however, is necessary for Russia, too, otherwise one can comprehend neither what this leap amounted to nor what its consequences were.

The matter can also be approached from another side (just as Lenin occasionally approached the dual power), and it can be said that Russia went through all three of Marx's stages—the first two, however, in an extremely telescoped, embryonic form. These 'rudiments', the stages of handicraft and manufacture—merely outlined in dots, so to speak—suffice to confirm the genetic unity of the economic process. Nevertheless, the quantitative contraction of the two stages was so great that it engendered an entirely new quality in the whole social structure of the nation. The most striking expression of this new ' quality ' in politics is the October Revolution.

What is most unbearable in this discussion is the ' theorising ' of Stalin, with the two trinkets which constitute his entire theoretical baggage : ' the law of uneven development ' and the ' non-skipping of stages'. Stalin does not understand to this day that the *skipping of stages* (or remaining too long at one stage) *is just what uneven development consists of*. Against the theory of the permanent revolution, Stalin, with inimitable seriousness, sets up the law of uneven development. Yet, the prediction that historically backward Russia could arrive at the proletarian revolution sooner than advanced Britain rests entirely upon the law of uneven development. However, to make this prediction one had to understand the historical unevenness in its whole dynamic concreteness, and not simply keep permanently chewing upon a 1915 quotation from Lenin, which is turned upside down and interpreted in the manner of an illiterate.

The dialectic of the historical 'stages' is relatively easy to understand in periods of revolutionary ascent. Reactionary periods, on the contrary, naturally become epochs of cheap evolutionism. Stalinism, this gross ideological vulgarity, the worthy daughter of the party reaction, has created a cult of its own of progress by stages, as a cover for its political tailism and haggling over rags. This reactionary ideology has now engulfed Radek too.

One stage or another of the historical process can prove to be inevitable under certain conditions, although theoretically not inevitable. And conversely, theoretically ' inevitable ' stages can be compressed to zero by the dynamics of development, especially during revolutions, which have not for nothing been called the locomotives of history.

For example, in our country the proletariat ' skipped ' the stage of democratic parliamentarianism, granting the Constituent Assembly only a few hours, and even that much only in the back yard. But the counter-revolutionary stage in China can in no way be skipped over, just as in Russia the period of the four Dumas could not be skipped over. The present counter-revolutionary stage in China, however, was historically in no sense ' unavoidable '. It is the direct result of the catastrophic policy of Stalin and Bukharin, who will pass into history as the organizers of defeats. But the fruits of opportunism have become an objective factor which can check the revolutionary process for a long time.

Every attempt to skip over real, that is, objectively conditioned stages in the development of the masses, is political adventurism. So long as the majority of the working masses have confidence in the Social Democrats, or let us say, the Kuomintang, or the trade union leaders, we cannot pose before them the task of the immediate overthrow of bourgeois power. The masses must be prepared for that. The preparation can prove to be a very long ' stage '. But only a tailist can believe that, ' together with the masses', we must sit, first in the Right and then in the Left Kuomintang, or maintain a bloc with the strike-breaker Purcell ' until the masses become disillusioned with their leaders '—whom we, in the meantime, uphold with our friendship.

Radek will hardly have forgotten that many ' dialecticians ' characterized the demand for withdrawal from the Kuomintang and the break with the Anglo-Russian Committee as nothing but a skipping over of stages, and besides that, as a breach with the peasantry (in China) and with the working masses (in Britain). Radek ought to remember this all the better since he himself was one of the ' dialecticians ' of this sorry type. Now he is merely deepening and generalizing his opportunist errors.

In April 1919, Lenin wrote in a programmatic article, ' The Third International and Its Place in History ':

' We should not be mistaken if we say that it is precisely this contradiction between the backwardness of Russia and its ' leap' to the higher form of democracy, its leap across bourgeois democracy to Soviet, or proletarian democracy, that it was precisely this contradiction that was one of the reasons . . . which, in the West, particularly hindered, or retarded, the under-standing of the rôle of the Soviets' (XVI, 183).*

Lenin says here directly that Russia made a ' leap across bourgeois democracy '. To be sure, implicit in Lenin's statement are all the necessary qualifications: after all, the dialectic does not consist of each time repeating all the concrete conditions ; the writer takes it for granted that the reader himself also has something in his head. The leap across bourgeois democracy remains in spite of that, and makes difficult, according to Lenin's correct observation, the understanding of the rôle of the Soviets by all dogmatists and

---

*4th ed., XXIX, 281-282. *Selected Works*, Eng. Ed., X, 31-32.

schematists—not only 'in the West', but also in the East.

And here is how this question is dealt with in the foreword to *The Year 1905*, which now suddenly causes Radek such disquiet :

'Already in 1905, the Petersburg workers called their Soviet a proletariat government. This designation passed into the everyday language of that time and was completely embodied in the programme of the struggle of the working class for power. At the same time, however, *we set up against Tsarism an elaborated programme of political democracy* (universal suffrage, republic, militia, etc.). We could act in no other way. Political *democracy is a necessary stage in the development of the working masses—* with the highly important reservation that in one case this stage lasts for decades, while in another, the revolutionary situation permits the masses to emancipate themselves from the prejudices of political democracy even before its institutions have been converted into reality.' (Trotsky, *The Year 1905*, foreword, page 7.)

These words, which, by the way, are in complete accord with the ideas of Lenin quoted by me above, sufficiently explain, I think, the necessity of setting up against the dictatorship of the Kuomintang an 'elaborated programme of political democracy'. But it is precisely at this point that Radek swings to the left. In the epoch of the revolutionary ascent he opposed the withdrawal of the Chinese Communist Party from the Kuomintang. In the epoch of the counter-revolutionary dictatorship, he resists the mobilization of the Chinese workers under democratic slogans. This amounts to wearing furs in summer and going naked in winter.

7. WHAT DOES THE SLOGAN OF THE DEMOCRATIC DICTATORSHIP MEAN TODAY FOR THE EAST ?

Losing his way in the Stalinist—evolutionary, philistine, and not revolutionary—conception of historical ' stages ', Radek, too, endeavours now to sanctify the slogan of the democratic dictatorship of the proletariat and the peasantry for the whole East. Out of the ' working hypothesis ' of Bolshevism, which Lenin adapted to the course of development of a specific country ; which he changed, concretized and at a certain stage cast aside—Radek constructs a supra-historical schema. On this point he persistently repeats the following in his articles :

' This theory, as well as the tactic derived from it, is applicable to all countries with a youthful capitalist development, in which the bourgeoisie has not liquidated the problem that the preceding social-political formations have left behind as a heritage.'

Just reflect upon this formula : Is it not a solemn justification of Kamenev's position in 1917 ? Did the Russian bourgeoisie ' liquidate' the problems of the democratic revolution after the February Revolution ? No, they remained unsolved, including the most important of them, the agrarian problem. How could Lenin fail to comprehend that the old slogan was still ' applicable '? Why did he withdraw it ?

Radek answered us on this point before : because it had already ' been accomplished '. We have examined this answer. It is completely untenable, and doubly untenable in the mouth of Radek, who holds the view that the essence of the old Leninist slogan does not at all lie in the forms of power but in the actual liquidation of serfdom by the collaboration of the proletariat and the peasantry. But this is precisely what Kerenskyism did not produce. From this it follows that Radek's excursion into our past for the purpose of solving the most acute question of the day, the Chinese question, is altogether absurd. It is not what Trotsky understood or failed to understand in 1905 that should have been investigated, but rather what Stalin, Molotov and especially Rykov and Kamenev did not grasp in February-March 1917 (what Radek's position was in those days I do not know). For if one believes that the democratic dictatorship was ' realized ' to such an extent in the dual power as to require an immediate change of the central slogan, then one must recognize that the ' democratic dictatorship ' in China was realized much more fully and completely through the régime of the Kuomintang, that is, through the rule of Chiang Kai-shek and Wang Ching-wei, with Tang Ping-shan as append-age.* It was all the more necessary, therefore, to change the slogan in China.

But after all, is the ' heritage of the preceding social-political formations ' not yet liquidated in China ? No, it is not yet liqui-dated. But was it liquidated in Russia on April 4, 1917, when Lenin declared war upon the whole upper stratum of the ' old Bolsheviks '? Radek contradicts himself hopelessly, gets muddled and reels from side to side. Let us remark in this connection that it is not entirely accidental that he uses so complicated an expres-sion as 'heritage of the formations', plays variations upon it, and obviously avoids the clearer term, ' remnants of feudalism, or of serfdom', Why? Because Radek only yesterday denied these remnants most decisively and thereby tore away any basis for the slogan of the democratic dictatorship. In his report in the Com-munist Academy, Radek said :

' The sources of the Chinese Revolution are no less deep than were the sources of our revolution in 1905. One can assert with certainty that the alliance of the working class with the peasantry

---

* Chiang Kai-shek is the leader of the Right Wing, and Wang Ching-wei of the Left Wing of the Kuomintang. Tang Ping-shan served as a Com-munist Minister, carrying out the line of Stalin and Bukharin in China.— L.T.

will be stronger there than it was with us in 1905, *for the simple
reason that it will not be directed against two classes, but only
against one, the bourgeoisie.*'

Yes, ' for the simple reason '. What, when the proletariat,
together with the peasantry, directs its fight against one class, the
bourgeoisie—not against the remnants of feudalism, but against
the bourgeoisie—what, if you please, is such a revolution called ?
Perhaps a democratic revolution ? Just notice that Radek said
this not in 1905, and not even in 1909, but in March 1927. How
is this to be understood ? Very simply. In March 1927, Radek
also deviated from the right road, only in another direction. In its
theses on the Chinese question, the Opposition inserted a most
important correction to Radek's one-sidedness of that time. But
in the words just quoted there was nevertheless a kernel of truth :
there is almost no estate of landlords in China, the landowners
are much more intimately bound up with the capitalists than in
Tsarist Russia, and the specific weight of the agrarian question in
China is therefore much lighter than in Tsarist Russia ; but on the
other hand, the question of national liberation bulks very large.
Accordingly, the capacity of the Chinese peasantry for *independent*
revolutionary political struggle for the democratic renovation of
the country certainly cannot be greater than was the Russian
peasantry's. This found its expression, among other things, in the
fact that neither before 1925 nor during the three years of the
revolution in China, did a Narodnik (Populist) party arise, inscrib-
ing the agrarian revolution upon its banner. All this taken together
demonstrates that for China, which has already left behind it the
experience of 1925-27, the formula of the democratic dictatorship
presents a much more dangerous reactionary snare than in Russia
after the February Revolution.

Still another excursion by Radek, into an even further distant
past, turns just as mercilessly against him. This time, it is the
matter of the slogan of the permanent revolution which Marx
raised in 1850 :

' With Marx,' writes Radek, ' there was no slogan of a democratic dictatorship, while with Lenin, from 1905 to 1917, it was
the political axis, and formed a component part of his conception

of the revolution *in all* [? !] *countries* of incipient [?] capitalist development.'

Basing himself upon a few lines from Lenin, Radek explains this difference of positions by the fact that the central task of the German revolution was *national unification,* while in Russia it was the *agrarian revolution.* If this contrast is not made mechanically, and a sense of proportion is maintained, then it is correct up to a certain point. But then how does the matter stand with China ? The specific weight of the national problem in China, a semi-colonial country, is immeasurably greater in comparison with the agrarian problem than it was even in Germany in 1848-50 ; for in China it is simultaneously a question of unification and of liberation. Marx formulated his perspectives of the permanent revolution when, in Germany, all the thrones still stood firm, the Junkers held the land, and the leaders of the bourgeoisie were tolerated only in the antechamber of the government. In China, there has been no monarchy since 1911, there is no independent landlord class, the national-bourgeois Kuomintang is in power, and the relationships of serfdom are, so to speak, chemically fused with bourgeois exploitation. The contrast between the positions of Marx and Lenin undertaken by Radek thus tells entirely against the slogan of the democratic dictatorship in China.

But Radek does not even take up the position of Marx seriously, but only casually, episodically, confining himself to the circular of 1850, *in which Marx still considered the peasantry the natural ally of the petty-bourgeois urban democracy.* Marx at that time expected an independent stage of democratic revolution in Germany, that is, a temporary assumption of power by the urban petty-bourgeois radicals, supported by the peasantry. There's the nub of the question ! That, however, is just what did not happen. And not by chance, either. Already in the middle of the last century, the petty-bourgeois democracy showed itself to be powerless to carry out its own independent revolution. And Marx took account of this lesson. On April 16, 1856—that is, six years after the circular mentioned—Marx wrote to Engels :

' The whole thing in Germany will depend on the possibility of covering the rear of the proletarian revolution by a second edition of the Peasants' War. Then the affair will be splendid.'

THE PERMANENT REVOLUTION

248

These remarkable words, completely forgotten by Radek, constitute a truly precious key to the October Revolution as well as to the whole problem that occupies us here, in its entirety. Did Marx skip over the agrarian Revolution ? No, as we see, he did not skip over it. Did he consider the collaboration of the proletariat and the peasantry necessary in the coming revolution ? Yes, he did. Did he grant the possibility of the leading, or even only an independent, rôle being played by the peasantry in the revolution ? No, he did not grant this possibility. He proceeded from the fact that the peasantry, which had not succeeded in supporting the bourgeois democracy in the independent democratic revolution (through the fault of the bourgeois democracy, not of the peasantry), would be in a position to support the proletariat in the proletarian revolution. ' Then the affair will be splendid.' Radek apparently does not want to see that this is exactly what happened in October, and did not happen badly at that.

With regard to China, the conclusions following from this are quite clear. The dispute is not over the decisive rôle of the peasantry as an ally, and not over the great significance of the agrarian revolution, but over whether an independent agrarian democratic revolution is possible in China or whether ' a second edition of the Peasants' War ' will give support to the proletarian dictatorship. That is the only way the question stands. Whoever puts it differently has learned nothing and understood nothing, but only confuses the Chinese Communist Party and puts it off the right track.

In order that the proletariat of the Eastern countries may open the road to victory, the pedantic reactionary theory of Stalin and Martynov on ' stages ' and ' steps ' must be eliminated at the very outset, must be cast aside, broken up and swept away with a broom. Bolshevism grew to maturity in the struggle against this vulgar evolutionism. It is not to a line of march marked out *a priori* that we must adapt ourselves, but to the real course of the class struggle. It is necessary to reject the idea of Stalin and Kuusinen—the idea of fixing an order of succession for countries at various levels of development by assigning them in advance cards for different rations of revolution. One must adapt oneself to the real course of the class struggle. An inestimable guide for this is Lenin; but the *whole* of Lenin must be taken into consideration.

When in 1919 Lenin, especially in connection with the organization of the Communist International, unified the conclusions of the period that had gone by, and gave them an ever more finished theoretical formulation, he interpreted the experience of Kerenskyism and October as follows : In a bourgeois society with already developed class antagonisms there can only be either the dictatorship of the bourgeoisie, open or disguised, or the dictatorship of the proletariat. There cannot be any talk of an intermediate régime. Every democracy, every ' dictatorship of democracy ' (the ironical quotation marks are Lenin's) is only a veil for the rule of the bourgeoisie, as the experience of the most backward European country, Russia, showed in the epoch of its bourgeois revolution, i.e., the epoch most favourable to the ' dictatorship of democracy'. This conclusion was taken by Lenin as the basis for his theses on democracy, which were produced only as the sum of the experiences of the February and October Revolutions.

Like many others, Radek also separates mechanically the question of democracy from the question of the democratic dictatorship. This is the source of the greatest blunders. The ' democratic dictatorship ' can only be the masked rule of the bourgeoisie during the revolution. This is taught us by the experience of our ' dual power ' of 1917 as well as by the experience of the Kuomintang in China.

The hopelessness of the epigones is most crassly expressed in the fact that even now they still attempt to contrast the democratic dictatorship to the dictatorship of the bourgeoisie, as well as to the dictatorship of the proletariat. But this means that the democratic dictatorship must be of an intermediate character, that is, have a petty-bourgeois content. The participation of the proletariat in it does not alter matters, for in nature there is no such thing as an arithmetical mean of the various class lines. If it is neither the dictatorship of the bourgeoisie nor the dictatorship of the proletariat, then it follows that the petty-bourgeoisie must play the *determining* and *decisive* rôle. But this brings us back to the very same question which has been answered in practice by the three Russian and the two Chinese revolutions ; is the petty-bourgeoisie today, under the conditions of the world domination of imperialism, capable of playing a leading revolutionary rôle in capitalist countries, even when it is a question of backward countries which are still confronted with the solution of their democratic tasks?

There have been epochs in which the lower strata of the petty-bourgeoisie were able to set up their revolutionary dictatorship. That we know. But those were epochs in which the proletariat, or precursor of the proletariat, of the time had not yet become differentiated from the petty-bourgeoisie, but on the contrary constituted in its undeveloped condition the fighting core of the latter. It is quite otherwise today. We cannot speak of the ability of the petty-bourgeoisie to direct the life of present-day, even if backward, bourgeois society, insofar as the proletariat has already separated itself off from the petty-bourgeoisie and is pitted antag-onistically against the big bourgeoisie on the basis of capitalist development, which condemns the petty-bourgeoisie to nullity and confronts the peasantry with the inevitable political choice between the bourgeoisie and the proletariat. Every time the peasantry decides for a party which on the surface seems petty-bourgeois, it actually offers its back as a support for finance capital. While in the period of the first Russian Revolution, or in the period between the first two revolutions, there could still exist differences of opinion over the *degree of independence* (but only the degree!) of the peasantry and the petty-bourgeoisie in the democratic revolution, now this question has been decided by the whole course of events of the last twelve years, and decided irrevocably.

It was raised anew in practice after October in many countries and in all possible forms and combinations, and everywhere it was settled the same way. A fundamental experience, following that of Kerenskyism, has been, as already mentioned, the Kuomintang experience. But no less importance is to be attached to the experience of fascism in Italy, where the petty-bourgeoisie, arms in hand, snatched the power from the old bourgeois parties in order to surrender it immediately, through its leaders, to the financial oligarchy. The same question arose in Poland, where the Pilsudski movement was aimed directly against the reactionary bourgeois-landlord government and mirrored the hopes of the petty-bourgeois masses and even of wide circles of the proletariat. It was no accident that the old Polish Social Democrat, Warski, out of fear of 'underestimating the peasantry', identified the Pilsudski revolution with the ' democratic dictatorship of the workers and peasants'. It would lead us too far afield, if I were to analyse here the Bulgarian experience, that is, the disgracefully confused policy of the Kolarovs and Kabakchievs towards the party of Stambulisky, or the shameful experiment with the Farmer-Labour Party in the United States, or Zinoviev's romance with Radić, or the experience of the Communist Party of Rumania, and so on and so forth without end. Some of these facts are analysed, in their essentials, in my *Criticism of the Draft Programme of the Communist International.* The fundamental conclusion of all these experiences fully confirms and strengthens the lessons of October—namely, that the petty-bourgeoisie, including the peasantry, is incapable of playing the rôle of leader in modern, even if backward, bourgeois society, in revolutionary no less than in reactionary epochs. The peasantry can either support the dictatorship of the bourgeoisie, or serve as prop to the dictatorship of the proletariat. Intermediate forms are only disguises for a dictatorship of the bourgeoisie, which has begun to totter or which has not yet recovered its feet after disturbances (Kerenskyism, Fascism, Pilsudski's régime).

The peasantry can follow either the bourgeoisie or the proletariat: But when the proletariat attempts to march at all costs with a peasantry which is not following it, the proletariat proves in fact to be tailing after finance capital : the workers as defenders of the fatherland in Russia in 1917 ; the workers—including the Communists as well—in the Kuomintang in China ; the workers in the Polish Socialist Party, and also the Communists to some extent, in Poland in 1926, etc.

Whoever has not thought this out to the end, and who has not understood the events from the fresh trail they have left behind, had better not get involved in revolutionary politics.

The fundamental conclusion which Lenin drew from the lessons of the February and the October Revolutions, and drew exhaustively and comprehensively, thoroughly rejects the idea of the 'democratic dictatorship'. The following was repeated by Lenin more than once after 1918 :

' The whole of political economy, if anybody has learned anything from it, the whole history of revolution, the whole history of political development throughout the nineteenth century, teaches us that the peasant follows the worker or the bourgeois . . . . If you do not know why, I would say to such citizens . . . . consider the development of any of the great revolutions of the eighteenth and nineteenth centuries, the political history of any country in the nineteenth century. It will tell you why. The economic structure of capitalist society is such that the ruling forces in it can only be capital or the proletariat which overthrows it. There are no other forces in the economic structure of that society.' (XVI. 217).*

It is not a matter here of modern England or Germany. On the basis of the lessons of any one of the great revolutions of the eighteenth or the nineteenth centuries, that is, of the *bourgeois* revolutions in the *backward* countries, Lenin comes to the conclusion that only the dictatorship of the bourgeoisie or the dictatorship of the proletariat is possible. There cannot be a ' democratic ', that is, an intermediate dictatorship.

*   *   *   *

His theoretical and historical excursion is summed up by Radek, as we see, in the rather thin aphorism that the bourgeois revolution must be distinguished from the socialist. Having descended to this ' step ', Radek straightway stretches out a finger to Kuusinen who, proceeding from his one lone resource, that is, ' common sense ', considers it improbable that the slogan of the proletarian dictatorship can be raised in both the advanced and the backward countries. With the sincerity of a man who understands nothing, Kuusinen convicts Trotsky of having ' learned nothing ' since 1905. Following Kuusinen, Radek also becomes ironical : for Trotsky, ' the peculiarity of the Chinese and Indian revolutions consists precisely of the fact that they are in no way distinguished from

---

* ' The Deception of the People by Slogans of Freedom and Equality', May 1919. 4th ed., XXIX, 338. An English version was published in pamphlet form in the *Little Lenin Library* in 1934 : see pp. 35-36 of this pamphlet.

the western European revolutions and must, therefore, in their first steps [? !] lead to the dictatorship of the proletariat.'

Radek forgets one trifle in this connection : The dictatorship of the proletariat was not realized in a Western European country, but precisely in a backward Eastern European country. Is it Trotsky's fault that the historical process overlooked the ' peculiarity ' of Russia ?   Radek forgets further that the bourgeoisie— more accurately, finance capital—rules in *all* the capitalist countries, with all their diversity in level of development, social structure, traditions, etc., that is, all their ' peculiarities '. Here again, the lack of respect for this peculiarity proceeds from historical development and not at all from Trotsky.

Then wherein lies the distinction between the advanced and the backward countries ? The distinction is great, but it still remains within the limits of the domination of capitalist relationships. The forms and methods of the rule of the bourgeoisie differ greatly in different countries. At one pole, the domination bears a stark and absolute character : *The United States*. At the other pole finance capital adapts itself to the outlived institutions of Asiatic mediævalism by subjecting them to itself and imposing its own methods upon them : *India*. But the bourgeoisie rules in both places. From this it follows that the dictatorship of the proletariat also will have a highly varied character in terms of the social basis, the political forms, the immediate tasks and the tempo of work in the various capitalist countries. But to lead the masses of the people to victory over the bloc of the imperialists, the feudalists and the national bourgeoisie—this can be done only under the revolutionary hegemony of the proletariat, which transforms itself after the seizure of power into the dictatorship of the proletariat.

Radek fancies that when he has divided humanity into two groups—one which has ' matured ' for the socialist dictatorship, and another which has ' matured ' only for the democratic dictatorship—he has by this alone, in contrast to me, taken into consideration the alleged ' peculiarity ' of the individual countries. In reality he has turned out a lifeless stereotype which can only divert the Communists from a genuine study of the peculiarity of a given country, i.e., the living interpenetration of the various steps and stages of historical development in that country.

The peculiarities of a country which has not accomplished or completed its democratic revolution are of such great significance that they must be taken as the basis for the programme of the proletarian vanguard. Only upon the basis of such a *national* programme can a Communist party develop its real and successful struggle for the majority of the working class and the toilers in general against the bourgeoisie and its democratic agents.

The possibility of success in this struggle is of course determined to a large extent by the rôle of the proletariat in the economy of the country, and consequently by the level of its capitalist development. This, however, is by no means the only criterion. No less important is the question whether a far-reaching and burning problem ' for the people ' exists in the country, in the solution of which the majority of the nation is interested, and which demands for its solution the boldest revolutionary measures. Among problems of this kind are the agrarian question and the national question, in their varied combinations. With the acute agrarian problem and the intolerable national oppression in the colonial countries, the young and relatively small proletariat can come to power on the basis of a *national democratic* revolution sooner than the proletariat of an advanced country on a purely *socialist* basis. It might have seemed that since October there should be no necessity to prove this any more. But through the years of ideological reaction and through the theoretical depravity of the epigones, the elementary conceptions of the revolution have become so rank, so putrid and so . . . . Kuusinified, that one is compelled each time to begin all over again.

Does it follow from what has been said that all the countries of the world, in one way or another, are already today ripe for the socialist revolution ? No, this is a false, dead, scholastic, Stalinist-Bukharinist way of putting the question. World economy in its entirety is indubitably ripe for socialism. But this does not mean that every country taken separately is ripe. Then what is to happen with the dictatorship of the proletariat in the various backward countries, in China, India, etc.? To this we answer : History is not made to order. A country can become ' ripe ' for the dictatorship of the proletariat not only before it is ripe for the independent construction of socialism, but even before it is ripe for far-reaching socialization measures. One must not proceed from a preconceived harmony of social development. The law of uneven development still lives, despite the tender theoretical embraces of Stalin. The force of this law operates not only in the relations of countries to each other, but also in the mutual relationships of the various processes within one and the same country. A reconciliation of the uneven processes of economics and politics can be attained only on a world scale. In particular this means that the question of the dictatorship of the proletariat in China cannot be considered exclusively within the limits of Chinese economics and Chinese politics.

It is precisely here that we come up against the two mutually exclusive standpoints : the international revolutionary theory of the permanent revolution and the national-reformist theory of socialism in one country. Not only backward China, but in general no country in the world can build socialism within its own national limits : the highly-developed productive forces which have grown beyond national boundaries resist this, just as do those forces which are insufficiently developed for nationalization. The dictatorship of the proletariat in Britain, for example, will encounter difficulties and contradictions, different in character, it is true, but perhaps not slighter than those that will confront the dictatorship of the proletariat in China. Surmounting these contradictions is possible in both cases only by way of the international revolution. This standpoint leaves no room for the question of the ' maturity ' or ' immaturity ' of China for the socialist transformation. What remains indisputable here is that the backwardness of China makes the tasks of the proletarian dictatorship extremely difficult. But we repeat : History is not made to order, and the Chinese proletariat has no choice.

Does this at least mean that every country, including the most backward colonial country, is ripe, if not for socialism, then for the dictatorship of the proletariat ? No, this is not what it means. Then what is to happen with the democratic revolution in general— and in the colonies in particular ? Where is it written—I answer the question with another question—that every colonial country is ripe for the immediate and thoroughgoing solution of its national democratic tasks ? The question must be approached from the other end. Under the conditions of the imperialist epoch the national democratic revolution can be carried through to a victorious end only when the social and political relationships of the country are mature for putting the proletariat in power as the leader of the masses of the people. And if this is not yet the case ? Then the struggle for national liberation will produce only very partial results, results directed entirely against the working masses. In 1905, the proletariat of Russia did not prove strong enough to unite the peasant masses around it and to conquer power. For this very reason, the revolution halted midway, and then sank lower and lower. In China, where, in spite of the exceptionally favourable situation, the leadership of the Communist International prevented the Chinese proletariat from fighting for power, the national tasks found a wretched, unstable and niggardly solution in the régime of the Kuomintang.

When and under what conditions a colonial country will become ripe for the real revolutionary solution of its agrarian and national problems cannot be foretold. But in any case we can assert today with full certainty that not only China but also India will attain genuine people's democracy, that is, workers' and peasants' democracy, only through the dictatorship of the proletariat. On that road there may still be many stages, steps and phases. Under the pressure of the masses of the people the bourgeoisie will still take steps to the left, in order then to fall all the more mercilessly upon the people. Periods of dual power are possible and probable. But what there will not be, what there cannot be, is a genuine democratic dictatorship that is not the dictatorship of the proletariat. An ' independent ' democratic dictatorship can only be of the type of the Kuomintang, that is, directed entirely against the workers and the peasants. We must understand this at the outset and teach it to the masses, without hiding the class realities behind abstract formulas.

Stalin and Bukharin preached that thanks to the yoke of imperialism the bourgeoisie could carry out the national revolution in China. The attempt was made. With what results ? The proletariat was brought under the headman's axe. Then it was said : The democratic dictatorship will come next. The petty-bourgeois dictatorship proved to be only a masked dictatorship of capital. By accident ? No. ' The peasant follows either the worker or the bourgeois.' In the first case, the dictatorship of the proletariat arises ; in the other the dictatorship of the bourgeoisie. It would seem that the lesson of China is clear enough, even if studied from afar. ' No,' we are answered, ' that was merely an unsuccessful experiment. We will begin everything all over again and this time set up the " genuine " democratic dictatorship.' ' By what means ?' ' On the social basis of the collaboration of the proletariat and the peasantry.' It is Radek who presents us with this latest discovery. But, if you will permit, the Kuomintang arose on that very same basis : workers and peasants ' collaborated '—to pull the chestnuts out of the fire for the bourgeoisie. Tell us what the political mechanics of this collaboration will look like. With what will you replace the Kuomintang ? What parties will be in power ? Indicate them at least approximately, at least describe them ! To this Radek answers (in 1928 !) that only people who are completely done for, who are incapable of understanding the complexity of Marxism, can be interested in such a secondary technical question as which class will be the horse and which the rider ; whereas a Bolshevik must ' abstract ' himself from the political superstructure, focusing his attention on the class foundation. No, permit me, you have already had your joke. You have already ' abstracted ' enough. More than enough ! In China, you ' abstracted ' yourself from the question of how class collaboration expressed itself in party matters, you dragged the proletariat into the Kuomintang, you became infatuated with the Kuomintang to the point of losing your senses, you furiously resisted withdrawal from the Kuomintang ; you shrank from political questions of struggle by repeating abstract formulas. And after the bourgeoisie has very concretely broken the skull of the proletariat, you propose to us : Let us try all over again ; and as a beginning let us once more ' abstract ' ourselves from the question of the parties and the revolutionary power. No ! These are very poor jokes. We will not allow ourselves to be dragged back !

All these acrobatics, as we have perceived, are presented in the interest of an alliance of the workers and peasants. Radek warns the Opposition against an underestimation of the peasantry and cites the struggle of Lenin against the Mensheviks. Sometimes, when one observes what is being done with quotations from Lenin, one resents bitterly such offences against the dignity of human thought. Yes, Lenin said more than once that denial of the revolutionary rôle of the peasantry was characteristic of the Mensheviks. And that was right. But in addition to these quotations, there also was the year 1917, in which the Mensheviks spent the eight months which separated the February from the October Revolution in an unbroken bloc with the Socialist Revolutionaries. In that period the Socialist Revolutionaries represented the overwhelming majority of the peasantry awakened by the revolution. Together with the S.R.s, the Mensheviks called themselves the revolutionary democracy and remonstrated with us that they were the very ones who based themselves upon the alliance of the workers with the peasants (soldiers). Thus, after the February Revolution the Mensheviks expropriated, so to speak, the Bolshevik formula of the alliance of the workers and peasants. The Bolsheviks were accused by them of wanting to split the proletarian vanguard from the peasantry and thereby to ruin the revolution. In other words, the Mensheviks accused Lenin of ignoring, or at least of underestimating the peasantry.

The criticism of Kamenev, Zinoviev and others directed against Lenin was only an echo of the criticism of the Mensheviks. The present criticism of Radek in turn is only a belated echo of the criticism of Kamenev.

The policy of the epigones in China, including Radek's policy, is the continuation and the further development of the Menshevik masquerade of 1917. The fact that the Communist Party remained in the Kuomintang was defended not only by Stalin, but also by Radek, with the same reference to the necessity of the alliance of the workers and peasants. But when it was 'accidentally' revealed that the Kuomintang was a bourgeois party, the attempt was repeated with the 'Left' Kuomintang. The results were the same. Thereupon, the abstraction of the democratic dictatorship, in distinction from the dictatorship of the proletariat, was elevated above this sorry reality which had not fulfilled the high hopes—a fresh repetition of what we had already had. In 1917, we heard a hundred times from Tsereteli, Dan and the others : 'We already have the dictatorship of the revolutionary democracy, but you are driving toward the dictatorship of the proletariat, that is, toward ruin.' Truly, people have short memories. The ' revolutionary-democratic dictatorship' of Stalin and Radek is in no way distinguished from the ' dictatorship of the revolutionary democracy' of Tsereteli and Dan. And in spite of that, this formula not only runs through all the resolutions of the Comintern, but it has also penetrated into its programme. It is hard to conceive a more cunning masquerade and at the same time a more bitter revenge by Menshevism for the affronts which Bolshevism heaped upon it in 1917.

The revolutionists of the East, however, still have the right to demand a definite answer to the question of the character of the ' democratic dictatorship ', based not upon old, *a priori* quotations, but upon facts and upon political experience. To the question : What is a ' democratic dictatorship '?—Stalin has repeatedly given the truly classical reply : For the East, it is approximately the same as 'Lenin conceived it with regard to the 1905 Revolution'. This has become the official formula to a certain extent. It can be found in the books and resolutions devoted to China, India or Polynesia. Revolutionists are referred to Lenin's ' conceptions' concerning *future* events, which in the meantime have long ago become *past* events, and in addition, the hypothetical ' conceptions' of Lenin are interpreted this way and that, but never in the way that Lenin himself interpreted them *after* the events.

'All right,' says the Communist of the East, hanging his head, ' we will try to conceive of it exactly as Lenin, according to your words, conceived of it before the revolution. But won't you please tell us what this slogan looks like in actuality ? How was it realized in your country ?'

' In our country it was realized in the shape of Kerenskyism in the epoch of dual power.'

' Can we tell our workers that the slogan of the democratic dictatorship will be realized in our country in the shape of our own national Kerenskyism ?'

' Come, come ! Not at all ! No worker will adopt such a slogan ; Kerenskyism is servility to the bourgeoisie and betrayal of the working people.'

' But what, then, must we tell our workers? ' the Communist of the East asks despondently.

' You must tell them,' impatiently answers Kuusinen, the man on duty, 'that the democratic dictatorship is the one that Lenin conceived of with regard to the future democratic revolution.'

If the Communist of the East is not lacking in sense, he will seek to rejoin :

' But didn't Lenin explain in 1918 that the democratic dictatorship found its genuine and true realization only in the October Revolution which established the dictatorship of the proletariat ? Would it not be better to orient the party and the working class precisely toward this prospect ?'

' Under no circumstances. Do not even dare to think about it. Why, that is the per-r-r-manent r-r-r-evolution ! That's Tr-r-r-otskyism ! '

After this harsh reprimand the Communist of the East turns paler than the snow on the highest peaks of the Himalayas and abandons any further craving for knowledge. Let whatever will happen, happen !

And the consequences ? We know them well : either contemptible grovelling before Chiang Kai-shek, or heroic adventures.

8. FROM MARXISM TO PACIFISM

What is most alarming, as a symptom, is a passage in Radek's article which, to be sure, seems to stand apart from the central theme that interests us, but which is intimately bound up with this theme by the uniformity of Radek's shift toward the present theoreticians of centrism. I refer to the somewhat disguised advances he makes toward the theory of socialism in one country. One must dwell on this, for this ' side-line ' of Radek's errors can surpass all the other differences of opinion in its further development, revealing that their quantity has definitively turned into quality.

Discussing the dangers that threaten the revolution from without, Radek writes that Lenin ' . . . . was conscious of the fact that *with the level of economic development in Russia in 1905* this [the proletarian] dictatorship can maintain itself only if the Western European proletariat comes to its aid'. (My emphasis—*L.T.*).

One mistake after another ; above all, a very crude violation of the historical perspective. In reality Lenin said, and that more than once, that the democratic dictatorship (and not at all the proletarian) in Russia would be unable to maintain itself without the socialist revolution in Europe. This idea runs like a red thread through all the articles and speeches of Lenin in the days of the Stockholm party congress in 1906 (polemic against Plekhanov, questions of nationalization, etc.). In that period, Lenin did not even raise the question of a proletarian dictatorship in Russia before the socialist revolution in Western Europe. But it is not there that the most important thing lies for the moment. What is the meaning of ' with the level of economic development of Russia in 1905 '? And how do matters stand with the level in 1917 ? It is on this difference in levels that the theory of socialism in one country is erected. The programme of the Comintern has divided the whole globe into squares which are ' adequate ' in level for the independent construction of socialism and others which are ' inadequate '; and has thus created for revolutionary strategy a series of hopeless blind alleys. Differences in economic levels can undoubtedly be of decisive significance for the political power of the working class. In 1905, we could not raise ourselves to the dictatorship of the proletariat, just as, for that matter, we were unable to rise to the democratic dictatorship. In 1917 we set up the dictatorship of the proletariat, which swallowed up the democratic dictatorship. But with the economic development of 1917 just as with the 1905 level the dictatorship can maintain itself and develop to socialism only if the Western European proletariat comes opportunely to its assistance. Naturally, this ' opportuneness ' cannot be calculated *a priori* ; it is determined in the course of development and struggle. As against this *fundamental* question, determined by the *world* relationship of forces, which has the last and decisive word, the difference between levels of development of Russia in 1905 and in 1917, however important it is in itself, is a factor of the secondary order.

But Radek does not content himself with the ambiguous reference to this difference of levels. After referring to the fact that Lenin saw the connection between the internal problems of the revolution and its world problems (well, now !) Radek adds :

' But Lenin did not *sharpen* only the concept of this connection between the maintenance of the socialist dictatorship in Russia and aid from the Western European proletariat, as it was *excessively sharpened by Trotsky's formulation,* namely, that it must be *state* aid, that is, the aid of the already victorious Western European proletariat.' (My emphasis—*L.T.*).

Frankly, I did not trust my eyes when I read these lines. To what end did Radek require this worthless weapon from the arsenal of the epigones ? This is simply a shamefaced rehash of the Stalinist banalities which we always used to make such thorough game of. Apart from everything else, the quotation shows that Radek has a very poor notion of the fundamental landmarks of Lenin's path. Lenin, unlike Stalin, not only never contrasted the pressure of the European proletariat upon the bourgeois power to the capture of power by the proletariat; on the contrary, he formulated the question of revolutionary aid from without much more sharply than I. In the epoch of the first revolution, he repeated tirelessly that we should not retain democracy (not even democracy!) without the socialist revolution in Europe. Generally speaking, in 1917-18 and the years that followed, Lenin did not consider and estimate the fate of our revolution in any way other than in connection with the socialist revolution that had begun in Europe. He asserted openly, for example: 'Without the victory of the revolution in Germany, we are doomed.' He said this in 1918, that is, *not* with the 'economic level' of 1905; and he had in mind not future decades, but the period immediately ahead, which was a matter of a few years, if not months.

Lenin declared dozens of times: If we have held out 'the reason . . . . was that a fortunate combination of circumstances protected us for a short time from international imperialism' (for a short time!—*L.T.*). And further: 'International imperialism could not under any circumstances, on any condition, live side by side with the Soviet Republic. . . . . In this sphere conflict is inevitable.' And the conclusion? Isn't it the pacifist hope in the 'pressure' of the proletariat or in the 'neutralization' of the bourgeoisie? No, the conclusion reads: 'Here lies the greatest difficulty of the Russian Revolution . . . . the necessity of calling forth an international revolution.' (XV, page 126).* When was this said and written? Not in 1905, when Nicholas II negotiated with Wilhelm II on the suppression of the revolution and when I advanced my 'sharpened' formula, but in 1918, 1919 and the following years.

Here is what Lenin said, looking back, at the Third Congress of the Comintern:

'It was clear to us that without the support of the international world revolution the victory of the proletarian revolution [in

---

* 'Speech on the Question of War and Peace,' 7 March, 1918, 4th edn., XXVII, 69-70. *Selected Works,* Eng. ed., VII, 288.

Russia—*L.T.*] was impossible. Before the revolution and even after it, we thought : Either revolution breaks out in the other countries, in the capitalistically more developed countries, immediately, or at least very quickly, or we must perish. Notwithstanding this conviction, we did all we possibly could to preserve the Soviet system under all circumstances, come what may, because we knew that we were working not only for ourselves but also for the international revolution. We knew this, we repeatedly expressed this conviction before the October Revolution, immediately afterward, and at the time we signed the Brest-Litovsk Treaty. *And, speaking generally, this was correct.* In actual fact, however, events did not proceed along as straight a line as we expected.' (*Minutes of the Third Congress of the Comintern,* page 354, Russian edition).*

From 1921 onward, the movement began to proceed along a line that was not so straight as I, together with Lenin, had expected in 1917-19 (and not only in 1905). But it nevertheless did develop along the line of the irreconcilable contradictions between the workers' state and the bourgeois world. One of the two must perish ! The workers' state can be preserved from mortal dangers, not only military but also economic, only by the victorious development of the proletarian revolution in the West. The attempt to discover two positions, Lenin's and mine, on this question, is the height of theoretical slovenliness. At least re-read Lenin, do not slander him, do not feed us with stale Stalinist mush !

But the plunge downward does not stop even here. After Radek inventing the story that Lenin considered adequate the ' simple ' (in essence, reformist, Purcellian) aid of the world proletariat, while Trotsky ' exaggeratedly demanded ' only state aid, that is, revolutionary aid, Radek continues :

' Experience showed that *on this point, too,* Lenin was right. The European proletariat was not yet able to capture power, but it was strong enough, during the intervention, to prevent the **world** bourgeoisie from throwing substantial forces against us.

---

* Verbatim Rport of 3rd Congress of Communist International, Petrograd, 1922. Lenin's speech of 5th July, 1921. 4th ed. XXXII, 456. *Selected Works,* Eng. ed., **IX,** 227.

Thereby it helped us maintain the Soviet power. Fear of the labour movement, along with the antagonisms in the capitalist world itself, was the main force that has guaranteed the maintenance of peace during the eight years, since the end of the intervention.'

This passage, while it does not sparkle with originality against the background of the exercises written by the literary functionaries of our time, is nevertheless noteworthy for its combination of historical anachronisms, political confusion and the grossest errors of principle.

From Radek's words it would follow that Lenin in 1905 foretold in his pamphlet *Two Tactics* (this is the only work to which Radek refers) that the relationship of forces between states and classes after 1917 would be such as to exclude for a long time the possibility of a large-scale military intervention against us. In contrast to this, Trotsky in 1905 did not foresee the situation that would necessarily arise after the imperialist war, but only reckoned with the realities of that time, such as the mighty Hohenzollern army, the very strong Hapsburg army, the mighty French Bourse, etc. This is truly a monstrous anachronism, which becomes even more complicated by its ridiculous inner contradictions. For, according to Radek, my principal mistake consisted precisely of the fact that I did put forward the prospect of the dictatorship of the proletariat 'with the level of development of 1905'. Now the second mistake becomes plain : I did not consider the prospect of the dictatorship of the proletariat put forward by me on the eve of the 1905 Revolution in the light of the international situation which arose only after 1917. When Stalin's usual arguments look like this, we don't wonder about it, for we know well enough his ' level of development ', in 1917 as well as in 1928. But how did Radek fall into such company ?

Yet even this is not yet the worst. The worst lies in the fact that Radek has skipped over the boundary that separates Marxism from opportunism, the revolutionary from the pacifist position. It is a question of nothing less than the struggle against war, that is, of *how and with what methods war can be averted or stopped ; by the pressure of the proletariat upon the bourgeoisie or by civil war to overthrow the bourgeoisie?* Radek has unwittingly introduced a fundamental question of proletarian policy into the controversy between us.

Does Radek want to say that I ' ignore ' not only the peasantry but also the pressure of the proletariat upon the bourgeoisie, and have taken into consideration the proletarian revolution exclusively ? It is hardly to be assumed that he will defend such an absurdity, worthy of a Thaelmann, a Semard or a Monmosseau. At the Third Congress of the Comintern, the ultra-lefts of that time (Zinoviev, Thalheimer, Thaelmann, Bela Kun, etc.) advocated tactics of putschism in the West in order to save the USSR. Together with Lenin, I explained to them as popularly as possible that the best possible assistance they could render us would be systematically and in a planned way to consolidate their positions and prepare themselves for the capture of power, instead of improvising revolutionary adventures for our sakes. At that time, regrettably enough, Radek was not on the side of Lenin and Trotsky, but on the side of Zinoviev and Bukharin. But Radek surely recollects—at any rate, the minutes of the Third Congress recollect it—that the essence of the argument of Lenin and myself consisted precisely of assailing the irrationally ' sharpened formulation ' of the ultra-lefts. After we had explained to them that the strengthening of the party and the pressure of the proletariat are very serious factors in internal and international relations, we Marxists added that ' pressure ' is only a function of the revolutionary struggle for power and depends entirely upon the development of this struggle. For this reason, Lenin delivered a speech at the end of the Third Congress, at a big private session of the delegates, which was directed against tendencies to passivity and waiting upon events, and closed with approximately the following moral : Engage in no adventures, but, dear friends, please do not tarry, for with ' pressure ' alone we cannot last long.

Radek refers to the fact that the European proletariat was not able to take power after the war, but that it prevented the bourgeoisie from crushing us. I also had more than one occasion to speak of this. Nevertheless, the European proletariat succeeded in preventing our destruction only because the pressure of the proletariat coincided with the very grave objective consequences of the imperialist war and the world antagonisms aggravated by it.

It is impossible to say which of these elements was of more decisive
significance : the struggle within the imperialist camp, the economic
collapse, or the pressure of the proletariat ; but the question cannot
be put in that way. That peaceful pressure alone is inadequate
was demonstrated too clearly by the imperialist war, which came
in spite of all ' pressure '. And finally, and this is most important,
if the pressure of the proletariat in the first, most critical years of
the Soviet Republic proved to be effective enough, then it was
only because at that time for the workers of Europe it was not a
question of exerting pressure, but of struggling for power—and
this struggle repeatedly assumed the form of civil war.

In 1905, there was neither a war nor an economic collapse in
Europe, and capitalism and militarism were in full-blooded frenzy.
The ' pressure ' of the Social Democrats of that time was absolutely
incapable of preventing Wilhelm II or Franz Josef from marching
into the Kingdom of Poland with their troops, or, in general, from
coming to the aid of the Tsar. And even in 1918, the pressure of
the German proletariat did not prevent Hohenzollern from occupy-
ing the Baltic provinces and the Ukraine, and if he did not get as
far as Moscow then it was only because his military forces were
not adequate. Otherwise, how and why did we conclude the Brest
peace ? How easily yesterday is forgotten ! Lenin did not confine
himself to hope for ' pressure ' by the proletariat, but repeatedly
asserted that without revolution in Germany we should certainly
perish. This was correct in essence, although a greater period of
time has intervened. Let there be no illusions ; we have received
an undated moratorium. We live, as before, under the conditions
of a ' breathing-space '.

A condition in which the proletariat is as yet unable to seize
power, but can prevent the bourgeoisie from utilizing its power
for a war, is a condition of unstable class equilibrium in its highest
expression. An equilibrium is called unstable precisely when it
cannot last long. It must tip toward one side or the other. Either
the proletariat comes to power or else the bourgeoisie, by a series
of crushing blows, weakens the revolutionary pressure sufficiently
to regain freedom of action, above all in the question of war and
peace.

Only a reformist can picture the pressure of the proletariat upon the bourgeois state as a permanently increasing factor and as a guarantee against intervention. It is precisely out of this conception that arose the theory of the construction of socialism in one country, given the *neutralization* of the world bourgeoisie (Stalin). Just as the owl takes flight at twilight, so also did the Stalinist theory of the neutralization of the bourgeoisie by the pressure of the proletariat arise only when the conditions which engendered this theory had begun to disappear.

The world situation underwent abrupt changes in the period when the falsely interpreted postwar experience led to the deceptive hope that we could get along without the revolution of the European proletariat by substituting for it 'support' in general. The defeats of the proletariat have paved the way for capitalist stabilization. The collapse of capitalism after the war has been overcome. New generations have grown up that have not tasted the horrors of the imperialist slaughter. The result is that the bourgeoisie is now freer to dispose of its war machine than it was five or eight years ago.

As the working masses move to the Left, this process will undoubtedly, as it develops further, once more increase their pressure upon the bourgeois state. But this is a two-edged factor. It is precisely the growing danger from the side of the working class that can, at a later stage, drive the bourgeoisie to decisive steps in order to show that it is master in its own house, and to attempt to destroy the main centre of contagion, the Soviet Republic. *The struggle against war is decided not by pressure upon the government but only by the revolutionary struggle for power.* The 'pacifist' effects of the proletarian class struggle, like its reformist effects, are only by-products of the revolutionary struggle for power; they have only a relative strength and can easily turn into their opposite, that is, they can drive the bourgeoisie to take the road to war. The bourgeoisie's fear of the labour movement, to which Radek refers so one-sidedly, is the most substantial hope of all social-pacifists. But 'fear' of the revolution alone decides nothing. The revolution decides. For this reason, Lenin said in 1905 that the only guarantee against the monarchist restoration, and, in 1918, against the restoration of capitalism, is not the pressure of the proletariat but its revolutionary victory in

Europe. This is the only correct way of putting the question. In spite of the lengthy character of the ' breathing-space ', Lenin's formulation retains its full force even today. I, too, formulated the question in the very same way. I wrote in *Results and Prospects* in 1906 :

' It is precisely the fear of the revolt of the proletariat that compels the bourgeois parties, even while voting monstrous sums for military expenditure, to make solemn declarations in favour of peace, to dream of International Arbitration Courts and even of the organization of a United States of Europe. These pitiful declamations can, of course, abolish neither the antagonism between states nor armed conflicts.' (*Our Revolution*, ' Results and Prospects', page 283.)*

The basic mistake of the Sixth Congress lies in this, that in order to save the pacifist and national-reformist perspectives of Stalin-Bukharin, it ran after revolutionary-technical recipes against the war danger, separating the struggle against war from the struggle for power.

The inspirers of the Sixth Congress, these alarmed builders of socialism in one country—in essence, frightened pacifists—made the attempt to perpetuate the ' neutralization ' of the bourgeoisie through intensified ' pressure ' methods. But since they couldn't help knowing that their leadership up to now in a series of countries had led to the defeat of the revolution and had thrown the international vanguard of the proletariat far back, they endeavoured first of all to jettison the ' sharpened formulation ' of Marxism, which indissolubly ties up the problem of war with the problem of the revolution. They have converted the struggle against war into a self-sufficient task. Lest the national parties oversleep the decisive hour, they have proclaimed the war danger to be permanent, unpostponable and immediate. Everything that happens in the world happens for the purpose of war. War is now no longer an instrument of the bourgeois régime ; the bourgeois régime is an instrument of war. As a consequence, the struggle of the Communist International against war is converted into a system of ritualistic formulas, which are repeated automatically

---

* See page 112 of the present volume.

on every occasion and, losing their effectiveness, evaporate. Stalinist national socialism tends to convert the Communist International into an auxiliary means of 'pressure' upon the bourgeoisie. It is just this tendency, and not Marxism, that Radek helps with his hasty, slovenly, superficial criticism. He has lost the compass and has got into a strange current that may carry him to far different shores.

Alma-Ata, October 1928

9. EPILOGUE

The prediction, or apprehension, which I expressed in the concluding lines of the previous chapter was, as the reader knows, confirmed a few months later. The criticism of the permanent revolution only served Radek as a lever to push himself away from the Opposition. Our whole book proves, we hope, that Radek's passage into the camp of Stalin did not come to us unexpectedly. But even apostasy has its gradations, its levels of debasement. In his declaration of repentance, Radek completely rehabilitates Stalin's policy in China. This means plumbing the lowest depths of betrayal. It only remains for me to quote an extract from my reply to the declaration of penitence by Radek, Preobrazhensky and Smilga, which puts them on the black list of political cynics :

'As befits all self-respecting bankrupts, the trio has not of course failed to take cover behind the permanent revolution. The most tragic experience of the whole recent history of the defeats of opportunism—the Chinese Revolution—this trio of capitulators seeks to dismiss with a cheap oath guaranteeing that it has nothing in common with the theory of the permanent revolution.

' Radek and Smilga obstinately defended the subordination of the Chinese Communist Party to the bourgeois Kuomintang, not only up to Chiang Kai-shek's coup d'état but also afterwards. Preobrazhensky mumbled something inarticulate, as he always does when political questions are involved. A remarkable fact :

all those in the ranks of the Opposition who defended the subordination of the Communist Party to the Kuomintang turned out
to be capitulators. Not a single Oppositionist who remained true
to his banner bears this mark, which is a mark of notorious shame.
Three-quarters of a century after the appearance of the *Communist
Manifesto,* a quarter of a century after the founding of the party
of the Bolsheviks, these ill-starred " Marxists" considered it possible
to defend the keeping of the Communists in the cage of the
Kuomintang ! In his answer to my charges, Radek already then,
just as in his letter of repentence today, tried to frighten us with
the " isolation " of the proletariat from the peasantry in the event
of the Communist Party's withdrawing from the bourgeois Kuomintang. Shortly before that, Radek called the Canton government
a peasants' and workers' government and thereby helped Stalin to
disguise the subordination of the proletariat to the bourgeoisie.
With what are these shameful deeds, the consequences of this
blindness, this stupidity, this betrayal of Marxism, to be covered ?
With what, indeed ! With an indictment of the permanent
revolution !

'As far back as February 1928, Radek, who was already looking
for pretexts for his capitulation, adhered promptly to the resolution
on the Chinese question adopted by the February 1928 Plenum of
the Executive Committee of the Comintern. This resolution brands
the Trotskyists as liquidators because they called defeats defeats,
and were not willing to consider the victorious Chinese counter-
revolution as the highest stage of the Chinese Revolution. In this
February resolution the course towards armed uprising and Soviets
was proclaimed. For every person not entirely devoid of political
sense and tempered by revolutionary experience, this resolution
constituted an example of the most revolting and most irresponsible
adventurism. Radek adhered to it. Preobrazhensky approached
the matter no less ingeniously than Radek, only from the opposite
end. The Chinese Revolution, he wrote, is already defeated, and
defeated for a long time. A new revolution will not come soon.
Is it worth while squabbling about China with the centrists ? On
this theme, Preobrazhensky sent out lengthy epistles. When I
read them in Alma-Ata, I experienced a feeling of shame. What
did these people learn in the school of Lenin ? I asked myself

over and over again. Preobrazhensky's premises were diametrically
opposed to Radek's premises, yet the conclusions were the same :
both of them were inspired by the great desire for Yaroslavsky
to embrace them fraternally through the good offices of Menzhinsky.* Oh, of course, they did it for the good of the revolution.
These are not careerists. Not at all. They are simply helpless,
ideologically bankrupt individuals.

‘ To the adventurist resolution of the February Plenum of the
ECCI (1928) I already then counterposed a course towards the
mobilization of the Chinese workers under democratic slogans,
including the slogan of a Constituent Assembly for China. But
here the ill-starred trio fell into ultra-leftism ; that was cheap and
committed them to nothing. Democratic slogans ? Never. “ This
is a gross mistake on Trotsky's part ”. Only soviets for China—
not a farthing less ! It is hard to conceive of anything more
senseless than this—by your leave—position. The slogan of
soviets for an epoch of bourgeois reaction is a baby's rattle, i.e., a
mockery of soviets. But even in the epoch of revolution, that is,
in the epoch of the direct building of soviets, we did not withdraw
the democratic slogans. We did not withdraw them until the real
soviets, which had already conquered power, clashed before the
eyes of the masses with the real institutions of democracy. This
signifies in the language of Lenin (and not of the philistine Stalin
and his parrots) : not skipping over the democratic stage in the
development of the country.

‘ Without the democratic programme—constituent assembly,
eight-hour day, confiscation of the land, national independence of
China, right of self-determination for the peoples living within it—
without this democratic programme, the Communist Party of
China is bound hand and foot and is compelled to surrender the
field passively to the Chinese Social-Democrats who may, with
the aid of Stalin, Radek and company, assume the place of the
Communist Party.

‘ Thus : although following in the wake of the Opposition,

---

* Menzhinsky was at that time the head of the GPU; Yaroslavsky was
one of the heads of the Central Control Commission of the party and was
especially active in attacking the Opposition and expelling many of its
adherents from the party.

Radek nevertheless missed what was most important in the Chinese Revolution, for he defended the subordination of the Communist Party to the bourgeois Kuomintang. Radek missed the Chinese counter-revolution, supporting the course toward armed uprising after the Canton adventure. Radek today skips over the period of the counter-revolution and the struggle for democracy by waving aside the tasks of the transition period in favour of the most abstract idea of soviets outside of time and space. But in return Radek swears that he has nothing in common with the permanent revolution. That is gratifying. That is consoling. . . . .

' The anti-Marxist theory of Stalin and Radek means for China, India and all the countries of the East, an altered but not improved repetition of the Kuomintang experiment.

' On the basis of all the experience of the Russian and Chinese Revolution, on the basis of the teachings of Marx and Lenin, tested in the light of these revolutions, the Opposition affirms :

' That the new Chinese revolution can overthrow the existing régime and transfer the power to the masses of the people only in the form of the dictatorship of the proletariat :

' That the " democratic dictatorship of the proletariat and the peasantry", in contrast to the dictatorship of the proletariat which leads the peasantry and realizes the programme of democracy, is a fiction, a self-deception, or what is worse still—Kerenskyism or Kuomintangism.

' Between the régime of Kerensky and Chiang Kai-shek, on the one hand, and the dictatorship of the proletariat on the other, there is no half-way, intermediate revolutionary régime and there can be none. Whoever puts forward the bare formula of such a régime is shamefully deceiving the workers of the East and is preparing new catastrophies.

' The Opposition says to the workers of the East : Bankrupted by the inner-party machinations, the capitulators are helping Stalin to sow the seeds of centrism, to throw sand in your eyes, to stop up your ears, to befuddle your heads. On the one hand, you are rendered helpless in the face of stark bourgeois dictatorship by being forbidden to engage in a struggle for democracy. On the other hand, there is unrolled before you a panorama of some sort of saving, non-proletarian dictatorship, which facilitates a fresh reincarnation of the Kuomintang in the future, that is, further defeats for the workers' and peasants' revolution.

' Such preachers are betrayers. Learn to distrust them, workers of the East; learn to despise them, learn to drive them out of your ranks! ....'

10. WHAT IS THE PERMANENT REVOLUTION?

BASIC POSTULATES

I hope that the reader will not object if, to end this book, I attempt, without fear of repetition, to formulate succinctly my principal conclusions.

1. The theory of the permanent revolution now demands the greatest attention from every Marxist, for the course of the class and ideological struggle has fully and finally raised this question from the realm of reminiscences over old differences of opinion among Russian Marxists, and converted it into a question of the character, the inner connexions and methods of the international revolution in general.

2. With regard to countries with a belated bourgeois development, especially the colonial and semi-colonial countries, the theory of the permanent revolution signifies that the complete and genuine solution of their tasks of achieving *democracy and national emancipation* is conceivable only through the dictatorship of the proletariat as the leader of the subjugated nation, above all of its peasant masses.

3. Not only the agrarian, but also the national question assigns to the peasantry—the overwhelming majority of the population in backward countries—an exceptional place in the democratic revolution. Without an alliance of the proletariat with the peasantry the tasks of the democratic revolution cannot be solved, nor even

seriously posed. But the alliance of these two classes can be realized in no other way than through an irreconcilable struggle against the influence of the national-liberal bourgeoisie.

4. No matter what the first episodic stages of the revolution may be in the individual countries, the realization of the revolutionary alliance between the proletariat and the peasantry is **conceivable only** under the political leadership of the proletarian vanguard, organized in the Communist Party. This in turn means that the victory of the democratic revolution is conceivable only through the dictatorship of the proletariat which bases itself upon the alliance with the peasantry and solves first of all the tasks of the democratic revolution.

5. Assessed historically, the old slogan of Bolshevism—'the democratic dictatorship of the proletariat and peasantry'—expressed precisely the above-characterized relationship of the proletariat, the peasantry and the liberal bourgeoisie. This has been confirmed by the experience of October. But Lenin's old formula did not settle in advance the problem of what the reciprocal relations would be between the proletariat and the peasantry within the revolutionary bloc. In other words, the formula deliberately retained a certain algebraic quality, which had to make way for more precise arithmetical quantities in the process of historical experience. However, the latter showed, and under circumstances that exclude any kind of misinterpretation, that no matter how great the revolutionary rôle of the peasantry may be, it nevertheless cannot be an independent rôle and even less a leading one. The peasant follows either the worker or the bourgeois. This means that the 'democratic dictatorship of the proletariat and peasantry' is only conceivable as a *dictatorship of the proletariat that leads the peasant masses behind it.*

6. A democratic dictatorship of the proletariat and peasantry, as a régime that is distinguished from the dictatorship of the proletariat by its class content, might be realized only in a case where an *independent* revolutionary party could be constituted, expressing the interests of the peasants and in general of petty-bourgeois democracy—a party capable of conquering power with

this or that degree of aid from the proletariat, and of determining
its revolutionary programme. As all modern history attests—
especially the Russian experience of the last twenty-five years—an
insurmountable obstacle on the road to the creation of a peasants'
party is the petty-bourgeoisie's lack of economic and political
independence and its deep internal differentiation. By reason of
this the upper sections of the petty-bourgeoisie (of the peasantry)
go along with the big bourgeoisie in all decisive cases, especially
in war and in revolution ; the lower sections go along with the
proletariat ; the intermediate section being thus compelled to
choose between the two extreme poles. Between Kerenskyism and
the Bolshevik power, between the Kuomintang and the dictatorship
of the proletariat, there is not and cannot be any intermediate
stage, that is, no democratic dictatorship of the workers and
peasants.

7. The Comintern's endeavour to foist upon the Eastern countries
the slogan of the democratic dictatorship of the proletariat and
peasantry, finally and long ago exhausted by history, can have
only a reactionary effect. Insofar as this slogan is counterposed
to the slogan of the dictatorship of the proletariat, it contributes
politically to the dissolution of the proletariat in the petty-bourgeois
masses and thus creates the most favourable conditions for the
hegemony of the national bourgeoisie and consequently for the
collapse of the democratic revolution. The introduction of this
slogan into the programme of the Comintern is a direct betrayal
of Marxism and of the October tradition of Bolshevism.

8. The dictatorship of the proletariat which has risen to power
as the leader of the democratic revolution is inevitably and very
quickly confronted with tasks, the fulfilment of which is bound up
with deep inroads into the rights of bourgeois property. The
democratic revolution grows over directly into the socialist revolution and thereby becomes a *permanent* revolution.

9. The conquest of power by the proletariat does not complete
the revolution, but only opens it. Socialist construction is conceivable only on the foundation of the class struggle, on a national
and international scale. This struggle, under the conditions of an

overwhelming predominance of capitalist relationships on the world arena, must inevitably lead to explosions, that is, internally to civil wars and externally to revolutionary wars. Therein lies the permanent character of the socialist revolution as such, regardless of whether it is a backward country that is involved, which only yesterday accomplished its democratic revolution, or an old capitalist country which already has behind it a long epoch of democracy and parliamentarism.

10. The completion of the socialist revolution within national limits is unthinkable. One of the basic reasons for the crisis in bourgeois society is the fact that the productive forces created by it can no longer be reconciled with the framework of the national state. From this follow, on the one hand, imperialist wars, on the other, the utopia of a bourgeois United States of Europe. The socialist revolution begins on the national arena, it unfolds on the international arena, and is completed on the world arena. Thus, the socialist revolution becomes a permanent revolution in a newer and broader sense of the word ; it attains completion only in the final victory of the new society on our entire planet.

11. The above-outlined sketch of the development of the world revolution eliminates the question of countries that are ' mature ' or ' immature ' for socialism in the spirit of that pedantic, lifeless classification given by the present programme of the Comintern. Insofar as capitalism has created a world market, a world division of labour and world productive forces, it has also prepared world economy as a whole for socialist transformation.

Different countries will go through this process at different tempos. Backward countries may, under certain conditions, arrive at the dictatorship of the proletariat sooner than advanced countries, but they will come later than the latter to socialism.

A backward colonial or semi-colonial country, the proletariat of which is insufficiently prepared to unite the peasantry and take power, is thereby incapable of bringing the democratic revolution to its conclusion. Contrariwise, in a country where the proletariat has power in its hands as the result of the democratic revolution, the subsequent fate of the dictatorship and socialism depends in the last analysis not only and not so much upon the national productive forces as upon the development of the international socialist revolution.

12. The theory of socialism in one country, which rose on the yeast of the reaction against October, is the only theory that consistently and to the very end opposes the theory of the permanent revolution.

The attempt of the epigones, under the lash of our criticism, to confine the application of the theory of socialism in one country exclusively to Russia, because of its specific characteristics (its vastness and its natural resources), does not improve matters but only makes them worse. The break with the internationalist position always and invariably leads to national *messianism*, that is, to attributing special superiorities and qualities to one's own country, which allegedly permit it to play a rôle to which other countries cannot attain.

The world division of labour, the dependence of Soviet industry upon foreign technology, the dependence of the productive forces of the advanced countries of Europe upon Asiatic raw materials, etc., etc., make the construction of an independent socialist society in any single country in the world impossible.

13. The theory of Stalin and Bukharin, running counter to the entire experience of the Russian revolution, not only sets up the democratic revolution mechanically in contrast to the socialist revolution, but also makes a breach between the national revolution and the international revolution.

This theory imposes upon revolutions in backward countries the task of establishing an unrealizable régime of democratic dictatorship, which it counterposes to the dictatorship of the proletariat. Thereby this theory introduces illusions and fictions into politics, paralyses the struggle for power of the proletariat in the East, and hampers the victory of the colonial revolution.

The very seizure of power by the proletariat signifies, from the standpoint of the epigones' theory, the completion of the revolution (' to the extent of nine-tenths ', according to Stalin's formula) and the opening of the epoch of national reforms. The theory of the kulak growing into socialism and the theory of the ' neutralization ' of the world bourgeoisie are consequently inseparable from the theory of socialism in one country. They stand or fall together.

By the theory of national socialism, the Communist International is down-graded to an auxiliary weapon useful only for the struggle against military intervention. The present policy of the Comintern, its régime and the selection of its leading personnel correspond entirely to the demotion of the Communist International to the rôle of an auxiliary unit which is not destined to solve independent tasks.

14. The programme of the Comintern created by Bukharin is eclectic through and through. It makes the hopeless attempt to reconcile the theory of socialism in one country with Marxist internationalism, which is, however, inseparable from the permanent character of the world revolution. The struggle of the Communist Left Opposition for a correct policy and a healthy régime in the Communist International is inseparably bound up with the struggle for the Marxist programme. The question of the programme is in turn inseparable from the question of the two mutually exclusive theories : the theory of permanent revolution and the theory of socialism in one country. The problem of the permanent revolution has long ago outgrown the episodic differences of opinion between Lenin and Trotsky, which were completely exhausted by history. The struggle is between the basic ideas of Marx and Lenin on the one side and the eclecticism of the centrists on the other.

Also By Leon Trotsky

	Cloth	Paper
The Age of Permanent Revolution: A Trotsky Anthology (ed. by Isaac Deutscher and George Novack)		$ 95
The Basic Writings of Trotsky (ed. by Irving Howe)		1.95
The Case of Leon Trotsky (verbatim transcript of Trotsky's testimony before the Dewey Commission)	$10.00	
The Chinese Revolution: Problems and Perspectives		.50
The Death Agony of Capitalism and the Tasks of the Fourth International ("Transitional Program")		.35
Diary in Exile	4.00	1.45
The Essential Trotsky		1.50
Fascism: What It Is and How To Fight It (a revised compilation)		.50
The First Five Years of the Communist International, Vol. II	5.95	
Flight from Siberia		.80
History of the Russian Revolution, 3 vols., boxed		5.00
Complete in one volume	14.50	
Abridged		1.95
In Defense of Marxism	5.95	2.45
The Kirov Assassination		.25
Literature and Revolution	3.75	1.85
The New Course		.95
On Black Nationalism and Self-Determination		.95
On the Labor Party in the United States		.50
On the Suppressed Testament of Lenin (includes On the Trade Unions		.95
Permanent Revolution: Results and Prospects		2.45
Problems of the Chinese Revolution	6.00	3.25
The Revolution Betrayed	5.95	2.95
Stalin: An Appraisal of the Man and His Influence	10.00	
The Stalin School of Falsification		3.00
Stalinism and Bolshevism		.35
Stalin's Frame-Up System and the Moscow Trials		1.00
Terrorism and Communism		1.95
Their Morals and Ours (with essays by John Dewey and George Novack)		.95
The Trotsky Papers, Vol. I (Lenin-Trotsky correspondence 1917-22; facing pages of Russian and English)	28.50	
Where is Britain Going?		1.50
Whither France?	4.95	1.45
On Engels and Kautsky		.50
Military Writings	5.95	1.95
Writings of Leon Trotsky (1939-40)		2.45
Writings of Leon Trotsky (1938-39)		2.95

MERIT PUBLISHERS 873 BROADWAY NEW YORK, N.Y. 10003

(write for free catalog)

DATE DUE